the Dry Creek Chronicles

Nineteenth Century Idaho Farm Life

Claudia Druss

Basin & Range Publishing
P.O. Box 1696
Longmont, CO 80502

Cover photos: P.L. Schick farmhouse circa 1874 & 1890,
courtesy of Dry Creek Historical Society

Cover design: Emilie Druss

Copyright © 2015 Basin & Range Publishing, First Edition

ISBN-10: 0692306714
ISBN-13: 978-0692306710

Acknowledgments

This book stands in gratitude to the scores of volunteers who worked tirelessly with the Dry Creek Historical Society to preserve for posterity the 1860s Schick-Ostolasa Farmstead in the Dry Creek Valley of southwestern Idaho.

My thanks and appreciation to those who made this book possible: to Lorraine Gross and Aimée Noonan who took the time to review and offer comments, and to Celeste Killeen, Keith Peterson, Celeste Rush, and Linda Winer for their encouragement and advice. A special thanks to the descendants of the Dry Creek and Green Meadow settlers who generously shared their ancestors' photos: Linda Bianchi, Vance Day, Rebecca Farley, Michael Harris, Sharon Ketchum, and Michele Randall.

Thank you also to the Developers of Hidden Springs for permitting part of this research to take place during the course of preserving the Farmstead; and to the Ada County Board of Commissioners who accepted the gift of the Farmstead and worked with the Dry Creek Historical Society in its management.

Table of Contents

Preface

The *Dry Creek Chronicles* arose in the process of documenting the historical significance of the National Register-listed Schick-Ostolasa Farmstead in the heart of the Dry Creek Valley of southwestern Idaho. Understanding the Farmstead's early history also meant telling the story of the other ranch families in the valley and those with whom they interacted in the nearby community of Green Meadow along the Boise River. While one community remained rural and the other gradually grew more urbanized, the two settlements were inextricably linked by marriage and by shared economic fortune and experience in similar agricultural environments.

Histories regularly recognize the major political and economic players in a community. Too often, they neglect to name the names of those who farmed the land and managed the forces of nature and economics on a daily basis to produce food for the community. These chronicles recognize the first farm families of Dry Creek and Green Meadow as they went about their daily lives in the late nineteenth century. Some few are well known, but most are not. Others have been missed by history and may be remembered, if at all, in the stories told by their descendents.

The Dry Creek and Green Meadow community histories are chronicled as they are known from the records of the U.S. Census Bureau, the U.S. General Land Office, Boise City and Ada County records, cemetery records, newspapers, and state and local histories. Family and individual photographs are from the Idaho State Historical Society archives, the Dry Creek Historical Society archives, state and local history books from the late nineteenth and early twentieth century, and those posted online by family members at genealogy websites. Undoubtedly more could be learned about each of the families through personal interviews with their descendents, but that is beyond the scope of this book.

The stories of the lives of the farm families in these two communities provide a personal insight into the nineteenth century settlement and development of Ada County at the edges of the growing towns of Boise City and Eagle. As the farm families labored to feed and educate themselves and others, they helped lay the agricultural groundwork for what would become the state of Idaho.

1 The Lay of the Land

Southwestern Idaho's Dry Creek Valley was a lush, thriving crossroads of farms, roads, and commerce in the late nineteenth century. It linked socially and economically to a similar agricultural settlement, known informally as Green Meadow, about three miles to the south near the Boise River. This is the story of the farming communities of the Dry Creek Valley and Green Meadow from their early settlement in the 1860s until the dawn of the twentieth century when the first homesteaders passed the land to a new generation. Although the two communities were similar in size and settlement early on, their paths diverged over the decades as the Green Meadow farms subdivided to become part of Boise City's residential settlement and Dry Creek remained a farming community with its 160-acre homesteads consolidating into ever-larger ranches.

Settlers arrived in this part of Idaho Territory from the California gold fields or by wagon train on the Overland Trail to take advantage of free land offered by the U.S. government, and to escape the aftermath of the Civil War. Clusters of homesteads grew up along the roads, creeks, and rivers—all bound by ties of kinship, economics, and geography. Families united in a network of agricultural production, transportation, marriage, family, and social ties settled the fertile mountain valleys, the dry foothills, and the floodplain of the Boise River, pioneering the use and governance of the land. They mined the creeks and hills, grew and harvested crops and livestock, cut and milled timber, developed transportation and irrigation systems, and built schools and churches to provide for the well being of themselves and their families.

Local commerce and settlement proceeded northwest from Boise City along the Valley Road, a segment of the Overland Trail (today's State Street), through the farms of Green Meadow and west to what would become the towns of Eagle, Star, and Middleton. The Hill Road, formed by Goodale's Cutoff of the Overland Trail,[1] took travelers from Boise City through Green Meadow and northwest to the mines of Willow Creek and then to Emmettsville and Payette. A cutoff led north to the Dry Creek Valley with an alternate road to Shafer Creek and the Boise Basin mines.

At its western edge, the Dry Creek Valley opened out onto the plain of the Boise River near the old road to Horseshoe Bend and today's Highway 55. To the east of the

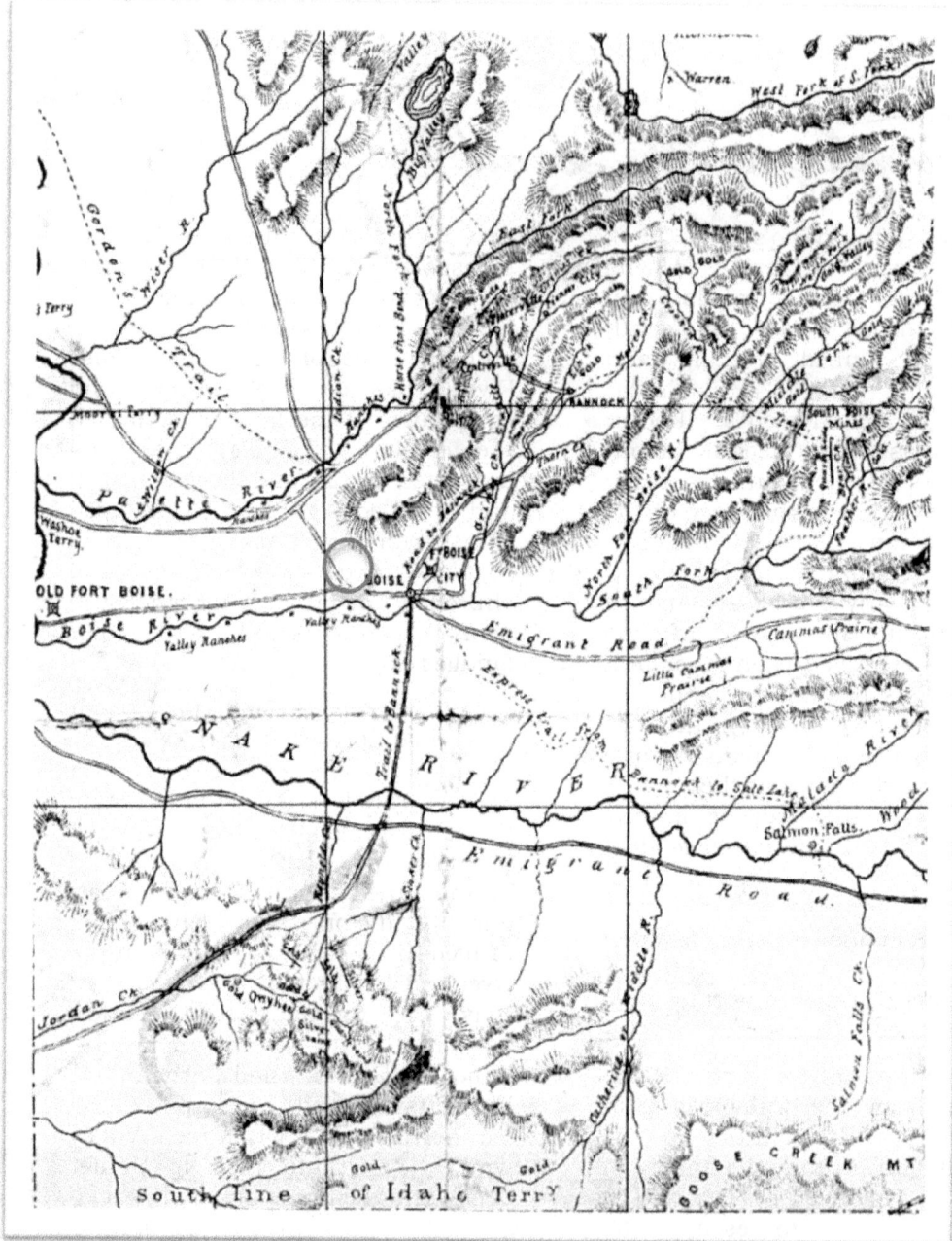

1864 map of southwestern Idaho showing the Dry Creek Valley/Green Meadow area (black circle).

highway were the farms of the upper Dry Creek Valley, extending into the foothills to Pierce Gulch. To the north, feeding into Dry Creek, were the homesteads of Spring Valley Creek, also known as Little Dry Creek. To the south of the Dry Creek Valley was Green Meadow, with its farms at the edge of the foothills between the Hill Road and the Boise River, connected to Dry Creek by old Horseshoe Bend Road and trails in Seaman Gulch and Pierce Gulch.

For this history, the area referred to as the Dry Creek Valley includes the valley itself and the surrounding foothills, as well as the open flats at the mouth of the valley as far south as the Dry Creek Canal. The Green Meadow community includes the farms between the foothills and the Boise River from Samuel Aiken's Green Meadow Ranch at the mouth of Pierce Gulch, northwestward to the farms flanking the old road to Horseshoe Bend, ending approximately at Edgewood Road in today's town of Eagle.

The Migration

In the two decades between 1840 and 1860, about 53,000 emigrants made their way west on the Overland Trail to Oregon in a journey that took about seven months. Few stopped in the seemingly inhospitable lands of southern Idaho, but many later backtracked to Idaho after spending time in Oregon or Washington. By the 1860s, Boise City was a hub of activity along the trail and along the roads to the Boise Basin mines in the mountains to the north.

Large wagon trains of settlers arrived from Missouri and Arkansas in 1863 fleeing the Civil War.[2] In the summer of 1864, the *Idaho Statesman* (August 2) reported that the streets of Boise City were crowded with emigrant wagons, farmers with loads of hay and other produce, long lines of ox teams loaded with lumber, and others with goods from Salt Lake City, Utah, and the Columbia River. Many of the emigrants set up tents at the edge of town while they checked out the opportunities in the area. The newspaper reported that they were less attracted by mining now than in the past, and more interested in homesteading.

Pack trains from Salt Lake City initially supplied the fledgling town of Boise City and other towns in Washington and Oregon. The *Statesman* (September 15, 1864) reported that a train of twenty-five four-mule wagons arrived in Boise City from Salt Lake, loaded with potatoes, barley, oats, butter, eggs, and 1,800 brooms. A large ox train of general merchandise would arrive soon. Flour, however, was very scarce in Idaho that year, and was sometimes stolen from pack trains, stores, or homes.

The need for a local source of food for Boise City and the nearby mines presented an opportunity for farmers working their newly acquired homestead land. Not only could they sell crops and meat to thousands of hungry miners and to the residents of Boise City, but also to the military at nearby Fort Boise.

The Mines

Gold discoveries in the Boise Basin,

northeast of the Dry Creek Valley, brought an influx of miners and others to the region from California and Oregon in a migration so massive that prices in The Dalles, Oregon, through which the migration passed, increased 400 percent from 1862 to 1863.[3] By 1863, Idaho City had more than 6,000 residents.[4] An extremely dry winter in northern California in 1864 resulted in thousands more miners heading for the Boise Basin. Five to six hundred miners arrived in the region each week.[5] By the end of 1863, the Boise Basin had a population of 16,000.

Miners from the Boise Basin naturally ventured south to explore the Dry Creek waterways for their mineral potential. However, they encountered very little placer gold on Dry Creek compared to the creeks in the Boise Basin. Eventually they worked some placer claims at the western end of the valley toward Willow Creek where the mining community of Pearl was later established.

In 1867, the proprietor of the Dry Creek stage station near the mouth of the valley found good quartz specimens from two substantial veins on Willow Creek.[6] One hundred feet on one of the veins sold for $400. After limited work at the Red Warrior claim in 1870, the Willow Creek area was quiet until the return of gold mining during the economic panic of 1893.[7]

The Lumber Mills

Sawmills constructed along the mountain creeks north of the Dry Creek Valley supplied the large quantities of lumber needed by the mines, farms, and towns. Some of the lumber used in the Dry Creek Valley, as well as in Boise City, came from Alexander Rossi's mill on Shafer Creek in Boise County, about twenty miles from Boise City. Rossi also owned a ranch in Dry Creek and sold lumber from there, among other locations.

The Shafer Creek Mill operated from 1869 to 1877 at its original location before it moved two miles upstream to follow the timber.[8] Three teams of oxen—with five yoke of oxen to a team—pulled timber down the mountainside to the mill. The owners quickly rebuilt the mill after it burned in 1881. This new steam mill had two rotary saws; a shingle saw edger; and a planer for cutting siding, matched lumber, and molding. It also produced picket fencing and a wide range of rough lumber—1.5 million board feet. Advertisements in the *Statesman* (1869, 1870) featured lumber for sale by Rossi and his partner A.H. Robie at their Dry Creek ranch. Lumber sold for $40 per 1,000 feet, and shingles for $9 per 1,000 shingles. Buyers could also haul their own lumber from the mill for a lower price. After Robie's death in 1878, Rossi partnered with William Ridenbaugh and continued his interest in the Shafer Creek Mill.[9]

Travel & Freight

The road from Walla Walla and Umatilla, Washington, to the Boise Basin mines followed the Payette River from the Snake River to Horseshoe Bend, then up Shafer Creek to Placerville. Cutoffs led to the Dry Creek Valley and Boise City.

Shafer Creek Mill, early 1880s (Elliott 1884).

Horse- and mule-drawn freight trains traveled the route to supply the mines and other locations along the way.

John Hailey, who later ranched in Green Meadow, ran a saddle train from Walla Walla to Boise City in 1863. That winter his train of thirty mules and thirty packhorses made a hazardous trip across the Blue Mountains carrying supplies to Idaho. Despite the difficulties, Hailey made about $2,000 on the trip.[10] As more freighters, including some who lived in the Dry Creek Valley, began making similar trips, the cost of shipping goods dropped from ten to twelve cents a pound, initially, to six to eight cents a pound in 1864.[11]

Stage lines quickly replaced saddle trains as soon as wagon roads cut across the landscape. Stage operations relied on mail contracts and passengers to pay the bills. Hailey's operation began carrying the mail from Boise to Oregon and Washington in 1866. In 1868, his stage line made three trips a day between Boise City and Oregon, often with thousands of dollars in gold from the Idaho mines.[12] Hailey ran multiple successful stage operations over the years, notably selling his Ogden-to-The Dalles route in 1870 for $130,000.[13] Although the stage line was eventually abandoned, the route remained an active freight line between Utah and Oregon.

Generally, the stages made three trips a week, passing through eastern Idaho, the Snake River Valley and Boise City, and then heading west to the Columbia River. There were more than a dozen passenger coaches pulled by four to six horses each. Summer fare was $40 and winter $60, with an extra charge for baggage that weighed more than twenty-five pounds.[14] Roadhouses served travelers in 1863 at Horseshoe Bend, Shafer, and at the mouth of the Dry Creek Valley, among other locations. These stops generally offered plain fare consisting of bread and bacon or other cheap meat with coffee, for a dollar.[15]

Today's north / south road to Horseshoe Bend may not have been a major route of travel during the nineteenth century. Maps from the 1860s through the 1890s show roads leading north to Horseshoe Bend via Cartwright Road and from the mouth of the Dry Creek Valley northwest across the foothills to Willow Creek and the Payette River. In 1868, the Boise City-to-Payette road crossed the Dry Creek Valley near the mouth of Goose Creek and continued northwest into the foothills.

Rossi and Robie completed a toll road to the Shafer Creek Mill in 1869. The road came up through Raymond and Stewart Gulches and over the divide into the Dry Creek drainage where it ran for more than four miles to the mill. One branch of the road led up what was later Cartwright Road, and the other went from the Robie/Rossi ranch in Dry Creek north through the foothills. Rossi finished the toll road as far as the Hawkins Toll Road (later Harris Creek Road) and operated it until July of 1880. Thomas Healy, who came to Boise in 1879 after the mines at Atlanta closed, purchased the Rossi toll road and sawmill in the 1880s and ran the operation until 1909.[16]

Before 1881, most roads in Idaho Territory were toll roads. In 1881, a legislative act forbade the granting of any new toll road franchises and designated all roads as county (free) roads. With the change in law in 1881, Healy received a license from the Ada County Commissioners to maintain the existing toll road from Dry Creek crossing to the mill at Shafer Creek. The toll road became a county road in 1913 after five years of public use.

Waist-High Grasses & Fertile Bottomlands

The Dry Creek Valley extends in an arc from a narrow defile in the foothills near Daniels Creek, northward and westward for about six miles to where it opens onto the floodplain of the Boise River. Dry Creek drains the Boise foothills from its headwaters in Boise County near Bogus Basin to the Boise River near the town of Eagle. Shingle Creek, Daniels Creek, Currant Creek, McFarland Creek, and Spring Valley Creek feed it on the north.

In the 1870s, Dry Creek reportedly ran fifteen to twenty inches of water during the dry season from springs scattered throughout the area, and two to three times that amount of water in the spring season according to the *Statesman* (September 1873). The newspaper reported that the creek was so high in 1865 that the mail wagon driver had to swim his horses across it first and then haul the wagon over with a rope line.

The Dry Creek Valley offered a lush opportunity for farming. A U.S. government surveyor described the valley bottom soil as "first rate" in the spring of 1868, while the surrounding foothills were "covered with good grass" but considered "unfit for settlement and cultivation."[17] The *Statesman* noted that the eastern valley was nearly a mile wide at its widest point, with rich black soil several feet deep. Oral tradition in the Yaryan family, whose ancestor Phillip L. Schick settled in the valley in 1863, tells of Schick finding the valley when a team of oxen escaped from him on the road to Boise City. Schick tracked the oxen to a fertile valley of waist-high grasses as far as the eye could see.[18]

Folks came out to the valley from Boise City to camp, hunt, and fish for trout. Boise City pioneer Henry C. Riggs introduced quail into Dry Creek in the spring of 1871. The quail arrived in four crates ordered from Independence, Missouri, and shipped on the stage from Kelton, Utah, at a cost of more than $100. Thirty-six quail were released in the valley that year, and more in succeeding years, including a shipment from California.[19]

Meanwhile, just over the foothills south of Dry Creek, on the rich soils of the Boise River floodplain between the river and the foothills, the farms

Henry C. Riggs
(Hawley 1920 Vol II).

of Green Meadow lay on the bottomland north of the river where water rose to just below the surface. These fertile, and sometimes boggy, fields were cultivated early on in tandem with the Dry Creek bottomlands. When the floodplain land was taken, hopeful farmers laid claim to the nearby sagebrush-covered plain, between the Valley Road and the Hill Road, and gradually changed the desert to farmland.

The Farms & Ranches

Homesteaders claimed the fertile bottomlands of the Boise River Valley and its tributaries, like Dry Creek, beginning in the early 1860s. For the rest of the century, the rich soil of the valley farms produced food and livestock for miners, the military, and residents of newly-platted Boise City. Enthusiasm for food production was in the air during the early days. Newspapers urged homesteaders to plant fruit trees instead of shade or ornamental trees. Farmers were encouraged to try to double their crop production each year and to send to Portland, Oregon, for the latest in mowers and reapers to cultivate more land.

The bleak winter of 1864/1865, with its heavy snow and cold, only briefly dampened the excitement. Although large numbers of livestock died and beef was not available on the local market for a time,[20] farmers and ranchers had recovered by the end of 1865 and agriculture boomed once again. John Hailey, in his history of Idaho, described the life of area farmers in the 1860s:

> The farmers had a hard time for some years, building houses, fencing their fields, making stables, corrals, sheds, etc., and grubbing out sage brush and plowing the land. The most of the seed for the new land was packed or hauled from eastern Oregon, which made it very expensive. It was very expensive getting water and building ditches. The crops were light, and last, but not least of the annoyances to the farmers, were the grasshoppers, which would come and sweep the fields clean after all the farmers' hard work. But the farmers persevered, and in a few years had very comfortable homes.[21]

The 1860s represented change in agriculture throughout the U.S. as farmers shifted from the use of hand power to horses for plowing, planting, and harvesting. Gang plows, sulky plows, and spring-tooth harrows for seedbed preparation increased field production. The latest in new technology, the Wilson Gangplow, came to Boise in 1867. A *Statesman* review (March 2, 1867) described the gangplow's three twelve-inch plows combined on a single frame to increase field efficiency.

Along with their use of the latest technology, local farmers often worked together for the common good to solve problems, to address the needs of the agriculture community, and to celebrate their successes. In 1866, the Idaho Territorial Legislature established the first local agricultural society with membership fees of $5 per person.[22] A second agricultural society incorporated in 1869. This time, incorporators included two active and successful farmers from the Green Meadow area, Samuel Aiken and Seth Bixby, among others. Ada County tasked the society with purchasing forty acres for a county fairground, and the first agricultural fair took place in the fall of 1869.[23]

The number of farms in the Boise area increased considerably from 1867 to 1870, but the demand for farm goods began to drop in the late 1870s. Most of the easily accessible gold was gone from the Boise Basin placer mines, and merchants closed up shop to head for the next potentially lucrative location. With fewer miners to feed, agricultural prices dropped. However, farmers still had to pay high costs for their own necessities including farm implements. Fruit and livestock growing, however, continued to provide a good income. As Hailey observed:

Under this state of affairs, upon the whole, the farmers could not, as a rule, be considered prosperous during these four years. A few of them, who had set out fruit trees early, began to get considerable fruit, which commanded a very good price. Stock raising, cattle and horses increased to a considerable extent in these four years, and the market price for beef, horses, and mules kept up at good figures.[24]

During the early 1870s, farmers throughout the U.S. began to explore the benefit of forming associations to address transportation needs, middleman profiteers, and other agriculture-related issues. Locally, the *Statesman* (September 7, 1872) reported on a newly formed Farmer's Club that included Dry Creek and Green Meadow farmers Aiken, A.J. (Jack) Wyatt, and William Gainey, among others. The clubs eventually became Idaho Territory Subordinate Granges, including the Dry Creek Grange.[25]

Acquiring the Land

Transfer of land from the U.S. government to private citizens in the American West took place under the authority of several nineteenth century land laws intended to encourage easterners to move west. The U.S. General Land Office (GLO) issued title patents[1] to settlers proving their ownership of the lands. Some settlers bought their land for cash, while others

---

[1] *A land patent issued by the U.S. government established title to the land for the patent holder.*

homesteaded the land or obtained it through other acts of Congress.

The claimants filled out entry forms to select the land and then paid the filing fees or fees for the claim itself. The local land office sent the paperwork to Washington D.C. where the land patent (certificate of ownership) was confirmed. Because of the extensive acreage sold in the late 1800s, the GLO had a paperwork backlog so large that several years often passed between the time a settler purchased land from a local land office and the time the patent was signed in Washington D.C.

The Land Act of 1820 permitted cash purchase of public land for $1.25 an acre with a down payment of $100 for eighty acres of land. Fourteen of the thirty-three ranches in the Dry Creek area, and twelve of the twenty-three Green Meadow ranches were originally cash purchases under this act.

The Scrip Warrant Act of 1855 authorized the U.S. government to issue scrip as payment for military or other services. Scrip could be used to purchase federal land. One 160-acre ranch on Dry Creek was purchased under this act in 1875.

The Homestead Act of 1862 permitted settlement of up to 160 acres of public land if the settlers lived on it for five years and grew crops or made improvements. The land was free except for a $15 filing fee, and homesteading was open to men twenty-one years of age or older who were U.S. citizens or planned to become citizens. Women over age twenty-one who were heads of households (single women, widows, or those with disabled husbands) were also eligible to receive homestead patents. Families and individuals settled seventeen of the thirty-three ranches in the Dry Creek area under this Act. Ten of the first Green Meadow ranches were homesteaded.

The Timber Culture Act of 1873 allowed citizens to acquire up to 160 acres of land if they planted trees on twenty-five percent of the acreage. Residence on the land was not required. One 80-acre property in the Green Meadow area was purchased in this way in 1892.

The Desert Land Act of 1877 encouraged the economic development of arid public lands. This Act offered 640 acres of land to a married couple for $1.25 per acre and the promise that they would irrigate it within three years. A single man could receive half that amount of acreage. One 240-acre property on the plain between the Dry Creek Valley and Green Meadow was purchased under this Act in 1894, evidently planning to receive irrigation from the Farmer's Union Canal about a mile to the south.

The 1866 Mining Act also affected land use in the Dry Creek Valley by declaring all public mineral lands free and open to exploration and settlement. Miners could file a claim on a mineral vein or lode for $5 an acre. Further, the Placer Mining Act of 1870 permitted the sale of placer mining lands for $2.50 an acre.

Folks began filing land claims in the eastern Dry Creek Valley as early as 1863. Homestead records and deeds document eight land claims in the Dry Creek Valley by 1864. All the early claims were on the fertile valley floor along the creek. Most changed hands very quickly in a complicated series of moneymaking schemes, in much the same way as mining claims were bought and sold. Eventually folks who actually intended to farm the land acquired the claims.

Acquiring the Water

Farmers in southwestern Idaho learned quickly that successful crop production on high desert lands required applications of irrigation water to supplement the limited rainfall in the region. Farmers first diverted irrigation water from the Boise River in 1864.

The New Union Ditch Company Canal irrigated farms in the Green Meadow area beginning in the spring of 1865.[26] Green Meadow landowners Seth Bixby, John Carpenter, and John Patterson led construction of the ditch that ran through their farms along the Valley Road. Irrigators enlarged the ditch in 1866 and it remained about same size for more than 100 years. Nearby, the Farmer's Union Ditch Company began building a diversion in 1894. They completed twenty-four miles of ditch along the Hill Road through Green Meadow to the Eagle area by 1899.

Well water was plentiful and accessible in the Dry Creek Valley, with its high water table and multitude of springs. Several settlers in the eastern valley found artesian wells or warm springs on their properties. P.L. Schick acquired the first right to divert water from Dry Creek in 1868. The Schick Water

Right consisted of 2.8 cubic feet per second (cfs) for 140 acres, at two diversion points on both sides of the creek.[27] In the early years, rock and brush diversion structures on the creek required rebuilding every year.

Major irrigation works in the lower Dry Creek drainage were built by the Dry Creek Ditch Company, which began construction of a canal on lower Dry Creek in 1879. By 1900, the thirteen-mile-long canal irrigated about 3,000 acres of land in lower Dry Creek,[28] but did not reach the upper Dry Creek Valley.

The People

The men in Dry Creek and Green Meadow were most often farmers or miners in their thirties when they arrived in Idaho. Some came from the gold fields of California and Colorado, while others brought their families west on the Overland Trail to Oregon, Washington, or Utah. In some cases, they had children or spouses who died along the trail. Many single men married the daughters of families they met on the trail or in Oregon. Others married in Idaho or returned to their home state for a bride.

Most of the landowners were born in the southern and eastern U.S. or in northern Europe. Southerners arrived in large numbers during and after the Civil War, resulting in a political majority of so-called 'Secessionist' Democrats in southwestern Idaho. However, Democrats and Republicans settled Dry Creek and Green Meadow in about equal numbers. Later elections, in which votes were approximately evenly split between the two parties, reflect these numbers.

The majority of landowners of European descent were born in Ireland and arrived in the area in the 1860s. A few were German, English, Swiss, Welsh, Danish, and French. Among the service workers and laborers in the area were a few Chinese and French cooks, and Mexican and Spanish farm laborers.

Dry Creek & Green Meadow Landowners Born Outside the U.S.

Landowner, 1860s	Born in	Landowner, 1870s	Born in
Robert C. Aiken	Canada	Jacob Bash	Germany
Samuel D. Aiken	Canada	John W. Case	Canada
John Atwell	Ireland	William Daniel	England
Patrick Ayers	Ireland	Thomas Healy	Canada
Mary M. Carpenter	England	Jacob & Anna Jensen	Denmark
Robert M. Crawford	Ireland	Eliz. Stewart	Ireland
Felix Johnson	Ireland		
		Landowner, 1880s	
Thomas H. Kingsbury	Ireland	John W. Case	Canada
Patrick McFarland	Ireland	Christopher H. Frank	Germany
Patrick McFarland	Ireland	William M. Jones	Wales
Henry & Regina Miller	Switz.	John Lemp	Germany
Phillip Paul	Germany	Joseph C. McIntyre	Canada
Barrett & Eliz. Williams	Wales	Levi S. Smith	Canada
		Landowner, 1890s	
		Lydia Clark	Canada
Source: U.S. Census 1870-1900.		Joseph & Jeanne Jullion	France

Dry Creek & Green Meadow Landowners Born in the Southern U.S.

Landowner, 1860s	Born in	Landowner, 1870s	Born in
John Blagg	North Carolina	Robert T. Barnes	Missouri
William H. Casner	Virginia	Thomas H.B. Breshears	Missouri
Henry B. Conway	Missouri	William & Bradford Hurt	Virginia
Reuben Cox	Tennessee	Thomas Morrison	North Carolina
William B. Dobson	Tennessee	William H. Smith	Virginia
William H. Gainey	Kentucky		
		Landowner, 1880s	
John M. Glenn	Tennessee	James C. Corder	Missouri
John M. Hailey	Tennessee	William T. Daly	Missouri
Charles Hurt	Virginia	Benton Garrett	Kentucky
John Keller	Virginia	Charles T. Glenn	Indiana
Richard S. Lipscomb	Kentucky	John H. Hall	Arkansas
Jacob Motto	Virginia	Gardner P. Harvey	Kentucky
John B. Pierce	Kentucky	Elizabeth McGinnis	Kentucky
William A. Rash	Alabama	John B. Pierce	Kentucky
Levi Read	Tennessee	John B. Wood	Tennessee
Andrew Rutledge	Tennessee		
		Landowner, 1890s	
T. Hugh Rutledge	Alabama	Mathew E. Duncan	Arkansas
Elizabeth Shubert	Missouri	William Goodall	Missouri
Taswell G. Wright	Alabama	William M. Huckba	Missouri
		Newton A. Morgan	Missouri
		David S. Potter	Missouri
		Samuel W. Swan	Kentucky
Source: U.S. Census 1870-1900.		William M. Huckba	Missouri

Dry Creek & Green Meadow Landowners Born in the Northern U.S.

Landowner, 1860s	Born in	Landowner, 1880s	Born in
James C. Baldwin	New Jersey	Martin S. Cobb	Indiana
George H. Banker	New York	William P. Coppock	Ohio
Seth Bixby	New York	Harmon Cox	Iowa
Peter E. Brown	Michigan	Henry Dickman	Ohio
Theodore Burmester	Ohio	Andrew J. Fessenden	Illinois
John Carpenter	New York	George B. Fisher	Ohio
David Clemmens	Indiana	George W. Fry	Iowa
Jacob Diehl	Penn.	John S. & Adrian J. Gary	Indiana
William B. Francis	Ohio	Ansel L. Goure	Wisconsin
David E. Heron	Penn.	William B. Hammer	Penn.
Neri Jack	Iowa	Thomas A. Mann	Rhode Isl.
John E. Miller	Iowa	William J. Marlatt	Illinois
John Patterson	Ohio	James J. Pettigrew	New York
Godfrey F. Rhodes	Ohio	Hiram G. Saxton	New York
Albert H. Robie	New York	Charles C. Smith	Iowa
George Rockhill	Ohio	Charles A. Stanton	Michigan
Phillip L. Schick	New York	John V. Wilson	Indiana
Edward J. Smith	Iowa		
		Landowner, 1890s	
Anneas J. Wyatt	Illinois	Martin M. Burd	Penn.
Andrew H. Wiley	Ohio	Charles B. Frank	Penn.
George W. Williams	Indiana	Samuel P. Glenn	Michigan
		Alphonse J. Lambrigger	Illinois
Landowner, 1870s			
John Robert Carpenter	New York	Edward K. Lewis	Illinois
John A. Owings	Indiana	Alexander Mencer	Penn.
Elizabeth Shoffner	Ohio	George Nibler	Minnesota
James M. Stewart	Ohio	James J. Rodgers	Illinois
Halley Vincen	Illinois	Forrest W. See	Wisconsin
		Samuel W. Stillwell	Kansas

Source: U.S. Census 1870-1900.

Endnotes

1 Bureau of Land Management (BLM), *Emigrant Trails of Southern Idaho*, Idaho Cultural Resource Series Number 1 (Boise: BLM Idaho State Office), 63.
2 William J. McConnell, *Early History of Idaho* (Caldwell: Idaho State Legislature, 1913), 189.
3 Eugene B. Chaffee, "Early History of the Boise Region 1811-1864" (M.A. Thesis, University of California, 1927), 57.
4 Carlos A. Schwantes, *In Mountain Shadows: A History of Idaho* (Lincoln: University of Nebraska Press, 1996), 52.
5 Idaho State Historical Society (ISHS), "Placer Mining in Southern Idaho, 1862-1864" (Reference Series Number 166, 1980).
6 ISHS, "Placer Mining in Southern Idaho."
7 Ibid.
8 Wallace W. Elliott, *History of Idaho Territory* (San Francisco: Wallace W. Elliott & Co., 1884), 192.
9 ISHS, "Alexander Rossi" (Reference Series Number 597, 1981).
10 *Illustrated History of the State of Idaho* (Chicago: The Lewis Publishing Company, 1899), 32.
11 Hiram T. French, *History of Idaho. A Narrative Account of Its People and Its Principal Interests, Volume I* (Chicago: The Lewis Publishing Company, 1914), 406.
12 Oregon Historical Society, "News Article, State Robbery," (The Oregon History Project, 2012). www.ohs.org/education/oregonhistory/historical_records
13 *Illustrated History of the State of Idaho*, 32.
14 Ibid.
15 McConnell, *Early History of Idaho*, 188-189.
16 James H. Hawley, *History of Idaho Volumes II & III* (Chicago: S.J. Clarke Publishing Company, 1920).
17 U.S. Geological Survey, *Surveyor's Field Notes* T5N, R2E (March 1868), 526.
18 Del Yaryan, Personal recollection of Del Yaryan told to Claudia Druss (2009).
19 S.J. Clarke Publishing Co., *Idaho Deluxe Supplement*, "Hon. Henry Chiles Riggs" (Chicago, 1920), 289.
20 Annie Laurie Bird, *Boise, the Peace Valley.* Canyon County Historical Society (Caldwell, Idaho: Caxton Printers, Ltd., 1975), 214.
21 John Hailey, *The History of Idaho* (Boise: Syms-York Company, Inc., 1910), 140.
22 Hawley, *History of Idaho Volume I*, 470.
23 Ibid.
24 Hailey, *History of Idaho, 143.*
25 Ezra S. Carr, *The Patrons of Husbandry on the Pacific Coast* (San Francisco: A.L. Bancroft and Company, 1875), 289.
26 ISHS, "New Dry Creek Ditch Company," Reference Series Number 529 (1974).
27 Idaho Department of Water Resources (IDWR), Adjudication Claim Report 63-383 (2004).
28 ISHS, "New Dry Creek Ditch Company."

2 Bottomlands: Dry Creek 1860s

The arrival of miners in southwestern Idaho raised local prices for hay and provisions, opening a profitable market for Dry Creek and Green Meadow farmers and ranchers. Homesteaders claimed the fertile bottomlands of the Boise River Valley and its tributaries, such as Dry Creek, beginning in the early 1860s. For the rest of the century, the rich soil of the valley farms produced food and livestock for miners, the military, and residents of Boise City.

Settlers first claimed land in the Dry Creek Valley around 1863 when about twenty householders established themselves. Among the first Ada County homesteaders to receive patents on their land were Dry Creek settlers John M. Glenn, Thomas Kingsbury, and Phillip L. Schick.

The name "Dry Creek" appeared in the local press at least as early as 1865 and probably earlier. Commissioners divided newly created Ada County into ten precincts including the Dry Creek Precinct. The first election judges in the new precinct were E.R. Stephens, S.B. Reed and a Mr. Parker—none of whom figured in the homesteading of Dry Creek. That same year, settlers laid out Dry Creek Cemetery in the foothills between the Dry Creek Valley and what became known as the Green Meadow community.

Roads and trails entered the valley from Boise City and points south via Stewart Gulch, Pierce Gulch, Seaman Gulch, the Hill Road, and the Valley Road, all converging on Dry Creek Road and the routes north to Shafer Creek and the Boise Basin mines. As more settlers moved into the area, their cooperative efforts improved the local transportation routes that served as economic lifelines.

Residents planned to improve the road connecting Boise City and the Payette River where it crossed Dry Creek as early as 1865. The *Idaho Statesman* (October 5, 1865) reported that this route was four miles shorter than other local routes between Boise City and the Payette area. Early the next year, a newspaper notice (January 3, 1866) also described a new toll road constructed through the Dry Creek Valley to the Shafer Creek Mill.

Although the Boise Valley was rapidly filling with white settlers, native people still had a presence in the area in the 1860s. The Northern Paiute people made inroads into what had been Shoshone territory in the Boise River Valley during this decade. Prominent among them was a leader, known to the white settlers as Howluck, whose band ranged from southwestern Idaho to central Oregon. He was a tall man who reportedly had very large feet and was called "Bigfoot" by white settlers in the region.

Howluck, like many native people, opposed the influx of miners into native-held lands.[1] When U.S. Army General George Crook took over military operations in the Snake War late in 1866, he fought Howluck in his first battle on the Owyhee River, where Howluck was rumored to have died. However, he survived and was captured with his band in eastern Oregon in 1868 by the U.S. Army and a party of Willow Creek miners. After attending talks at Camp Warner in 1869, Howluck's band was settled on an Oregon reservation.

In a later "Bigfoot" story printed in the *Statesman* in 1878, Howluck was said to be a part-Cherokee desperado from Oklahoma who stole horses and robbed stages in Idaho and Oregon. This legend eventually appeared in Elliott's 1884 *History of Idaho Territory.*[2]

Dry Creek Valley oral tradition had it that Howluck and his men passed through the valley in the late 1860s when homesteader P.L. Schick was working to raise the main support beam for the roof of his large barn. The Indians stopped to help him and Howluck was able to single-handedly raise the crossbeam into place, much to Schick's gratitude.[3] Local oral tradition also reported a large Indian encampment at the

mouth of the Dry Creek Valley as late as the early 1880s.[4]

The U.S. General Land Office (GLO) conducted its first official survey of the Dry Creek Valley in the spring of 1868. Peter W. Bell surveyed the western end of the valley where most of the homestead claims were at the time. The survey extended about as far up the valley as the Schick homestead. John Owens and A.B. Plume were chainmen and Patrick McFarland was the axeman assisting the surveyor. McFarland later homesteaded in the valley.

Early in the settlement era, men speculated on land claims in the valley before moving on to other locations and pursuits. From 1865 to 1868, a number of names appeared briefly in land records as the claims changed hands quickly. Eventually, though, men who had been farmers before coming to Idaho put their talents to use growing crops and livestock on the homestead claims. Landholders either purchased their farms outright or gradually improved the land claim as a homestead.

Land acquisition in the Dry Creek Valley was about evenly divided between cash sales under the 1820 Land Act and homestead claims under the 1862 Homestead Act, with a few parcels acquired under other land acts. The 1870 U.S. Census referred to the occupation of the landowners as "Farmer" compared to "Farmworker" for non-landowners. Also living in the valley were freighters or teamsters who moved lumber and supplies along the Kelton Road, and to and from the Boise Basin. Near the western end of the valley, where it opened out onto the plain of the Boise River, was a stage station along the Boise-to-Payette road where stage drivers and livestock tenders lived.

The Landowners

Most households in the Dry Creek Valley consisted of a farmer / landowner and his family,

sometimes with farmworkers boarding in the same household. GLO records, U.S. Census records, local histories, and cemetery records document some of the stories of the homesteaders who arrived in the valley in the 1860s. Undoubtedly, however, some have been missed by history and may be known only to their descendents or to those who

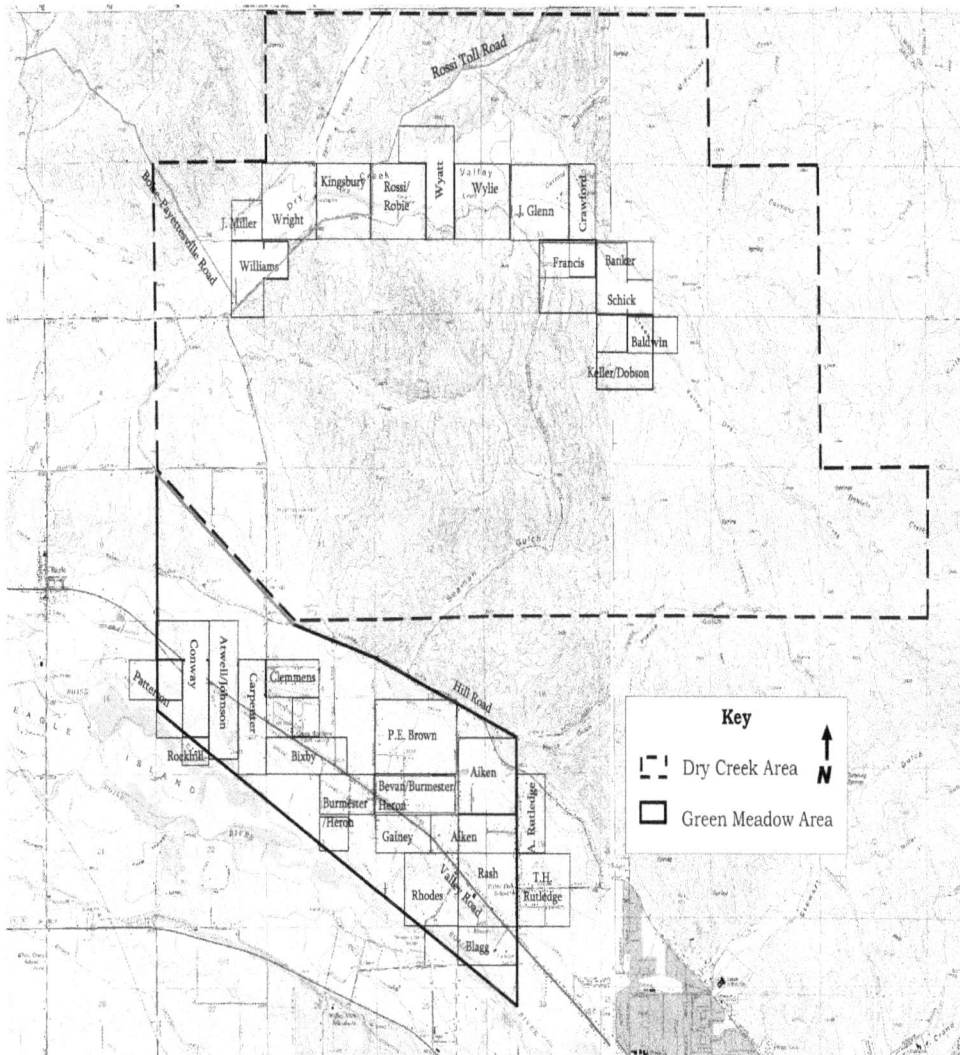

Dry Creek and Green Meadow homesteads, 1860s. *Sources: GLO Land Patent Records & Ada County Records.*

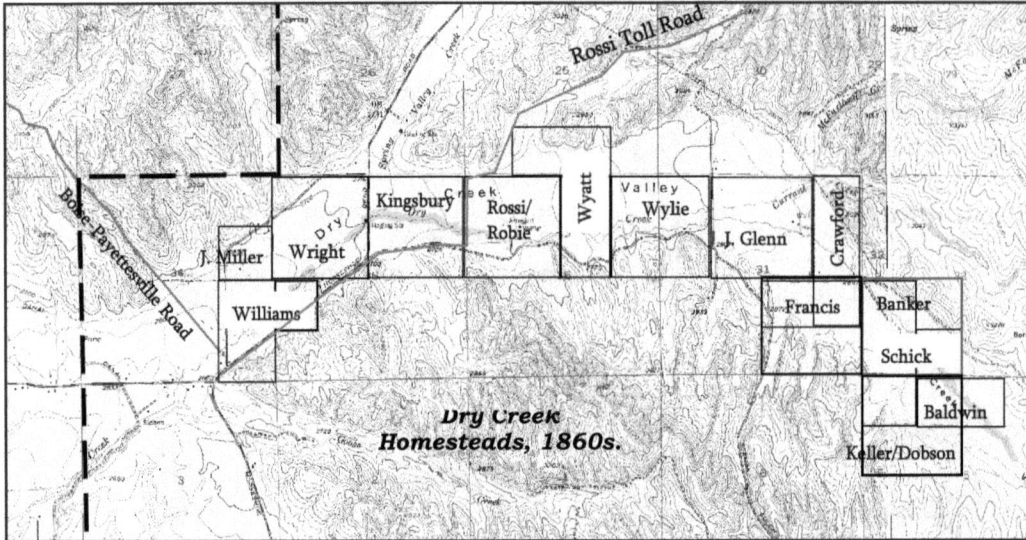

Dry Creek Homesteads, 1860s.

lived and worked beside them during that era. The families described here represent settlement from west to east up the Dry Creek Valley.

C. Elizabeth L. Alexander Shubert Freeman

In 1870, Elizabeth Shubert, formerly Elizabeth Alexander, was the housekeeper at the stage station near the mouth of Dry Creek. Born in Missouri around 1827, she married Albert Alexander at the age of twelve. Elizabeth was illiterate and the spelling of the name Shubert appears in various records as "Subart" and "Streetart." The Alexanders had seven children who survived to adulthood. Elizabeth's first son, Gabriel, was born when she was thirteen. After him were Minerva, Newton, Mary F. (Fannie), Reuben, and Elizabeth (Betty). Gabriel stayed in Missouri and may have died in the Civil War. Albert also may have died in the 1860s.

Elizabeth married Henry H. Shubert in Missouri in 1869. By 1870, she and her two younger daughters lived in Idaho without Shubert. She kept house at the stage station with Betty (age fourteen) and Fannie (age eighteen). At the time, Shubert's real estate was valued at $300.

Elizabeth married her third husband, Horace M. Freeman, at Boise City in 1871. She died in the Hull's Gulch area near Boise City in the spring of 1877 at the age of fifty and was buried in Pioneer Cemetery.

Taswell G. & Serafina Greer Wright

Alabama farmer Taswell Wright settled on a small farm in the western Dry Creek area. Serafina, born in Virginia, married Taswell in Missouri in 1852. They followed the gold rush to California where their first child, Emma, was born in 1857. By 1861, they lived in Oregon,

18

where Cornelia and Theodocia were born. The Wrights moved to Idaho sometime in the mid-1860s.

In 1870, Wright owned 160 Dry Creek acres valued at $500— suggesting he had one of the smaller farms in the area. His 100 acres of improved farmland produced 500 bushels of spring wheat, twenty-five bushels of oats, twenty-five bushels of barley, and ten tons of hay. Livestock consisted of two horses and two milk cows.[5] Also boarding at the Wright farm was a young farm worker, William G. Grow and a miner, William Cole.

Serafina died in 1868 at the age of thirty-eight, leaving Taswell to raise three young daughters. A Chinese man, Sam Hop, cooked for the family after she died. Wright and his children remained in Idaho for only a few years after Serafina died. They returned to California by the mid-1870s. Wright died in Arizona in 1899.

Barrett & Elizabeth Griffith Williams

At the mouth of the Dry Creek Valley, where it opened onto the broad plain of the Boise River, was the homestead of the venerable 'Uncle' Barrett Williams. In the 1860s, his place was called Gulch Ranch. Barrett Williams was born in 1803 in Wales. In 1840, he married Elizabeth Ann Griffith, born in 1812 in Wales. They were the elders among the first homesteaders in the Dry Creek Valley.

Barrett trained as a saddler in Wales, and learned to read and write at Sunday school.[6] The Williams family immigrated from Wales in

1841 and settled in New York according to the *Statesman* (December 24, 1899). Later they moved to Ohio and then to Wisconsin where Barrett farmed and earned a living as a merchant.[7] Along the way, Barrett and Elizabeth had eight children: John Barrett, Margaret, Thomas Barrett, Martha, Richard, Henry Barrett, Elizabeth Ann, and William O. The eldest was born in Wales; the others were born in the midwestern U.S. in the 1840s and 1850s before the family moved to Idaho.

Barrett and his sons Thomas and Richard headed west to Oregon on the Overland Trail with an ox team and wagon in 1861.[8] The next year, the Williams family backtracked to Idaho Territory and the gold fields of the Boise Basin. Barrett eventually found gold on Willow Creek to the west of Dry Creek. Throughout the 1860s, Barrett Williams & Co. worked placer claims on the creek, making a "clean up" of forty ounces of clean gold dust after a week's run in 1870 according to the *Statesman* (March 10, 1870).

Williams took to farming in the mid 1860s when "the rheumatism" set in.[9] He homesteaded 160 acres, maintained a stage stop along the Boise to Payette Road where it crossed his land, and raised crops and livestock for ten years. Like many local farmers, he also raced horses. In 1865, the *Statesman* (October 10) reported that his horse, Black Hawk, won at the races.

Barrett Williams gained respect in the local community early on and was elected Justice of the Peace for the Dry Creek Precinct in 1866 according to the *Statesman* (August 28, 1866). The first Ada County election in the Dry Creek Precinct was held at the Williams home at Gulch Ranch in 1865.

In 1870, the U.S. Census reported that five of the Williams' adult children lived with them at the ranch. That year, their sixteen-year-old daughter Elizabeth married an English brick mason, Charles May, who was twenty-one years her senior. All of the Williams children lived relatively long lives, surviving into the twentieth century, although none of them established farms in the Dry Creek Valley after they left home.

Along with the Williams family, five farm workers and their families lived at the ranch in 1870: Reuben L. and Martha Brown and their children Thomas and Elizabeth, James Chism, George Deitz, Thomas Wilson, and George Nightingale.

The U.S. Census Agricultural

Schedule for 1870 valued Williams' farm at $700. He had nine horses, one mule, five milk cows, six oxen, and forty cattle. The farm produced 110 bushels of spring wheat, fifty bushels of oats, 130 bushels of potatoes, and 200 pounds of butter. Williams completed the cash purchase of his Dry Creek ranch in 1872 and shortly thereafter sold it to Green Meadow pioneer David Clemmens.

In 1873, at the age of seventy, Uncle Barrett moved to Boise City and established a third career in lumber and real estate.[10] He purchased a block on Jefferson Street where he built and sold ten houses. Williams also had a lumber business for a number of years, constructing two sawmills that he later passed on to his sons.[11]

The records of Williams' lumber business in the 1870s not only document his business transactions, but also offer insight into his personality.[12] Williams'

Elizabeth Williams
(Idaho State Historical Society #3783).

Barrett Williams
(French 1914 Vol II).

handwriting was dramatic and ornate—in one accounting ledger, he practiced his signature, with its large, flowing capitals, several times on the front page. Although his handwriting was beautiful, his spelling was questionable. In an early ledger, his lists of supplies frequently included "batatoes," "flower," and "benes" as well as other staples like coffee, sugar, beef, pork, and butter. His customers' names, too, were frequently misspelled.

Williams sold lumber to a number of Dry Creek and Green Meadow residents over the years, including Albert H. Robie, Thomas Healy, Anneas J. Wyatt, David Heron, James Baldwin, David Clemmens, William Dobson, Samuel and Robert Aiken, Thomas Kingsbury, John Patterson, Godfrey Rhodes, and Seth Bixby. Folks sometimes traded goods or services to him for their lumber. One year, Kingsbury traded threshing services for lumber, and farmhand Jacob Drake worked for Williams for nineteen days in return for meals, tobacco, cash, and wooden shingles.[13]

'Uncle' Barrett retired in 1880 at Boise City. He was a member of Custer Encampment No. 6, Pioneers of the Pacific and a lifelong Democrat. In 1897, Williams and another man led a parade of more than 130 of the area's earliest settlers through downtown Boise City.

John E. & Julia A. Miller

John Miller made shingles in Iowa before moving west in the 1860s. He was born in Pennsylvania in 1820 and Julia in Ohio in 1822. John could not read or write. After the Civil War, the Millers headed west to Oregon from Iowa, eventually backtracking to Idaho. Their daughter Mary Ellen remained in the Midwest with her ten children until the early 1880s when her family also moved to Oregon.

The Millers settled on land at the mouth of Dry Creek north of the Williams place. The 1870 U.S. Census listed their property value as $700. John also farmed land worth $300 in the Green Meadow area while Julia remained at the ranch in Dry Creek. Twenty-two-year-old Mary Scheper, with her two young sons Samuel and George, kept house for John in 1870. Meanwhile, in Dry Creek, Julia's small operation had a horse, two mules, two milk cows, and produced 200 bushels of spring wheat according to the U.S. Census Agricultural Schedule.

The *Statesman* (July 10, 1892) reported that Julia died at Dry Creek from spotted fever. Ten years later (April 12, 1902), the newspaper noted that the Miller property in eastern Dry Creek sold to William T. Daly for $50. John died in 1904 and was buried in Dry Creek Cemetery.

Thomas H. & Elizabeth Wells Kingsbury

Prosperous farmer and freighter Thomas Kingsbury was born about 1831 in Ireland. He and Elizabeth married in Indiana in 1850 and had five children in Iowa before they headed west: Mary J., William G., Thomas J., Nancy J., and Daniel A.

Thomas first improved a land claim in Indiana before he and Elizabeth made the trip west on the Overland

Trail with mules, oxen, and a two-horse team to La Grande, Oregon. There he built a log house with canvas windows[14] and he and Elizabeth had another child, Elizabeth A. (Bettie).

After fifteen months in Oregon, the Kingsburys returned east to the Dry Creek Valley. In 1866, they homesteaded 160 acres on the lush valley floor at its widest point, where Spring Valley Creek enters Dry Creek. Kingsbury hauled the lumber to build his Dry Creek house from Silver City, sixty miles away, and paid $60 for it.[15] The Kingsburys had four more children in Idaho Territory: John T., Frederick, Margaret E., and Walter S., for a total of ten children.

Kingsbury's 160 acres were worth $800 in 1870. His 100 acres of improved farmland produced 275 bushels of spring wheat, 500 bushels of barley, 200 bushels of potatoes, and 300 pounds of butter. Kingsbury owned two horses, four mules, ten milk cows, three cattle, and three swine. He patented his Dry Creek homestead in 1874.

To house his dairy cattle, Kingsbury built a large new barn at the ranch in 1873. Painted white and called a "model barn" by the *Statesman* (September 23, 1873), it measured forty-six by sixty feet. The barn was designed and constructed by William Huntley, who also taught school in the area. In 1878, the *Statesman* (April 13) reported that Kingsbury's thirteen-year-old daughter Bettie was milking ten cows there each day, in addition to doing the farmstead housework.

Like many farmers, Kingsbury worked at other occupations to supplement his income. He did custom threshing at ranches in the area including at the Richards' ranch near Eagle, Idaho. In 1871, his former farmhand, Jacob Drake, shot Kingsbury in the back while he worked on a threshing job for Richards. Drake was a carpenter who had boarded in the Kingsbury household. Evidently, he and Kingsbury had a dispute over a several-hundred-dollar debt. Drake reportedly drew a revolver and fired three shots at Kingsbury, hitting him in the back and through the lungs, according to the *Statesman* (March 22, 1873).

Drake was charged with intent to commit murder. He pleaded not guilty and went to trial in October of 1871. The jury convicted Drake and the judge sentenced him to four years at hard labor in the Idaho Territorial Penitentiary. While in prison, he tried to commit suicide by cutting his own throat and stabbing himself in the chest with a pocketknife. Some of his Dry Creek friends, like A.J. Wyatt, noted that Drake was not of sound mind. The *Statesman* (March 22, 1873) reported that he had a "weak mind" because a loaded wagon had run over his head. After the suicide attempt, Governor Thomas Bennett granted Drake a full pardon and released him from prison.

Kingsbury survived the shooting and continued his threshing business. During the 1873 growing season, he threshed 58,000 bushels of grain with his machine and traded threshing services for lumber at Barrett Williams' mill. Among his customers was Jared Peck who ranched between Boise and Green Meadow. Kingsbury threshed ninety-six bushels of oats and 666 bushels of grain for Peck, an amount that was "considerably ahead of the estimated yield" according to the *Statesman* (September 9, 1873).

Kingsbury also regularly hauled wood from Rossi's Shafer Creek Mill to the Dry Creek Valley[16] and other locations. In April of 1878, the *Statesman* reported that he purchased Mr. Thurman's "cow-teams" and was prepared to begin freighting to the mines at Rocky Bar for the year. While he was gone, Kingsbury rented out eighty acres of his own land to a man named Thomas Farmer.

In addition to his many business operations, Kingsbury was an active Democrat, serving as a Dry Creek delegate to the state convention in 1876 according to the *Statesman* (August 8, 1876).

By 1880, Thomas, now aged forty-nine, was working as a freighter with his sons Daniel and John in Cassia County, Idaho, while running his ranch at Dry Creek with his wife. In 1880, their children Daniel, Bettie, John, Frederick, Margaret, and Walter lived at the ranch. William returned to Iowa in January of 1881 to marry and brought his new wife back to Idaho according to the *Statesman* (January 13).

Kingsbury's Dry Creek ranch had a good-sized orchard operation in the 1880s, producing 70,000 pounds of apples, 7,000 pounds of prunes, and many plums. The *Statesman* (November 3, 1881) reported that he took 10,000 pounds of apples to the

Wood River area to sell for a "good price" and advertised another 40,000 "choice winter apples" for sale at his ranch in Dry Creek.

The Wood River Valley must have held promise for the family because after eighteen years, the Kingsburys left Dry Creek for a 120-acre ranch near Hailey, Idaho, in 1884.[17] Their son Daniel moved with them, blacksmithing and working in the mines for twelve years. Daniel acquired 160 acres that grew to include 800 acres of grazing land and cultivated fields.

The Kingsburys remained at Hailey until 1891 when they sold their property and left for Oregon.[18] Elizabeth died in Oregon in 1907. After his wife's death, Thomas H. returned to Idaho to live out his life at Middleton where he died in 1913 at the age of seventy-nine.

Alexander & Adaline Seaman Mullen Rossi

Prominent Boise citizen Alexander Rossi was a German immigrant born in 1828 to an Italian father and French mother. He headed to California during the gold rush in the 1850s. By 1860, Rossi was running a machine shop in Oregon City, Oregon.[19] He later operated a sawmill and assay office[2] at Lewiston, Idaho, before moving to Idaho City in 1862 to oversee a sawmill and assay office.

Rossi arrived in Boise City around 1865, continuing a partnership with A.H. Robie in a series of sawmills and other ventures.[20] In September

---

[2] *An assay office tests and certifies the purity of mined metal ore.*

of 1867, the *Statesman* reported that the Rossi & Robie assay office at Boise City was nearly complete, with "beautifully plastered and ceiled" walls. The office was to open later that year, promising six-hour returns on new assays.[21] Rossi later donated a city block for the stone assay office building that stands in Boise today between Idaho and Main Streets.

Although he lived in Boise City, Rossi homesteaded 160 acres of Dry Creek bottomland, just east of Kingsbury's place, known as the Robie Ranch for his partner. Rossi & Robie completed a toll road through the valley between the ranch and Kingsbury's property "in the most direct line" to their Shafer Creek lumber mill according to their advertisements in the *Statesman* (May 1869).

An 1867 business directory also lists Robie as the proprietor of a sawmill on Dry Creek.[22] In December of 1868, he advertised the sale of one-inch-thick lumber for greenbacks at $50 per 1,000 feet at the lumberyard and $40 per 1,000 feet at the ranch on Dry Creek. Cattle and grain were also taken in trade for lumber. Rossi & Robie's enterprise was very successful and paid federal taxes on sales in excess of $50,000 in 1868. Rossi received title to the Dry Creek ranch in 1870. Robie ran the ranch and subsequently came to own it.

Rossi married Adaline Seaman Mullen in 1873. Adaline had two daughters from her previous marriage, and she and Rossi had three more children together: Alexander F., Kirk, and Anna. Only

Alexander Rossi
(French 1914 Vol II)

Alexander survived to adulthood. He, too, entered the lumber business.[23]

Rossi's prominence continued to grow in the 1870s. He participated widely in both business and civic affairs, including serving as an Ada County Commissioner from 1873 to 1881.[24] Although he maintained some connections with the ranch on Dry Creek, Rossi's diverse responsibilities required that he hire out the management of the ranch and livestock.

One of his lumber partnerships was Rossi & Lambing, which began in August of 1873. He took on Isaac P. Lambing, an Idaho City miner, as a partner in the Shafer Creek Mill. Their business owned the steam sawmill, planer, and shingle machine on Shafer Creek, along with the toll road from Dry Creek. Together they were valued at $8,500. Other assets included an extra saw ($200), an office and lots in Boise City ($1,500), twenty-five yoke of cattle and chains ($2,910), a wagon ($500), and lumber ($4,209). Of the total partnership assets of $24,800, Rossi's share was about $20,300, while Lambing's was only about $3,800. At year's end in 1873, their sales totaled more than $10,600.[25] The Rossi & Lambing partnership dissolved in 1874 and Rossi assumed full ownership of the Shafer Creek Mill according to the *Statesman* (October 3, 1874). The next spring, the newspaper reported that he had enough logs on hand to cut 300,000 board feet of lumber.

The 1880 U.S. Census identified Rossi as a lumber merchant living with his family on Main Street in Boise City. A few doors away lived Judge Henry E. Prickett and *Statesman* publisher and former Idaho Supreme Court Justice, Milton Kelly. In 1884, the Rossi family moved to Washoe, Idaho, near Payette, where Rossi ran a sawmill until he retired at Boise City in 1895. Rossi was respected in the Boise community as a man of intellect and kindness.[26] He died in March of 1906 at age seventy-six of an apparent heart attack and was buried in Pioneer Cemetery[3] in what was described by the *Payette Independent* newspaper as one of Boise City's largest funerals.

Albert H. & Martha Craig Robie

A successful businessman and rancher, Robie was born in New York around 1833. He headed to Washington Territory in 1853 with

---

[3] *Pioneer Cemetery, at the west end of Warm Springs Avenue, was first used as a burial ground in 1863, making it Boise's oldest continuously-used cemetery.*

Territorial Governor Isaac I. Stevens, employed as a "cook-boy"[27] and as quartermaster for the Oregon and Washington Volunteers.[28]

Robie was part of Stevens' entourage and a "non-tribal signer" of the Blackfeet Treaty of Fort Benton, Montana, in 1855. Stevens appointed him special agent for the Indian Department in Washington Territory in 1856, later assigning him to the Yakima District,[29] where he worked to improve the lot of the Yakima people. Robie's 1857 report from the Yakima District included a description of the Yakima people at the time:

> They were formerly a wealthy and prosperous tribe, some of them possessing large herds of horses and cattle, but they have become very much impoverished during the war, and in fact have lost nearly everything, or have given it away in hiring Indians who were friendly disposed to join them in hostilities.
>
> I have used every possible means to encourage them in laying up a good supply for the winter; notwithstanding, they will require some assistance during the coming autumn and winter; and should the fall run of salmon fail, of which there are some fears, they will be almost destitute, and, if government aid is not extended to them, they cannot escape starvation.[30]

Robie recommended the following support from the U.S government:

> Under the present condition of affairs, it is very difficult to form any correct estimates; but, in my opinion, there will be required thirty-eight thousand dollars ($38,000) for the maintenance of friendly relations and to supply the actual necessities of the Indians in the

A.H. Robie married Martha Craig at Walla Walla, Washington, in 1860. Martha was born in 1842 at Lapwai in Nez Perce Territory to renowned English mountain man William Craig[32] and his Nez Perce wife Isabel James Moses. The Robies had five children: Clara Rosa, Elizabeth, Albert Hugh, Mary Mollie, and Minnie. All but the eldest were born in Idaho after 1863.

After his government service, Robie moved to Lewiston where he ran a sawmill with Rossi. Rossi and Robie ended up in Boise City around 1863 and started the Shafer Creek Mill near Dry Creek, among many other enterprises. In October of 1866, the *Statesman* reported that Robie had made an advance in the manufacture of roof shingles that resulted in a smooth, uniform shingle—better than others on the market at the time did. His success in the lumber industry eventually made Robie a wealthy man with interests throughout the Northwest. He is believed to have started the first sawmill in Harney County, Oregon, in 1865. The mill provided lumber and shingles for the construction of Fort Harney. He sold the mill in 1877 for $44,000 for the equipment, lumber, buildings, and land.[33]

Robie also ran and owned the Rossi/Robie ranch on Dry Creek. The 1868 GLO survey map of his ranch shows a wagon road crossing east to west south of the creek. A building is depicted north of the creek where a cluster of ranch buildings stood well into the twenty-first century. The 1870 U.S. Census reported that Robie's land was worth $8,500. With his $45,000 in personal property, he was by far the most prosperous rancher on Dry Creek.

Like other area ranchers, Robie raised and sold horses and mules for the military. In 1875, General George Crook had the U.S. Army buy 200 Idaho pack mules from Robie to ship to him at Cheyenne, Wyoming, via Ogden, Utah.[34]

At the time of the 1870 Census, Robie was staying in Dry Creek with his farm workers. His wife and children may have been living at Lewiston where his two younger daughters were born in the early 1870s. The Robie household in Dry Creek included: Williston G. Osborn, John and Mary Sink with their son Michael, Phillip Paul, Alexander Montoya, and another farm worker.

Like many prominent businessmen of the time, Robie was also active in civic affairs and was a representative from Ada County to the Eighth Session of the Idaho Territorial Legislature.

In 1877, he sold his 42,000-acre Diamond A Ranch at Steens Mountain, Oregon, to Peter French.[35] At the outbreak of the Bannock War the next year, Robie and French were gathering horses from the ranch when the Shoshone attacked them. Robie survived the initial attack, but the experience ultimately proved fatal to him. He died from fatigue and exposure on July 26, 1878, shortly after returning to his home on Dry Creek. Robie was buried in Boise City's Masonic (Pioneer) Cemetery.

As a tribute to the well-regarded pioneer, the local Masons passed a special resolution printed in the *Statesman* (August 10, 1878):

> *Resolved, That by the untimely death of Bro. Robie at the early age of 46 years, the Territory has lost one of the most enterprising citizens, the community a true neighbor and friend, and upright and generous man, Shoshone Lodge a faithful and highly esteemed member, and his family a most kind and devoted husband and father.*

The *Statesman* (November 23, 1878) reported that Robie's estate, administered by his friend John Hailey, included the Dry Creek farm and implements, a 450-acre farm in nearby Spring Valley, and various lots in Boise City. His wife inherited half the estate and his children each received $1,315. Martha inherited $70,000, making her a very wealthy woman.[36] The Ada County Land Claim Records Index shows that a sum of $14,000 was tied up in a lawsuit with a neighbor, A.J. Wyatt, and another $13,000 was distributed elsewhere.

The autumn after Robie's death, Martha and her children moved into a house at the corner of Bannock and Seventh Streets in Boise City. Shortly after they moved in, a chimney fire damaged part of the house but they saved their belongings according to a *Statesman* report (October 12. 1878). While in Boise, Martha was a regular participant in Boise's social life, including appearing at a masquerade costumed as a young boy in February of 1879.

She eventually took up with notorious gunslinger and cattle rustler Henry Clay (Hank) Vaughan who, along with Billy Moody and Jim Alexander, were said to have used the Robie Ranch in Dry Creek as a base for raids into Boise City and the surrounding area.[37]

By 1880, the U.S. Census reported that Martha was living at Lewiston with her daughters Mary and Minnie. With her inheritance, she and Vaughan bought a ranch north of the Umatilla Reservation where Martha moved in 1882 to participate in the Indian Allotment Act that qualified her to claim 160 acres of reservation land.[38]

Hank and Martha frequently traveled by train between Umatilla and Boise City. Hank, ironically, was rewarded by the railroad with a lifetime pass for foiling train robbers on one of his trips. While married to Martha, Hank was also concurrently married to two other women, Lois McCarty (of a well-known Oregon outlaw family) and Louisa Jane Ditty, whom he subsequently divorced, making his marriage to Martha legal in 1888.[39]

Hank and Martha sold the Robie Ranch around 1886 and moved to Centerville, Washington. In 1893, Vaughan was crushed to death by a falling horse at Pendleton, Oregon.[40] When he died, he reportedly had the scars of thirteen bullet wounds from shootouts over the years. Martha died in Oregon in 1930.

Anneas J. (Jack) & Phoeba Chesnut Wyatt

A man of ever-changing interests, Jack Wyatt was born around 1832 in Illinois. He seems to have come to Idaho Territory by way of the

California gold fields. By 1863, "Jewsharp Jack"[4] as he was known, was running a livery stable at Placerville, Idaho.[41] In 1865, he married Phoeba Ann Chesnut who was born in Wisconsin in 1848. The Wyatts had three children in Idaho: Verina E., Jacob L., and William W.

Wyatt settled 160 acres on Dry Creek east of the Rossi/Robie place in September of 1869. The property was purchased using a U.S. government warrant assigned to Michael McNulty, a military teamster in the war with Mexico. According to GLO records, McNulty signed the warrant over to Wyatt to complete the land purchase in 1875. Wyatt patented his 160-acre ranch under the Scrip Warrant Act—the only one of the Dry Creek settlers to acquire ownership using this military benefit.

Wyatt was very active in business enterprises outside the valley. In December of 1866, the *Statesman* reported that he purchased a building on Main Street in Boise City and opened the Mount Hood Saloon with a partner, Joseph Forsythe, whom he had known in California. According to the newspaper a few months later in 1867, Wyatt treated his guests politely and served only the best liquor. Later that year, Wyatt "retired" from Forsythe & Wyatt. Forsythe refurbished and reopened the saloon as Forsythe & Co. Forsythe and Wyatt remained friends until Forsythe died of

consumption in 1878 at Wyatt's home on Dry Creek.

Wyatt was Ada County Constable in the Boise Precinct in 1866 and 1867 when he asked to be relieved of his post to leave the Territory to go back to the U.S.[42] The *Statesman* (February 1,1868) noted that on his return from Chicago early the next year, Wyatt described the city as a dull place and expressed no desire to remain there. He was elected Marshal of Boise City in 1869[43] and Ada County records show that he paid taxes on his land in Dry Creek in 1868 and 1869. An active Democrat, Wyatt was a regular delegate to the Territorial Democrat Convention from 1866 to 1882.

The 1870 U.S. Census reported that Wyatt's farm produced 200 bushels of spring wheat, 500 bushels of barley, 140 tons of hay, and 600 pounds of butter. He had nine horses, two mules, three milk cows, and three other cattle. Newspaper accounts described his operation as one of several prosperous farms in the Dry Creek Valley at the time. It included about 140 acres in a single large field, a twenty-acre pasture, and another five acres with a small orchard (including peaches) and a garden next to his house. The house had a running spring and a milk house, with another small house for hired help according to the *Statesman* (September 1873). Across the creek from the house were a barn, granary, stack yard,[5] and corrals.

Wyatt cut 180 tons of hay on

---

[4] *A Jew's harp is a musical instrument also known as a jaw harp or mouth harp. It has no particular connection with Jews or Judaism.*

[5] *A stack yard is an enclosure for stacking hay or grain.*

seventy-five to eighty acres in 1873, and 1,460 bushels of grain on another forty-four acres. He had also acquired more than thirty horses (although none were thoroughbreds), as well as three milk cows, and a number of other cattle. From his holdings, he expected to bring in $6,060 for the year, paying half in expenses, and leaving a profit of $3,030. The county charged him $300 in taxes in 1875.

By November of 1877, Wyatt was living in Boise City and considering whether to return to his Dry Creek ranch. Evidently, there were problems afoot because two years later, on September 11, 1879, he and his wife officially abandoned their 160-acre Dry Creek homestead.[44] Although the Wyatts had officially abandoned their homestead, they were still living in Dry Creek in 1880 on land valued at $8,000 in the U.S. Census. At that time, the Wyatts had four boarders: Claud and Clara Alexander (a saddler and musician) with their infant son, and Harry Gray, a laborer.

The year 1880 difficult for Wyatt. He spent the winter of 1879/1880 engaged in a lawsuit and jury trial against the estate of his neighbor, A.H. Robie, according to the *Statesman* (January 3, 1880). He was also ill for most of the year, and on December 7, the newspaper reported that Wyatt suffered from an attack of "erysipelas," a strep infection of the skin.

After years of ups and downs, Jack and Phoeba Ann began divorce proceedings in 1885 and finally left the Dry Creek Valley for good. Jack was the defendant in the proceedings. Phoeba Ann received half the value of their personal property in the settlement, while Jack received the real estate. She moved to Washington State with her three children and eventually married Benjamin Stafford. The Wyatt children also apparently split with their father. Verina married her stepfather's son, Frank Stafford, in 1889 and William married Stafford's daughter Ruby.

James A. Corder bought Wyatt's Dry Creek ranch in May of 1886.[45] Wyatt moved to Boise County where he was involved in freighting, among other businesses. In 1888, the Weiser, Idaho, newspaper (October 26) reported that he arrived in town with "the first wagon load of ore ever hauled from the Seven Devils, 2,760 pounds of copper ore from the Blue Jacket mine."

Wyatt married Elizabeth Yenny in 1890 and filed on a homestead on the west side of Payette Lake in Boise County in 1896, beginning yet another career as an entrepreneur in the early tourism trade. Wyatt built and operated a hotel and advertised his thirty-foot sailboat for use by visitors on Payette Lake.[46] He also built and operated a wood-powered steamboat that towed a dancing barge around the lake.[47] An 1898 advertisement in the *Statesman* (February 17) featured Wyatt. In the ad, Dr. Darrin, who practiced in Boise City, claimed to have cured Wyatt's hearing after years of deafness by using some sort of electromagnetic invention.

Wyatt died December 26, 1899,

leaving his homestead and estate to James Walton who sold it to noted Boise City attorney Samuel H. Hays. The land eventually became Payette Lake's first subdivision, laid out in 1914.[48]

Wyatt was apparently not on good terms with his adult children because he left them each the sum of one dollar in his will. After his death, his three children filed suit to claim his land, saying that because the homestead patent had not been finalized at the time of his death, he did not have the right to will it to Walton. The case went to the Idaho Supreme Court, which ruled against Wyatt's children.[49]

Andrew H. & Elizabeth Perkins Wiley

Farmer Andrew Wiley was born in Ohio in 1827. He homesteaded 160 acres east of Wyatt's place with his wife Elizabeth. The Wylies married in 1864 and moved to Washington Territory in the late 1860s. Their first two children, Oakland (Oakley) C. and Mary E., were born in Washington. They had three more daughters in Idaho (Annie H., Ida May, and Effie), suggesting that they moved to Idaho around 1869. An unnamed infant may have died in 1870.

That year, the Wiley's forty acres of improved land and livestock produced 1,000 pounds of butter, but livestock numbers were not tallied in the U.S. Census data. The property was valued at $1,000. By 1880, the Wiley family had moved to Green Meadow, probably while Andy continued to farm in Dry Creek.

Their daughter Annie married in 1886 at the age of fourteen. Mary died in 1887 at the age of twenty. By 1900, Elizabeth had died and seventy-two-year-old Andy was rooming with a group of servants in the Middleton area. He later moved back to Dry Creek where he worked as a farm hand. Wylie died in 1916.

George W. & Mary E. Glenn Williams

Stockman George Williams came to Idaho by way of Oregon in the 1860s. He was born in 1836 in Illinois where he married and had a son and daughter before moving west.

He was single again when he met Mary Glenn, daughter of Dry Creek homesteaders John and Elizabeth Glenn, in Oregon in 1863. They married and had eight children. The first two, John L. and Nancy E., were born in Oregon Territory. Hulah, who was six months old at the time of the 1870 Census, was born in Idaho. Hulah was not listed in later censuses suggesting that she may have died. Five more children were born in Idaho: George W., Jr., Hattie B., William W., Mary, and Elise.

George worked as a cattle broker in the Dry Creek Valley for several decades. In 1870, his personal property, presumably including livestock, was valued at $10,000. GLO records show that he completed the patent of 160 acres of land in the foothills off Seaman Gulch in 1889. The previous year, he and H.H. Sprague filed a lawsuit against his neighbor, P.L. Schick, in a failed dispute over the trade of nine horses. Schick won the suit.[50]

After Mary died in 1900, George Sr. moved to Pearl with his children William, Mary, and Elise. He died in 1909 at Sweet and was buried at Weiser, Idaho.

John M. & Elizabeth Thompson Glenn

The patriarch of one of Dry Creek's longest resident families, John Glenn, was a Tennessee farmer born around 1811. He and his wife Elizabeth (born in Kentucky in 1814) had ten children: Charles T., Riley J., James S., Alice J., Henry H., Sally Ann, Mary E., John T., Thomas, and William P. The five older children were born in Indiana, and the five younger in Iowa. In 1862, the Glenns headed west for the Salmon River region. When the roads proved too difficult, the family went to Oregon instead. Enroute, their son John T. served as an advance guard for the wagon train. The Glenns remained in Oregon for two years before returning east to Idaho in 1864.[51]

In Idaho Territory, they claimed 160 acres in central Dry Creek. Glenn's 150 acres of improved land produced 260 bushels of spring wheat, twenty bushels of corn, seventy bushels of barley, and thirty bushels of potatoes in 1870. He had seven horses, twenty milk cows, forty-nine other cattle, and produced 500 pounds of butter.[52] Glenn patented his land, valued at $1,000, in 1874.

John M. died in the spring of 1880 of heart disease and was buried in Dry Creek Cemetery.[53] Elizabeth inherited the farm and reported owning fifty-six horses, fourteen milk cows, and twenty beef cattle in

June of that year. The farm also produced 500 pounds of butter and 250 dozen eggs.[54]

Elizabeth died in 1892 and was also buried in Dry Creek Cemetery. Three of the Glenn children remained in the Dry Creek Valley: Alice, who married Dry Creek farmer E. James Smith in Iowa before moving to Idaho; Mary, who married George Williams in Oregon; and Charles, who purchased the original Glenn homestead from his mother.

Edward James & Alice Glenn Smith

E. James Smith was born in Iowa in 1837. He and Alice Glenn married in Iowa in 1857 and had five children there: Charles, Mary E., Ellen J., Florence, and Lucinda M. Smith seems to have settled in Dry Creek in 1869 or 1870. He began the decade working on a farm he did not own—probably on John Glenn's homestead where they lived with Alice's parents. In 1877, he acquired forty acres north of the Rossi/Robie ranch through a cash entry sale.

By 1880, he was also leasing the "Robie farms" according to the *Statesman* (March 16, 1880) and working the ranch with his four older children. Smith advertised stock grazing at his ranch and at the Robie Ranch for $2 per month. His *Statesman* ad (August 6, 1881) noted that teamsters could graze their stock for 12.5 cents per head per night with "good fence, good water and good pasture."

By 1900, the Smiths, now in their sixties, lived at Garden Valley, Idaho, with their daughters Florence and Lucinda. Alice died at Caldwell,

Idaho, in 1903 and James died there in 1924.[55] In the early twentieth century, James' grandson Edward C. Smith took over the ranch and still lived there into the mid-twentieth century.

William B. Francis

William Francis filed one of the earliest land claims in the Dry Creek Valley in 1864. For a short time, he owned 160 acres of agricultural land in the central valley—later the Crawford and Rodgers homesteads.[56] Francis was born in Ohio around 1830, but little else is known of his personal life from public documents.

Francis' short-term transactions over the years suggest that his activity in the area was more involved with land speculation than with farming. In 1866, Francis filed a lawsuit against his neighbors P.L. Schick, James B. Harris, and George H. Banker in which he tried to recover $1,500 in gold coin plus $50 in damages from each of them as payment for property he had sold them. The payment had been due in October of 1865 according to a report in the *Statesman* (July 28, 1866). Francis tried to attach some of Schick's property (four horses owned by Banker and Schick) in lieu of payment. However, the judge dismissed the case.[57]

Francis apparently left the valley after selling his land to Schick and Banker. In the 1870s and 1880s, he owned land and sold horses elsewhere in Ada County. He returned in 1894 to buy 240 acres in the foothills above Goose Creek between Dry Creek and Green Meadow under the Desert Land Act.

Again, not much seems to have happened with his land. Ada County sold the property for $44.81 in back taxes that same year. Francis died in 1898 and was buried in Pioneer Cemetery at Boise City.

Robert M. Crawford

Robert Crawford, one of the few unmarried landowners in the valley, homesteaded 160 acres in the central Dry Creek Valley to the west of P.L. Schick's place in the late 1860s. According to the 1868 Ada County tax assessment records, his house was located between houses owned by Schick and William Casner. Crawford was born in Ireland in 1830.

Crawford's thirty acres of improved farmland did not list crop production in the 1870 U.S. Census. His livestock consisted of three horses, a milk cow, and five other cattle on real estate valued at $500. Ada County taxed the property at $100 in 1875. Crawford patented his 160-acre homestead two years later—nearly ten years before he would become a citizen as required by U.S. law.

He worked the farm at least until 1880. That year his property was valued at $2,000. He had an acre in apple trees, some fifty horses, seven milk cows, and twenty beef cattle.[58] However, his focus on livestock and fruit apparently did not pay the bills. The wrap-up of the mining boom by the early 1880s affected many local farmers like Crawford. His land was among those farms reported in the *Statesman* (December 10, 1881) as having been sold for back taxes.

Crawford became a U.S. citizen in

1886[59] after leaving the valley. By 1900, he had retired to Oregon to live with his two elderly sisters. He died sometime after 1910.

William H. & Elizabeth Casner

The Casner family is well known in Idaho histories for their ranch on the road to Idaho City, although they lived in the Dry Creek Valley for a short time in the 1860s. William Casner was born in 1827 in Virginia. He and Elizabeth (born in 1853 in Ohio) married in 1871. At some point during the 1860s, the Casners lived in Dry Creek near Crawford's ranch. They had ten children, nine of whom survived: Jennett N. (Nettie), George W., Elizabeth, William H. Jr., Andrew A., Alexander G., Ephraim B., Mildred S., and John W.

By 1880, William, Sr. lived in Willow Creek, west of Dry Creek, near a group of Chinese miners. Between 1885 and 1891, the family moved to Idaho City, where they ranched on the Idaho City road into the twentieth century. William, Sr. died in 1922 at the age of ninety-four. Elizabeth died in 1930. She and William were both buried in the family plot at their ranch.

Neri Jack

Neri Jack was an Iowa farmer whose 160 acres was valued at $500 in 1870. That year, his ten acres of improved farmland produced thirty bushels of spring wheat and thirty bushels of potatoes according to the U.S. Census Agricultural Schedule. His only livestock were two horses. Jack left the area by 1880 and little else is know of his personal life from public documents.

George H. Banker

Banker was born in New York in 1826, the son of a carriage maker. By 1860, he lived in Shasta County, California, where he worked as a miner. Banker may have come to Idaho around the same time as P.L. Schick, with whom he later partnered on a land claim. Banker claimed a 160-acre homestead on November 23, 1865, adjoining on its west the William Francis land claim, which he later purchased.[60] Portions of that claim became the Schick and Coppock homesteads. In the late spring of 1866, the *Statesman* (June 7) reported that the first load of new hay for sale that year came from Mr. Banker's farm on Dry Creek.

Little else is known about George Banker from public documents—it is possible that he returned to New York in the late 1860s. His identity has not been confirmed in later U.S. Census or Ada County records.

John Keller

John Keller, born in Virginia around 1834, apparently speculated briefly in land claims in the Dry Creek Valley before moving on to mining activities. He claimed 160 acres on Dry Creek near the Banker/Schick place in 1863 and sold the property to William B. Dobson in 1866. By 1870, Keller was mining in the Idaho City area.

William B. & Eliza Paynter Hartley Dobson

William Dobson was born in Tennessee in 1840 and arrived in Idaho in the 1860s.[61] Early on, he was active in buying and selling land claims in the Dry Creek Valley. In 1868 and 1870, he also paid income tax on money he earned as a peddler in Boise City.[62] It is not clear exactly where Dobson lived in Dry Creek, but in 1869, he had six yoke of cattle, two mules, and a wagon.

Eliza Hartley, born in Virginia in 1840, had three children from a previous marriage to William C. Hartley. Clinton F., William F. and Elizabeth L. (Lizzie) were born in the 1860s. The Hartleys traveled west in a wagon train on the Overland Trail for three months in 1864 driving a yoke of cows for milk and a yoke of steers. Eliza began the trip with a two-year-old son and gave birth to her second son in Iowa as they headed west. Their daughter Lizzie was born in Idaho in 1867. The Hartleys farmed in Ada County until William died in 1871.

The next year, Eliza married William B. Dobson. Eliza and William B. had three more sons: Frank, Leonard, and Charles N., all born in the 1870s.

By 1877, the Dobsons lived in Stewart Gulch, but their children ranged the hills at the eastern end of Dry Creek. During the Bannock Wars (1877-1878), their son William F., then a young boy, recalled hunting for horses in the hills around Dry Creek when he saw an Indian riding quickly down the road on a pony. William F. was frightened given the context of the war, but later learned that the man was being chased by a white man and did not even notice him.[63] As an adult, William F. worked at various occupations in the Wood River area and farmed at Star.[64] He married Annie L. Morrison, daughter of Dry Creek farmers Thomas and Elizabeth Morrison.

Frank Dobson grew up in nearby Stewart Gulch and attended a school conducted by Picayune Smith[65] about four miles northwest of Boise City. Frank ended his schooling at age seventeen and cowboyed on Smith's Prairie where he had 500 head of cattle. Later he worked as a cattle buyer for C.W. Moore's Idaho Dressed Beef Company. Recognized as one of the top riders and ropers in Idaho, Frank won $100 in 1900 for roping and tying steers.[66] Eventually he owned a ranch near Star, Idaho. Len Dobson bought the old Cartwright Ranch on Shafer Creek in Boise County north of Dry Creek.

William B. and his four-year-old son Charles both died in 1882 and were buried in Dry Creek Cemetery. Eliza received the patent on their land at the mouth of Stewart Gulch, in the area of present-day Hillside Junior High School, in 1886. She eventually moved to Boise City to live with her son Len. Eliza died in 1922 and was buried in Dry Creek Cemetery.

Phillip L. & Mary Yaryan Schick

Long-time Dry Creek resident Phillip L (P.L.) Schick claimed 160 acres at the upper or eastern end of the Dry Creek Valley where the broad bottomlands begin to narrow into the foothills. He was born in New York in 1837, the eldest of seven children. His parents were from Germany, and his father served in the Civil War with the 17th New York Volunteers.[67]

In 1862, Schick traveled from California to Portland to The Dalles,

Oregon, by water, and then to Lewiston, Idaho, by ox team, before continuing south to the Boise Valley according to an account in the *Statesman* (July 26, 1892). Oral tradition in his family tells of Schick finding the Dry Creek Valley when an ox from his team wandered off, leading him to a wide valley of waist-high grasses.[68]

Schick partnered with George Banker to work a homestead in the valley. The sequence of their partnership transactions is unclear, but public records document the 1865 sale of 320 acres on Dry Creek to Schick and Banker by W.B. Francis and Philip Hull.[69] This acreage seems to have been at issue in Francis's 1866 lawsuit against them. At any rate, Schick and Banker paid taxes on the Dry Creek property from 1867 to 1870.[70]

In 1868, Schick paid $16 for a homestead application on about 159 acres along Dry Creek.[71] By this time, he was the sole owner of the property. His homestead application listed a house, stable, chicken house, and planted trees—improvements to the property worth $600. Schick patented his thriving homestead in 1874.

The 1870 U.S. Census reported that Schick's farm included seventy-five acres of improved land and eighty-two acres of unimproved land valued at $1,500. He had four horses and a milk cow. Crops included 200 bushels of spring wheat, 500 bushels of corn, 500 bushels of barley, thirty bushels of potatoes, ten bushels of beans, and ten tons of hay. Schick paid $100 in wages in 1869 to his farmhand,

Edward Lewis, who boarded at the farm.

In the fall 1870, Schick married twenty-two-year old Mary A. Yaryan, who had arrived in Idaho six months earlier, and brought her to his successful ranch. The *Statesman* (August 21, 1910) later recounted that her wedding dress was a gown of blue alpaca wool trimmed with blue silk fringe. The gold watch pinned to her chest was a wedding gift from her husband. Mary, born in Indiana, was the daughter of Andrew and Elizabeth Yaryan who farmed along the Boise River.

The Schick's daughter and only child, Clara, was born three years later. When she was six years old and ready to attend school, Schick built a school on Dry Creek Road at the nearby Glenn homestead with lumber from the Shafer Creek Mill according to a 1953 article in the *Statesman*. Clara attended the school through the eighth grade.

Schick's school became a center of civic life in the Dry Creek Valley. It was a polling place in nearly every election and the locus of the valley's political meetings. Newspaper reports in the 1880s and 1890s indicate that Phillip and Mary were very active in the Ada County Republican party. As a respected man in the community, Schick was regularly selected to serve on local juries. The newspaper reported that the Ada County Commissioners paid him $9 in 1878 for his work as a juror. Like other farmers in the valley, Schick also took on extra labor to earn cash. For example, in the spring of 1882, he earned $21 for six days of work on a county bridge according to the *Statesman*. He also kept sheep in Boise County, and in February of 1902, the newspaper reported that he received a refund of $28.60 in Ada County taxes for livestock kept outside the county.

By 1880, Schick farmed 160 acres, with thirty additional acres in meadow or orchard. The value of his farm had increased to $3,500. His livestock included thirty-four horses, six milk cows, seventy-five beef cattle, seven swine, and 130 poultry. At that time he had eleven acres in barley, ten acres in corn, twelve acres in oats, fourteen acres in wheat, and forty acres in hay.[72] He also had an orchard with apple, peach, and plum (prune) trees. Schick paid $500 in wages that year, possibly to Horatio Hills, a laborer who lived nearby with his wife Anny.

Over the decades, Schick continued his successful farming efforts, gradually acquiring more land as his neighbors died or left the valley. In the late 1870s, he expanded his simple one-room homesteader house with a grand two-story addition. He was touted in a March 1890 *Statesman* article as having "one of the most valuable ranches in the famous Boise Valley" and reportedly drove "to town in his own carriage and is happier than the Czar of Russia." Around that time, Schick had a portrait photograph taken of him in his carriage next to his Dry Creek home. In one of his last land purchases reported in the *Statesman* (November 16, 1898), he bought the 120-acre Goure homestead for $150 after the death of its owner that year.

Dry Creek Valley residents like Schick made regular use of the newspaper to spread the word about lost property. In July of 1880, Schick advertised finding two fully-grown white hogs on his property and asked the owner to claim them and pay the damages. In October of 1898, he lost a wallet containing a note and two county warrants, and offered a reward for its return.

The early 1890s brought a long

*Phillip and Mary Schick wedding photo, 1870
(Dry Creek Historical Society).*

string of court dates for Schick in the matter of water trespass by his upstream neighbor William Daly. Newspaper reports show that the case continued for two years before Schick was able to prove that he held the senior water right on Dry Creek.

By 1900, Phillip and Mary lived in one household at the Dry Creek farm, while Clara, her husband, and her son lived in another. Schick died an accidental death at the age of sixty-four on April 15, 1902 at his Dry Creek farmhouse. A story in the *Statesman* reported in detail the unusual accident that caused his death. On the afternoon of April 12, he and Mary were riding home in their open-spring wagon after a trip to Boise to pick up groceries.

> *There was a strong wind blowing which was full in their faces as they started down a hill about a half mile from home. As they rode down the hill, Mary glanced back over her shoulder and was alarmed to see that the back of the wagon seat was on fire. The flames were being whipped eight feet high by the wind and were swirling under the seat behind her husband and burning his back.*[73]

Mary removed her woolen shawl, threw it over her husband's back, and dragged him from the wagon as she tried to convince him he was on fire. Schick denied that he was on fire and insisted that she stop. Mary tried to get him into nearby Dry Creek, but he collapsed on the road. She finally put out the flames and found that her husband's back and much of the front of his body was terribly burned. Nothing was left of his clothing but the collars.

A neighbor who happened along the road helped Mary get her husband into what was left of the wagon and take him home. Mary escaped without burns, despite the fact that her husband burned alive beside her. He continued to insist that he was not injured until he passed out. A doctor came the next day and reported that Schick had serious burns over most of his body including his hands. His back was so badly burned that his bones were nearly visible. Despite the burns, Schick apparently never felt any pain. He died of the burns three days later at the farmhouse.

Schick was remembered as a kindly, good-hearted man. His *Statesman* death notice (April 17, 1902) referred to him as "one of the best known and popular farmers in Ada County." A Presbyterian minister presided over his burial at Dry Creek Cemetery. At the time of his death, the newspaper (May 27, 1902) reported that Schick's estate included nearly 400 acres of land— real estate valued at $12,000, as well as eleven horses, twenty-four cattle, 2,000 sheep, and personal property valued at $5,518. In addition to his original patented property, his landholdings included the former Daniel and Goure homesteads. His wife and daughter inherited the ranch.

After her husband's death, Mary Schick moved to Boise City. She advertised 300 acres of the ranch for sale in February of 1906. At that time, 200 acres were under cultivation and the ranch included "good springs" and "plenty of wood" with two houses and good outbuildings. She appears not to have found a buyer for the ranch as she eventually transferred 277 acres to her son-in-law Forrest See in 1919. In 1910, sixty-three-year-old Mary lived on State Street in Boise City where she had taken in lodgers. She died in 1926 and was buried next to her husband in Dry Creek Cemetery.

James C. & Sarah Coffey Baldwin & Emma Daniels Baldwin

James Baldwin was a blacksmith from New Jersey who was born in 1829. Sarah, born about 1835, was from Illinois. They had married and lived in Missouri by 1853. Their five older children Sarah, James Charles, John A., William R., and Mary E. were all born in Missouri. The younger two, May Belle and George E., were born in Idaho Territory after the Baldwins arrived in 1864. Young Sarah died in 1860 at the age of seven. John died of typhoid in 1879 at the age of twenty-one. Of the seven children, only James, Jr., May Belle, and George lived to see the new century with their parents.

James, Sr. worked as a blacksmith for a few years before taking up

ranching[74] in the Dry Creek Valley. In 1870, he and his sons farmed land valued at $3,000 to the east of Schick's place, probably the ranch that was later patented by William Daniel. Their eighty acres of improved farmland produced 640 bushels of spring wheat, twenty bushels of potatoes, 200 pounds of butter, and thirty tons of hay. Livestock included eight horses, four milk cows, six oxen and six other cattle according to the 1870 U.S. Census. Since James was a blacksmith by trade, he probably earned additional money performing these services for others in the valley.

James and Sarah Baldwin divorced around 1872. Sarah married farmer Jacob Bowers in 1875 and settled in Stewart Gulch. She died in 1917 and was buried in Boise's Pioneer Cemetery.

Meanwhile, James Baldwin moved back to Boise City where he owned a blacksmith shop on Main Street. He reportedly slept in the back of the shop, which almost burned down in the summer of 1875 according to a report in the *Statesman* (August 14, 1875). When James remarried in the late 1870s, he and his new wife Emma H. Daniels lived in Boise City with their two daughters Matilda and Emma. They divorced in 1898. James died in 1914 and Emma in 1922. Both were buried in Pioneer Cemetery.

Richard S. & Sarah Lipscomb

Richard Lipscomb was a farmer from Kentucky who worked 160 acres of land in the valley in 1870. His thirty acres of improved fields produced 450 bushels of barley. He and Sarah married in 1879 when he was thirty-six and she was fifteen years old. They boarded with the Baldwin family. Sarah died in the spring of 1880 at the age of sixteen while giving birth to her first child. After her death, Richard left the valley and moved to Utah.

The Farmworkers & Tradespeople

Few of the farmworkers from the 1860s ended up owning their own land in the valley. Most worked in the area for only a short time before moving on to other opportunities. Generally they boarded with landowner families, although some lived alone. Drivers and stock tenders lived at the stage station.

Isaac & Fannie Alexander Straight Flenner

Isaac Straight was a stage driver born around 1821, probably in Ohio. He worked as a farm laborer in Indiana, was married, and had three sons in the 1840s and 1850s. Isaac left his family in Indiana and headed west during the 1860s. Apparently, he never returned because by 1880, his first wife considered herself a widow.

In 1870, Straight was driving on the stage line that passed near the mouth of the Dry Creek Valley. Although he was forty-nine years of age at the time, he was newly married to eighteen-year-old Fannie Alexander, the daughter of Elizabeth Shubert. Isaac and Fannie eventually had seven children: Alice, James T., Elizabeth K., Horace L., Frances G., Minnie M. and William I.

By 1880, the Straights had left Dry Creek for Boise City where Isaac worked as a laborer. He died in 1891 and was buried in Boise City's Pioneer Cemetery. Fannie married John D. Flenner sometime after 1900. Flenner died in 1916 and Fannie lived into the 1920s.

The End of a Decade

By the end of the 1860s, the Dry Creek Valley floor was well settled and improved. After some initial land speculation, farmers who intended to earn their livelihood by working the land mostly owned the farms. Absentee professionals and investors who hired farm managers owned a few of the farms. Although farmers sometimes worked additional jobs to earn cash, most thrived as their diverse production supplied the mines of the Boise Basin, the residents of Boise City, and the livestock needs of the military at Fort Boise. The coming decade of the 1870s would bring technological advances in farm production, increased crop diversity, and the controversial introduction of sheep ranching into the valley.

Endnotes

[1]Gregory Michno, *The Deadliest Indian War in the West: The Snake Conflict 1865-1868.* (Caldwell, Idaho: Caxton Press, 2007), 219.

[2]Idaho State Historical Society (ISHS), "Bigfoot" (Reference Series Number 40, 1970).

[3]Del Yaryan, Personal recollection of Del Yaryan told to Claudia Druss (2009).

[4]Ronald J. Baker, *A Brief History of Eagle, Idaho* (Eagle, Idaho: Eagle Public Library, 2005), 6.

[5]U.S. Federal Census, Ada, Idaho Territory, Agricultural Schedule, 1870.

[6]*An Illustrated History of the State of Idaho* (Chicago: The Lewis Publishing Company, 1889), 257.

[7]French, Hiram T. *History of Idaho. A Narrative Account of Its People and Its Principal Interests, Volume II* (Chicago: The Lewis Publishing Company, 1914), 742.

[8]Lewis Publishing Co., *Illustrated History of Idaho,* 258.

[9] Ibid.

[10]French, *History of Idaho,* 742.

[11]Lewis Publishing Co., *Illustrated History of Idaho,* 258.

[12]Barrett Williams, Ledgers of Business Transactions, 1872-1880, Volumes 1–5 (ISHS Archives).

[13]Ibid.

[14]James H. Hawley, *History of Idaho, Volume IV* (Chicago: S.J. Clarke Publishing Company, 1920), 514.

[15]Ibid.

[16]Rossi & Lambing. Daily Accounts Jurnal, 1873-1876 (ISHS Archives).

[17]Hawley, *History of Idaho,* 515.

[18]Ibid.

[19]French, *History of Idaho Volume 2,* 622.

[20]Ibid.

[21]ISHS, "The Boise City Assaying and Refining Works" (Reference Series Number 3, 1962).

[22]Henry G. Langley, *Pacific Coast Business Directory for 1867* (San Francisco: H.G. Langley, 1867), 338.

[23]French, *History of Idaho Volume 2,* 623.

[24]Roxann Gess Smith, "Boise City Elections 1867 to 1885" (City of Boise, 2000), gesswhoto.com/ idaho/ boise-elections.html.

[25]Rossi & Lambing, Daily Accounts Journal (ISHS Archives).

[26]French, *History of Idaho Volume 2,* 623.

[27]Hubert Howe Bancroft, *The Works of Hubert Howe Bancroft Volume XXXI, History of Washington, Idaho, and Montana 1845-1889* (San Francisco: The History Company, Publishers, 1890), 64.

[28]ISHS, "Albert H. Robie" (Reference Series Number 596, 1981).

[29]University of Washington, "*Report of A.H. Robie, special agent for the Indians between the Columbia River and the Cascade Mountains, July 31, 1857.*" (University of Washington Digital Collections, 2009).

[30]U.S. Office of Indian Affairs, *Annual report of the commissioner of Indian affairs, for the year 1857, Oregon and Washington Superintendency* (1858), 350.

[31]Ibid., 353.

[32]ISHS, "Albert H. Robie."

[33]Ibid.

[34]Max A. Delgado III, *Jesus Urquides: Idaho's Premier Muleteer.* (Master of Arts in History, Boise State University, 2010), 29.

[35]A.G. Ontko, *And the Juniper Trees Bore Fruit, Volume V* (Bend, Oregon: Maverick Publications, Inc., 1999), 181.

[36]Ibid.

[37]Merrill W. Beal, "Rustlers and Robbers: Idaho Cattle Thieves in Territorial Days," *Idaho Yesterdays* 7:1 (Spring 1963), 28.

[38]Ontko, *Juniper Trees,* 181.

[39]Ibid.

40Legends of America, "Hank Vaughn–An Unhappy Horse Thief" (2006). www.legendsofAmerica.com.
41Shelton Woods, ed., *Valley County Idaho Prehistory to 1920*, Valley County History Project (Donnelly, Idaho: Action Publishing, 2002), 306.
42Ada County Commissioners, Minutes of the meetings, January 3, 1866; January 10 and October 8, 1867, Idaho State Historical Society Archives.
43Smith, "Boise City Elections."
44Ada County Homestead Abandonment (1879).
45Ada County Deed Book 11, 599.
46Woods, *Valley County Idaho Prehistory, 306.*
47James Hockaday, *History, Payette National Forest* (USDA Forest Service Intermountain Region, 1968), 18.
48Woods, *Valley County Idaho Prehistory, 306.*
49Burdett A. Rich, and Henry P. Farnham, eds., *The Lawyers' Reports Annotated*, New Series Book 34 (New York: The Lawyers Co-operative Publishing Company, 1911), 400-404.
50Ada County Court Records, 1888 (ISHS Archives).
51Hawley, *History of Idaho Volume II*, 482-483.
52U.S. Census, 1870 Agricultural Schedule, Dry Creek Precinct.
53US Census Mortality Schedules and Dry Creek Cemetery Records.
54U.S. Census, 1880 Statistics of Agriculture.
55Idaho Death Index 1911-1951.
56Ada County Land Claims Book 1, 67.
57Ada County Court Records, 1866.
58U.S. Census, 1880 Statistics of Agriculture.
59Naturalization Index (2005). www.idahohistory.net/naturalization.html
60Ada County Land Claims Book 1, 229.
61Hawley, *History of Idaho Volume III*, 818.
62IRS Tax Assessment List, 1868.
63Hawley, *History of Idaho Volume IV*, 652.
64Ibid.
65Ibid.
66Ibid.
67National Park Service (NPS), "Civil War Soldiers & Sailors" (2005). www.itd.nps.gov/cwss
68Yaryan, Personal recollection.
69Ada County Deed Book, 1-383.
70Ada County Commissioners, Minutes of the meetings 1868–1870.
71Boise City Land Office Records Homestead Application No. 45, 1874.
72U.S. Census, 1880 Statistics of Agriculture.
73*Idaho Statesman*, April 15, 1902.
74Wallace W. Elliott, *History of Idaho Territory* (San Francisco: Wallace W. Elliott & Co., 1884), 265.

3 *Floodplain: Green Meadow 1860s*

When the U.S. Army arrived in the Boise River Valley in the summer of 1863, they were looking for a place to put a military post. The only signs of life visible from the emigrant road in the western valley were Nine-Mile House (the Maxon Ranch) where Dry Creek entered the Boise River[1] and an abundance of jackrabbits. A few years later in 1867, surveyors described it as rolling terrain with second-rate soil,[2] compared to the Dry Creek Valley's first-rate soil.

By the end of the decade, however, families had claimed farms on either side of the Valley Road all the way to Boise City. The area that came to be called Green Meadow, after Samuel Aiken's Green Meadow Ranch, lay along the Valley Road between the Hill Road and the Boise River about seven miles downstream from Boise City. There the farms at the mouth of Pierce Gulch, Seaman Gulch, and the old road to Horseshoe Bend constituted a broad community of social interaction with the Dry Creek Valley farms to the north.

Families homesteaded Green Meadow at the same time as Dry Creek. About twenty householders established themselves there in the 1860s, with the first homestead patented in 1869. Among the first to receive homestead patents in Ada County were Green Meadow farmers Samuel Aiken, Seth Bixby, John Blagg, John Carpenter, Henry Conway, and William Gainey. An August 1864 story in the *Idaho Statesman* observed that the diversity of crops grown in the Green Meadow and Eagle Island area included beans, potatoes, cabbage, corn, oats, and barley.

The proximity of Green Meadow to Boise City meant that Green Meadow farmers were often active in the politics and industry of the greater Boise Valley, more so than the Dry Creek Valley farmers who were simply further away. Bixby and Aiken were especially active. In 1868, they were part of an Ada County committee to organize an association "to promote the industry and general interest of the Territory." The next year they were on the invitation committee for the First Annual Ball of the Ada County Jockey Club advertised in the *Statesman* (October 23, 1869). Tickets for the ball were $10 in currency and included supper.

The Landowners

Like those in the Dry Creek Valley, landholders in the Green Meadow area either purchased their farms

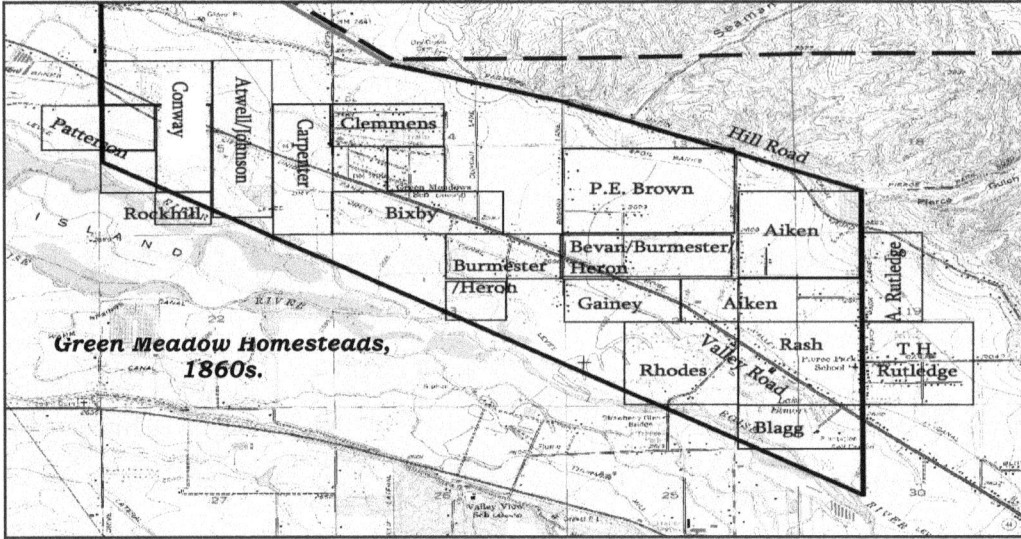

Green Meadow Homesteads, 1860s.

outright or were in the process of homesteading land claims. GLO records, the U.S. Census, and local histories and newspapers document much of their settlement. Nevertheless, some early settlers have undoubtedly been missed by written history and may be known only to their descendents or to those who lived and worked beside them during that era. The families described here represent settlement from west to southeast along the Valley Road toward Boise City.

John & Louisa B. Patterson

John Patterson was a prosperous farmer born in 1826 in Ohio. Louisa Burdge was born in New York in 1842. The Pattersons married in Iowa in 1863 and came to Idaho the next year on the Overland Trail via Lander's Cutoff according to the *Statesman* (July 26, 1892). They had two sons after they reached Idaho: John W. and George F.

Patterson settled 150 acres of

bottomland between the Valley Road and the Boise River at the far western edge of Green Meadow north of Eagle Island. He patented the homestead in 1869. According to the 1870 U.S. Census records, Patterson's ranch was valued at $3,000 and his personal property at $5,000, making him one of the more prosperous farmers in the area. Ada County assessed his assets at $6,095 in 1871.

The *Statesman* (May 17, 1877) reported that the Patterson family lived in an attractive, well-kept home visible from the Valley Road. Their apparently opulent home was described as a "well-built and beautiful-appearing building of the Elizabethan style." Inside, it was richly carpeted and curtained, and featured carved walnut bedsteads, embroidered pillows, and "luxurious chairs" according to the *Statesman* (November 23, 1876).

On a visit to his farm in 1877, a

writer observed a network of sloughs and ditches crossing Patterson's farm along the Boise River. The water was very near the surface, making for a marshy plot of land. At that time, Patterson's livestock included Morgan, Messenger, Leviathan, and Planter horses, as well as Brahma, China, Cochin, Poland, and Golden Pheasant poultry.

The Patterson family continued farming into the last decade of the century. At some point during the 1890s they divorced and John left the farm. He died in 1900 and was buried in Dry Creek Cemetery.

Louisa remained at the farm with her sons and their families. John W. married Lucinda Peck in 1890 and settled nearby.

Louisa died in 1915 leaving the second generation of the family to continue at the ranch well into the twentieth century.

Henry B. & Nancy Hedden Cobb Conway

The Conways were southerners, born in Kentucky. Henry was born in 1830 and Nancy in 1839. After bullet and saber wounds in the Mexican War (1846-1848), Conway received a medal of honor from General Scott according to his son's account.[3] Conway also served as guide on the Santa Fe Trail before heading for Oregon. He arrived in Idaho in 1862, setting up a livery business at Boise City. There he met widow Nancy Cobb whose husband John died that same year. Henry and Nancy married in 1863 and had two children: Mary Jane and William H.

The Conways homesteaded 158 acres northeast of Patterson's place around 1868. Conway's land extended from north of the Valley Road to the Boise River. He owned the stage station at the junction of the Valley Road and the road north to Horseshoe Bend.[4] In 1868, Conway paid taxes on $400 in assets according to Internal Revenue Service (IRS) tax assessment lists. By 1870, the Conways' real estate was valued at $2,000. They patented the homestead in 1874.

Henry was active in civic affairs and served as Ada County Coroner in

1867.[5] The next year he was paid $21 as an Ada County road supervisor according to the *Statesman* (January 20, 1870).

Nancy and Henry divorced in 1873 after ten years of marriage and she remained at the ranch with her children. After the divorce, part of the Conway property was owned by Thomas Hugh Aiken, brother of Samuel and Robert Aiken. Hugh Aiken figured prominently in the founding of the nearby town of Eagle. He married Conway's sixteen-year-old daughter Mary Jane in 1881. The Conway's son, William H., owned a ranch west of Green Meadow and was involved in various irrigation enterprises including the Thomas Aiken Ditch and the Conway-Hamming Ditch.[6] William married Frances Breshears and farmed in the Eagle area well into the twentieth century.

In the 1880s, a boarder named William Smith also lived at the Conway ranch. Smith was notable for having posted a newspaper notice in 1882 revealing that his real name was George W. Snowdon. According to a *Statesman* (January 21,1882) report, he was serving in the Confederate Army when taken prisoner by General Sherman's Union Army on its march to the sea. In order to avoid prison, he enlisted in the Union Army. When the war ended in 1865, he deserted the Army and took the name "Smith," his mother's maiden name. Snowdon later moved west, ending up in Idaho in 1878.

Henry Conway left Green Meadow after his divorce to pursue mining interests in nearby Washington County. In the early 1880s, he worked the Conway Ledge in the Heath Mining District about three miles from Ruthburg, Idaho. The *Statesman* (January 20, 1883) reported that the quartz from the ledge had a value of $16 per ton in gold and $4 per ton in silver. In 1900, Conway also located the seventeen-acre Homestake Lode in the Heath District.

By 1910, seventy-eight-year-old Henry was living in the Idaho Soldiers' Home in Boise City. He died later that year and was buried in Dry Creek Cemetery. Nancy Conway married her third husband, John B. Wood, in 1882 and remained at Green Meadow.

Felix Johnson
Farmer Felix Johnson was born in Ireland in 1828. He came to the U.S. as a teenager in 1845 and was unable to read or write. He may have owned the old Atwell ranch for a time. In 1870, his real estate was valued at about $1,000, the same as his neighbor John Carpenter's land. He had two fellow-Irishmen, George Welch and Dennis McCarty, boarding and working with him. Johnson left Idaho in the early 1870s for Oregon where he married and lived out his life.

John Atwell
John (Scotty) Atwell was born in Ireland in 1830. By May of 1865, he was living in Idaho Territory and had filed a homestead claim on a 154-acre property between the Valley Road and the Boise River. Later that year, he sold his surplus ditch water to his neighbor John Patterson.

46

In December of 1865, Atwell lost his ranch to Dr. John A. Raymond in a suit of ejectment relating to the law of prior possession on public lands. The *Statesman* (December 23, 1865) considered this one of the most important land cases in Ada County at that time. Atwell evidently lost the case, and the next summer, the *Statesman* (June 14, 1866) reported that his Green Meadow neighbor, lawyer Theodore Burmester, defended him on appeal.

Burmester received land on Eagle Island from Atwell in January of 1866—possibly in payment for services rendered. In 1866, Atwell owed $300 in Ada County taxes on his property. GLO records show that he received the patent to his land 1870, after he had left the ranch.

Atwell earned income selling liquor in Boise City in 1866, probably as part of a saloon operation.[7] Two years later, an advertisement in the *Statesman* (August 11,1868) was seeking Atwell to claim a sum of money left to him by his father who had died in Pennsylvania.

After leaving the ranch, Atwell pursued mining in the Brownlee, Idaho, area at the Weiser Mines. He and others established the quartz mining settlement of Ruthburg, according to the *Statesman* (June 6, 1876). In 1896, Atwell's body was found in Monroe Creek by a group of children. A coroner's jury ruled his death a suicide according to a newspaper story in April of that year.

John & Mary Mallems Carpenter

John Carpenter was born around 1822 in New York. Mary Mallems was born in England in 1827. They had two sons in New York in the 1840s: John Robert (Johnny) and a son listed in the U.S. Census as "W.C.," who may have died as a teenager.

John and his sons traveled west in 1859, intending to go to Pike's Peak, Colorado. Along the way, Carpenter changed plans, traded his horses for an ox team, and headed for California. At one point, his wagon train encountered Indians who Carpenter said tried to trade him some buffalo robes for one of his sons. Eventually the Carpenter men met up with Mary in California. She had traveled by ship around Cape Horn to San Francisco, and then by pack train to Yreka, California.[8] The Carpenters mined and ranched in California and Oregon for two years before relocating to Idaho City by ox team in 1863.

After settling in Idaho, John and Johnny headed back to Oregon in 1863 to buy supplies for the winter. On the trail, they were robbed of $500 while camped at Placerville, Idaho. During the struggle with the robbers, John saved much of his money by slipping it into his underwear. Johnny was shot in the right hand in the fracas and lost the use of two fingers[9]

The Carpenter family purchased the Saxon ranch east of Atwell's place along the Valley Road in the fall of 1865. The homestead was valued at $1,000 in 1870. Carpenter grew a wide range of crops on the fertile bottomland of the Boise River. He displayed onions, cabbage, chicory, vegetable oysters,[6] carrots, beets, squash, and radishes at the Ada County fair in 1873. Mary showed butter at the fair according to the *Statesman* (October 7). The farmstead was patented in 1874.

Like many households, the Carpenters usually had boarders who worked at their farm or at nearby farms. In 1870, for example, their household included Henry and Pauline Dickman with their daughter Louisa. The Dickmans later claimed their own homestead further east in Green Meadow.

John and Mary farmed the land until 1876, when they sold the ranch to their son and moved back east to Pennsylvania where John remained until his death in 1895.[10] Johnny went on to play a role in the founding of the town of Eagle west of Green Meadow in the early twentieth century.

Theodore & Arminta H. Burmester

Lawyer and rancher Theodore Burmester was born in Ohio in 1837 of German parents. His family was in Oregon by 1853 when he was sixteen. Arminta (Minnie) Hunsaker was born in Illinois in 1843 and lived in Oregon by 1850. She and Theodore, by then a lawyer, married in Oregon in 1861. They moved to Idaho around 1866, when he was admitted to practice law in Idaho Territory. He first advertised a law practice with Joseph Combs and later went into practice with S.L. Scaniker.[11]

---

[6] *Vegetable oyster, also known as salsify, is an herb with a long edible root.*

Burmester bought 139 acres, south of Bixby's place between the Valley Road and the Boise River, from John Hailey in 1868.[12] He also received other property from John Atwell in 1866.

The Burmesters had four children, two of whom died by 1869. Tragedy again struck the family in the spring of 1869 in an event reported as far away as New York. The *New York Times* (June 9, 1869) reported that a farmhand of Burmester's, John Konopeck, returned to the house from the field one day while Minnie and her two-year-old son Willie were home alone. Konopeck told her that he had cut his finger and wanted a bandage. When she went to get a bandage, he followed her inside and attacked her from behind. During the ensuing struggle, he headed upstairs to find a gun and she locked the door behind him. When he tried to return and found the door locked, he fired several shots through the door to open it.

By that time, Minnie also found a gun and tried to shoot him, but the gun did not go off. He then shot her in the abdomen and she fell to the ground pretending to be dead. At that point, Konopeck proceeded to set fire to the house.

Meanwhile Minnie managed to crawl outside where her son Willie was hiding in a wagon near the house. The flames were moving toward the wagon when a neighbor, John Bevan, arrived and pulled the wagon to safety. Other neighbors carried Minnie to Seth Bixby's house and sent for medical help as the house burned to the ground. Konopeck's burned remains were later found in the ruins. The *New York Times* called him a gypsy from Bohemia.

Despite medical treatment by a Boise doctor and nursing by Elizabeth Bixby, twenty-six-year-old Minnie died of her wounds. The *Statesman* (May 20, 1869) noted in her lengthy obituary the large community of friends and well-wishers who gathered at the funeral of this well-regarded young woman.

Trouble continued to follow Theodore Burmester. By the end of the year, he was charged with the murder of fellow lawyer Russell B. Morford. Burmester was allegedly seeing Morford's wife who was seeking a divorce from Morford. Mrs. Morford was seen a number of times in Burmester's company, sometimes alone, sometimes at night, and when he visited her during an illness. This led to ill will between Morford and Burmester. Eventually Burmester shot and killed Morford when both men drew guns on each other during an argument.

John Bevan, who farmed Burmester's ranch, testified at the trial that Burmester lived at the ranch only part time after the fire, spending the rest of the time in

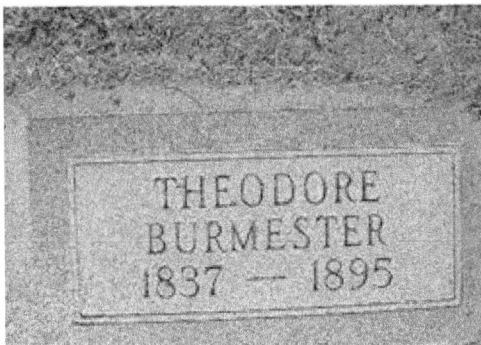

town. He also testified that Burmester came to the ranch alone with Mrs. Morford on occasion. The *Statesman* (December 28, 1869) reported that on one visit they left the ranch together after sundown in the direction of Dry Creek on what was then called the Dry Creek trail, probably up Pierce Gulch at the northeast corner of Aiken's ranch.

More than sixty witnesses were called—most gave testimony similar to Bevan's. Although the court of public opinion was clearly against Burmester, he was acquitted of murder after the jury deliberated for only about thirty minutes. A *Statesman* editorial later accused presiding Judge David Noggle of having instilled in the jury a bias to acquit Burmester despite all evidence.

Following the trial, Burmester sold his ranch back to John Hailey[13] and moved to Oregon with his sons Frank and William, who were cared for by their mother's family. William died at age six and Frank lived into the twentieth century.

GLO records show that Burmester received his land patent in 1870 after he moved to Oregon. He later remarried and practiced law in Oregon and Utah for many years, while continuing ranching. Burmester was active in organizing the short-lived Democratic Club of Utah in the 1880s. He died in Utah in 1895.

John M. & Louisa Griffin Hailey

Businessman, legislator, rancher, and historian, John Hailey was born in 1835 in Tennessee. He headed for Oregon country in 1853 and there fought in the Rogue Indian War of

1855/1856.[14]

In Oregon, he married Louisa M. Griffin, who was born in Kentucky in 1833. They married in 1857 and their first child, Jesse C., was born the following year. Four more children were born in Oregon in the 1860s: John M., Jr., Leona E., Thomas G., and Burrel B. Their sixth child, George C., was born in Idaho.

With reports of gold in the Boise Basin, Hailey financed his first packing venture to the area in 1862. That first venture led to a successful, long-lived hauling operation with lucrative mail-carrying and stagecoach contracts. Over the decade, he purchased a number of ranch properties in the Green Meadow area near his stage route.

In 1870, Hailey sold his hauling operation to fund livestock ranching. A visitor to his ranch in 1876 described seeing large, healthy herds of sheep crossed with Merino rams and a black Messenger stallion called Royal Sovereign. Royal Sovereign was:

> . . . *perfection and the artist, sculptor or critic can't find a single fault or failure. He is perfect as well as powerful and gigantic.*[15]

As a well-known and successful businessman, Hailey was elected to represent Idaho Territory in the U.S. House of Representatives from 1873 to 1875. After his first term in Congress, he returned to the stagecoach business briefly, just before the railroad moved into the area. During that time, he also invested in central Idaho mining operations and claimed the land

John M. Hailey, 1862
(Idaho State Historical Society #111A15).

Louisa Griffin Hailey
in later years
(Idaho State Historical Society #984-111-6).

that became the town of Hailey.

Hailey's interest in Idaho politics and government continued in the 1880s with his election to the Idaho Territorial Council and to another term in Congress from 1885 to 1887. In 1907, Hailey served as the first Secretary and Librarian of the Idaho Historical Society. His history of Idaho's early years was published in 1910.

Most of the Hailey children spent their adult lives in Oregon. Only Burrel remained in the northwest Boise area. Louisa died in 1918 and John in 1921. Both were buried in Boise's Pioneer Cemetery.

John S. Bevan

John Bevan (also spelled Bevin or Bevins) claimed 120 acres east of Burmester's place and north of the Valley Road around 1865. He sold the property to Burmester in April of 1869,[16] but continued to live there and work the ranch for Burmester. Bevan helped save Burmester's son during the 1869 fire and later testified at Burmester's murder trial.

Bevan received his ranch patent in 1871 after he sold the property to Burmester. It is difficult to track Bevan's later activities because of the many spellings of his name in the historical records. At any rate, by the twentieth century, two prominent local ranchers, David Heron and John Gary, owned the Bevan ranch.

David & Sarah Wilkinson Clemmens

David Clemmens was a native of Indiana born in 1836, the middle of ten children. Sarah E. Wilkinson was born in Indiana in 1838 and was one of the few Green Meadow-area residents who could not read or write. David and Sarah married in Iowa in 1861. They had twins, Catherine Lerah and Jesse E., and

two more children, Sabina E. and James M., in Iowa. David was registered for the Civil War draft in Iowa in 1863.

The Clemmens family set out on the Overland Trail in the summer of 1865 with two yoke of oxen and four children under the age of three. They traveled with a party of 125 wagons under Captain Bob Lockett.[17] Like many families on the trail, they first went to Oregon and then backtracked to Idaho.

In 1866, David Clemmens homesteaded 120 acres in the Green Meadow area adjoining the Bixby and Carpenter properties. The next year his livestock consisted of two cows, a hog, and a calf. Clemmens patented the land in 1871.

The Clemmens' daughter Ada A. was born at the Green Meadow homestead in 1867. Six-year-old Jesse died there in 1869. Seven-year-old Sabina, named for David's sister, died in 1871. Both were buried in Dry Creek Cemetery.

In 1870, the Clemmens family moved to Dry Creek where they bought the old Barrett Williams place, later known as Brookside, along the Boise City to Payette road. They lived in the house that had once been an inn on the stage line from Kelton, Utah, to Umatilla, Oregon. There, three more children were born: Ida, John W., and D.E. Six of the Clemmens' eight children lived to adulthood.

Seth & Elizabeth E. Coleman Bixby

Bixby was a rancher and livestock dealer born the son of a farmer in New York in 1831. He and Ellen

Coleman (also born in 1831) married in Ohio in 1851 and moved to Missouri where their first three children, Gilbert L., Phila Anna, and Emma I., were born. From Nebraska, they headed west on the Overland Trail in the spring of 1862. After four months on the trail, they reached Auburn, Oregon, where they spent the winter. In the spring of 1863, they backtracked to Idaho where the Bixby children were said to be the first children of white settlers brought into the Boise Basin. In 1864, the family moved to Boise City where they had two more children: James R. and Asa S.

Bixby claimed 160 acres south and east of the Clemmens place. He, along with Carpenter, Patterson, and others, built the first irrigation canal in the Green Meadow area in 1864. They completed the New Union Ditch Company Canal in the spring of 1865[18] from the Boise River to the northwest through the farms of the Green Meadow area.

In 1868, Bixby paid $10.40 in federal taxes on income of $208 according to IRS Tax Assessments records. By 1870, his property consisted of half interest in a mower, eight horses, two mules, oxen, seventeen cows, thirty-nine calves, five beeves, and twelve hogs.

Well respected in the area, Bixby was active in local politics and was elected Ada County Administrator in 1868.[19] He patented his homestead in 1874 and two years later sold the property to move to Sonoma County, California, and later to Oregon according to the *Statesman* (September 5, 1876).

Emma Bixby
(Idaho State Historical Society #90A4).

The Bixbys returned to Idaho in the 1880s. In 1888, the *Statesman* (May 8) reported that Elizabeth had eight tumors removed from her neck by Dr. Perrault and Dr. DuBois in Boise City. The tumors reportedly ranged in size from a walnut to a goose egg.

Seth died of a stroke in 1897 and Elizabeth in 1899, both in Payette where they lived with their daughter Anna and her family. Anna had married Peter Pence, president of the First National Bank of Payette and Payette's first mayor. The Bixbys were buried at Middleton, Idaho. All their children lived into the twentieth century.

Peter E. & Catherine E. Brown & G. Caroline Sexton Brown

Forty-niner Peter Brown was born in Michigan in 1830 and moved to Canada as a child. After his parents died, he sailed to the California gold fields in the 1840s by way of Cape Horn.[20] Brown mined in California for a number of years before moving to Idaho City in the early 1860s to work in the dairy business on Moore's Creek. Catherine was born about 1835 in New York.

The Brown's one child, Charles, was born in Idaho in 1868, the year they settled eighty acres east of Sam Aiken's place near what became the Bogart Station on the Boise & Interurban Railway line.[21] Brown's initial acreage was valued at $2,000 in 1870 (patented in 1875). He acquired an additional 160 acres around 1874 (patented in 1880).

In May of 1877, the newspaper reported that Brown was confined to his room with a bout of rheumatism. His young son Charles was "dangerously ill with lung fever" according to the *Statesman* (May 17, 1877), but survived.

Peter Brown was the first sheep grower in Green Meadow and initially the only sheep grower in the Boise River basin below Boise City according to the *Statesman* (May 4, 1876). He began with a band of 100 to 200 sheep. Three years later, his operation had grown immensely to include 1,500 sheep and 1,000 lambs. Brown raised sheep for about five years before switching to cattle in 1881.[22]

Peter E. Brown
(Hawley 1920 Vol III).

Peter and Catherine divorced in 1882. The next year he married Galena Caroline Sexton who had come to Idaho from Missouri in 1882.[23] Peter and Caroline had four children: Clarence Otis, Nora B., Ora L., and P. Ola before Peter died in 1896.

Peter left the Green Meadow farm to Caroline, who paid taxes on 340 acres of land in 1899 according to the *Statesman* (July 16, 1899). In 1900, she worked the farm with the help of a hired man, Abraham Miller, the son of Green Meadow farmers Henry and Regina Miller. Her parents and brother lived next door.

The property was valued at $5,475 by the Ada County Assessor in 1901. Part of the Brown farm was condemned in 1907 for the new trolley line that proceeded northwest along the Valley Road.[24] Caroline and her family remained in Green Meadow into the twentieth century. She died in 1929.

David E. & Fidelia Canfield Heron

Civil engineer David Heron was born in 1833 in Pennsylvania of Scottish parents. Fidelia Canfield was born in 1831 in Connecticut. After graduating college, David moved west to the Colorado mines in 1860 and then to Idaho's Boise Basin in 1863.[25]

He and Fidelia met at Central City, Colorado, where she was the community's first schoolteacher.[26] They married in 1861 and had a daughter, Mary T., while in Colorado. Their son Frank E. and daughter, Alice J., were born in Idaho. Alice later attended a teachers' college in Michigan and became the principal of Whittier Elementary School in Boise City.[27] By 1900, the Herons had adopted two more children: Zurah A., and David C.

David E. arrived in Idaho first, followed by Fidelia who traveled in a train of 120 wagons (about 400 emigrants) from Denver. During the trip Mrs. Heron was said to have "attracted the attention of an Indian chief, and he had made offers to induce her to leave the company, which of course she refused."[28]

In Idaho, Heron took up farming, first near Middleton, where he developed an 120-acre ranch that he sold before moving to the Green Meadow area. In 1869, he bought the 200+ -acre Burmester / Bevan / Hailey place, the site of the Hailey Stage Station,[29] from John Hailey for $2,500. This farm combined eighty acres of the Bevan homestead and 180 acres of the Burmester homestead.

On a visit to the Heron farm in 1877, a newspaper reporter noted that the Heron home was near the site of the house where the wife of Theodore Burmester was murdered in 1869. The Herons lived in their town home in Boise City by 1891.[30]

For many years, Heron was active in Ada County Republican politics. He was assistant Ada County Assessor for four years and held the following positions: Ada County Recorder (1881); Ada County Commissioner

David & Fidelia Heron (French 1914, Vol. II)

(1882); and Ada County Assessor (1885). His influential positions and status as a local pioneer with many admirers led to in his election to the Idaho Legislature in 1896 and 1898. Heron was honored in 1897 as one of the early Boise City pioneers in a parade of more than 130 of the earliest settlers through downtown Boise according to the *Statesman* (August 17, 1897).

David E. died in 1906. After his death, Fidelia sold the Green Meadow farm for $17,000. It was divided into ten-acre tracts according to the *Statesman* (August 3, 1906). Fidelia died in 1915 and was buried alongside her husband at Morris Hill Cemetery[7] in Boise City.

Frank Heron married in 1893 and lived in the White Cross Precinct southwest of Green Meadow, but later returned to Green Meadow where he farmed into the early twentieth century. Frank died in 1917 and was buried in Dry Creek Cemetery.

William H. & Jerusha Kilgore Gainey & Mahala C. Gainey

The Kilgore-Gainey family's chronicle offers a snapshot of a complex series of nineteenth century marriages, divorces, deaths, and remarriages. Jerusha Fields was born in 1825 in Missouri. At the age of fifteen, she married John I. Butler in Missouri. Butler may have died, and in 1847, Jerusha married J. Kilgore. The Kilgore's first child, Cordelia, was born in Iowa. The

---

[7] *Morris Hill Cemetery was established in 1882 by the City of Boise on the river valley bench south of the Boise River.*

family headed west for California where their daughter Lucinda Catherine (Kittie) was born in 1851. Kilgore died in California in 1852 and Jerusha gave birth to their third daughter, Paradine (Parry), the next year in Oregon.

William Gainey was born in 1830 in Kentucky. By 1854, he was living in Oregon where he met and married Jerusha Kilgore in the 1850s. The Gaineys moved to Idaho by 1865. William engaged in the retail liquor trade in the mining communities of Happy Camp and Rocky Bar. By 1866, he was in the Boise Valley where he reported an earned income of $900.[31] Gainey lived in Boise City at least until 1868.

In the late 1860s, he purchased a 160-acre farm along the Valley Road south of John Bevan's place that included fifty acres of woodland and was valued at $2,000 by 1870. That year the operation produced 100 bushels of spring wheat, 100 bushels of corn, 500 bushels of oats, 200 bushels of barley, 400 bushels of potatoes, and 400 pounds of butter. Gainey had nine cows and four oxen.[32] He patented his land in 1874 and may have sold it shortly thereafter.

Jerusha's daughter Kittie married John Ewing at Boise City in 1865 when she was fourteen. At eighteen, she married Ephraim B. Ball. After their divorce in 1879, Kittie lived alone, supporting herself as a seamstress, while her two young sons boarded with another family. Kittie later married two more times: William P. Ireland in 1882 at Rocky Bar, and John M.A. Wilson in 1884 at Boise City.

Meanwhile, Cordelia married Lucian Bonaparte (Lute) Lindsey in 1865. Lute kept a livery stable at Boise City and served as Ada County Sheriff. They had ten children and moved to Oregon by 1880. Paradine married Lute's brother Lavalette Lindsey, who was nineteen years her senior, in 1868. Both families lived together in Boise City for a time. Paradine and Lavalette had two children and were divorced by 1880.

Jerusha died in 1872 of "inflammation of the lungs" (possibly pneumonia) according to her obituary in the *Statesman* (January 4). Two years later, William married Mahala Ann Caylor. They had two children: William H.H., born in Idaho, and John F., born in California.

By 1880, the Gaineys were in Oregon where William remained until his death in 1888 at age fifty-eight. In the early twentieth century, Mahala returned to Idaho and lived in Canyon County. She died in 1908 at Emmett, Idaho, and was buried at Ola, Idaho.

Godfrey F. & E. Grace Watkins Rhodes

Long-time Green Meadow resident Godfrey Rhodes was a farmer born in Ohio in 1833 of German parents. He came to Idaho in the 1860s and settled on a small homestead in the Green Meadow area. By 1870, Rhodes owned about 100 acres valued at $400. It included twenty acres of woodland and thirty acres of improved farmland that produced 700 bushels of barley and sixty bushels of potatoes.[33] Rhodes received his land patent in 1875.

Godfrey married Grace Watkins, who was twenty-four years younger than he, in 1877. Grace came west from Ohio with her family in 1864 when she was a child of seven. Godfrey and Grace had five children: Fred W., Alice R., Margaret E., Marie K., and Theresa M. (Nessie). Margaret died at the age of three months and Marie lived to the age of ninety-nine years, dying just a few months before her 100th birthday.

By 1880, Rhodes' modest farm had increased in value to $2,000. It now included a little over 160 acres, most of which was tilled, along with thirty acres of woodland. The Rhodes' continued to farm in Green Meadow into the twentieth century with their son Fred. Godfrey died in 1917 of pulmonary congestion, and Grace in 1927 of influenza. They were both buried in Morris Hill Cemetery.

William A. & Mary Jane Baker Rash

William Rash was a freighter, miner, merchant, and farmer born in Alabama in 1825. Mary Jane Baker was born in Kentucky in 1834. They married in 1848 and had eight children. Their eldest child, Nancy E., was born in Missouri in 1850 before they headed west, reaching Oregon in the fall of 1851. In Oregon, John W., James, Mary, Susan, Ruby, Margaret, and Addie were born. Susan and Mary died as young children.

According to son John's recollections, William always chased the pot of gold at the end of the rainbow and moved his family around frequently, looking for the next best opportunity.[34] He headed for the gold diggings at Orofino, Idaho, in 1861 and from there to Idaho City before returning to La Grande, Oregon, in 1863 to set up a store. For the rest of the 1860s, the family continued to move around the Northwest, ending up in Idaho in 1869. In Idaho, William and John drove freight and ranched. John also drove for John Hailey's stageline during the Indian wars of the late 1870s.

William Rash's 160 acres in Green Meadow, including twenty acres of woods, was valued at $1,000 in 1870. He had six horses and three milk cows, and produced ninety bushels of spring wheat, 300 bushels of potatoes, and $1,000 worth of market garden produce.[35] In 1873, the *Statesman* (October 7) noted that Mrs. Rash showed three kinds of onions and a variety of early potatoes, as well as butter and homemade soap "as white as chalk" at the Ada County fair.

By 1880, the Rash family was on the move again and returned to Umatilla County, Oregon, where William and Mary ran a hotel. Ruby Rash remained in Idaho, having married John Carpenter's son, Johnny, in 1876 when she was fifteen. Addie married David C. Heron in 1889.

William died in 1885 in Montana and Mary Jane in 1899 in Oregon.

John & Judith Blagg

John and Judith (Juna) Blagg were both born in North Carolina in 1804 and 1805, making them the oldest of the early Green Meadow settlers. Their son and daughter, Martha A. and James R., were born in the 1830s in Tennessee. From there, the

family moved to Missouri and then to Idaho in 1864. Neither John nor Juna could read or write.

John owned about 160 acres north of the Boise River at the far southeastern corner of Green Meadow. In 1870, the Blagg's farm was valued at $1,500. He had fifteen acres of woodland and fifty acres of improved farmland that produced 200 bushels of spring wheat and twenty bushels of potatoes. Blagg owned two horses and four milk cows that produced 100 pounds of butter. He also had two swine.[36] Blagg patented his land in 1874.

Martha Blagg married James Cowsert in Missouri and had five children. The Cowsert family moved to Idaho in 1864, presumably with the Blaggs, and lived nearby between Green Meadow and Boise City. Martha died in 1868 and was buried in Boise's Pioneer Cemetery. After her death, John and Juna lived at the farm with their son-in-law and grandchildren.

Juna died in 1877 at age seventy-three. John died in 1878 at seventy-four, leaving his estate to his grandchildren. Both were thought to be quite elderly for the times. The *Statesman* (February 15, 1877) wrote of them the year before they died:

> *Mr. and Mrs. Blagg are probably the oldest people in our vicinity, he being a year the oldest. They are quite rugged for such old people. . .*

The Blaggs were buried in Boise City's Pioneer Cemetery. In 1907, their homestead became the location of Pierce Park, a destination for family picnics on the Boise & Interurban Trolley line.

George & Hannah C. Taylor Rockhill

George Rockhill, who worked one of Green Meadows' smaller farms, was born in Ohio in 1827. Hannah was born in Indiana in 1848. They had at least ten children, five of whom died before reaching adulthood: Rosa A., E. Franklin, Mary L. (died at age three), Emma A. (died at age ten), Florence B., John H. (died at age three), W. Elmer, George, Jr., Lillie M. (died at age two), and Adelaide (died at age four).

The Rockhills moved to Idaho sometime before 1866. George farmed about 110 acres, ten of which were in woodland and sixty in improved cropland. His land produced 1,000 bushels of spring wheat, 300 bushels of barley, and 300 bushels of potatoes.[37] Rockhill had a horse, a milk cow, and a meat cow. He also patented forty acres along the Boise River south of Conway's place in 1871.

Around 1877, the Rockhills sold their land and moved to Washington where they lived out their lives. In the fall of 1880, the *Statesman* posted a mysterious advertisement seeking George Rockhill, whose whereabouts were unknown, and stating that something to his advantage awaited his response.

Jacob & Laura M. McClellan Diehl

Farmer and saddler Jacob Diehl was born in Pennsylvania in 1817. Laura McClellan was born in Illinois in 1840. The Diehls migrated west by ox team and wagon to Oregon in 1863. There their first four children were born: Vianna M. (Annie),

Richard M., John M., and James J. They arrived in Idaho between 1868 and 1869. Four sons were born in Idaho: George W., Lewis E., Frederick W., and Frank M. Frank died in 1870 at the age of three months of "brain inflammation."[38] Lewis went on to partner in the Eagle store, Diehl & Mace.

At first, Jacob established a saddle store at Boise City.[39] He later sold the shop and took up farming. By 1870, Diehl owned 120 acres near Sam Aiken's farm. He had two horses, two milk cows and a hog. Diehl's 110 acres of improved ground produced 1,000 bushels of spring wheat, 200 bushels of oats, and 100 bushels of barley.[40]

After Laura died in 1877 at the age of thirty-eight, Diehl moved to Boise City where he ran a road sprinkling business and managed a toll bridge for William H. Ridenbaugh on an acre of land near the Boise River Bridge at Ninth Street. At the end of the 1880s, he advertised his sprinkling wagon and team of horses for sale in the *Statesman* (May 7, 1889). The business finally sold in 1893, after Diehl's land sold for back taxes.

Jacob Diehl died in 1894 and was buried in the Masonic section of Boise's Pioneer Cemetery.

Samuel D. & Angeline P. Aiken & Robert C. Aiken

Samuel (Sam) Aiken was arguably the most successful Green Meadow farmer in the late nineteenth century. He was born in 1829; his brother Robert was born in 1836. The brothers said they were born in Maine, although in the 1880s they were found to have hailed from Nova Scotia, Canada, and were not U.S. citizens at all. The Aiken brothers came to Idaho in 1863 after working in California and Oregon. Sam was said to have built the first carriage ever manufactured in Oregon.[41]

Robert Aiken claimed forty acres east of John Bevan's place in the early 1860s. Samuel claimed 131 acres at the mouth of Pierce Gulch in 1864 and called it Green Meadow Ranch. The name of his ranch eventually came to refer to the small community of ranches between the Hill Road and the Valley Road near the junction of the road to Dry Creek.

In 1870, Sam, a long-time bachelor, headed a household of farm workers, including his brother Robert, Eugene D. Whipple, Sackfield Dyre, Thomas J. Sconce, James C. Hudson, Patrick Carroll, and their French cook Emilie Blance. The value of his 295 acres of land, listed in the 1870 U.S. Census as $10,000, made him by far the wealthiest farmer in the Green Meadow area. That year, he had eleven horses and a milk cow, and produced 700 bushels of spring wheat, 200 bushels of rye, 400 bushels of oats, 700 bushels of barley, 300 bushels of potatoes, ten bushels of beans, eighty tons of hay, and other market-garden produce. Aiken also planted a 300-tree black walnut orchard from seed. The orchard began producing large quantities of walnuts in about seven years.

Aiken patented his ranch in 1874 and that year showed a variety of yellow flint corn at the county fair. The *Statesman* (October 7, 1873) opined that good farming practices such as his could result in a yield of seventy-five bushels of corn per acre. In October of 1875, the newspaper reported that Aiken's crops won three prizes from the Idaho Agricultural Park Association for best field corn, best beans, and best garden potatoes. Aiken had raised 6,000 bushels of grain and eighty tons of hay on 240 acres according to the newspaper (May 4, 1876).

By the late 1880s, Green Meadow Ranch consisted of 340 acres in the home farm and 160 acres along the river, irrigated by a ditch from the Boise River and by several natural springs. Aiken's farm machinery included a mower, seeder, thresher, and horse rakes. In 1876, he expected to harvest 8,000 bushels of grain according to the *Statesman* (May 4, 1876). He also grew timber, with 2,000 young trees and seedlings including walnut, hickory, maple, oak, and butternut, in addition to an orchard and shrubs near his house.

Aiken's diverse farming operation produced 1,440 gallons of milk from twelve milk cows and 328 dozen eggs from a flock of 500 chickens. He had twenty-four horses in 1880 and the farm had increased in value to $15,000.[42] Aiken figured he would harvest about 3,000 pounds of walnuts in 1882, making his walnut orchard more profitable than his apple orchard according to the *Statesman.*

Probably more than any other rancher in Green Meadow or Dry Creek, Aiken used newspaper advertising to enhance his business. He regularly advertised in the *Statesman* beginning in 1867 when he offered green grass and grain stubble grazing for horses and mules, along with "good water" at Green Meadow Ranch five miles from Boise City (September 24,1867). He advertised fifty tons of hay for sale at his ranch in January of 1868.

According to the *Statesman* (October 8, 1870), he also grew a certain variety of Norway oats that produced 200 bushels from 106 pounds of seed. In the early 1870s, he advertised the Norway oats and the seed for sale, including 300 bushels of oats in 1871.

Ten years later, Aiken was still advertising his hay at Green Meadow Ranch for one cent per pound, along with winter apples and grain. "...but don't forget the money," he said (April 23, 1881).

Aiken's advertising also extended to personal matters. In August of 1872, he offered a reward for the return of a black leather pocketbook he had lost. It evidently contained about $60 in currency and $500 in notes payable to him and was lost near a Boise City blacksmith shop or along the road between Boise City and his ranch.

After many years as a successful rancher, Sam Aiken married widow Angeline Parker in 1874. Angeline had four children with her first husband, Thomas Parker: Andrew, Elizabeth A., William J., and Tabitha. She and Sam are not known to have had children. Robert Aiken remained a bachelor. In 1880, he was sharecropping in Green Meadow and living by himself near the Rhodes family. Robert later moved to Washington County where he worked as a farmer. He died in 1924 and was buried in Pioneer Cemetery.

Along with local fame and prosperity came some serious setbacks for Sam Aiken. An 1884 story in a Montana newspaper recounted that throughout their years of homesteading, the Aiken brothers had not been U.S. citizens and were therefore not qualified to acquire lands under the Homestead Act. When this information was made public, three or four individuals tried to claim Sam's valuable ranch with its acres of black walnut and other timber. It was reported in the *Butte Montana Daily Miner* (November 14, 1884) to have cost Aiken $5,000 in lawyer's fees to fend off the land takeover and receive proper title from the U.S. government.

Sam Aiken's Green Meadow Ranch.
Freight wagon in foreground is on the Hill Road (Elliott 1884).

A few years later, a small spring or "water spout" above Green Meadow Ranch caused a landslide from the foothills to the north. The landslide covered a large area of ground near Aiken's house with one to two feet of soil. According to *Statesman* reports (February 28, 1888), uneven places were covered four to ten feet deep.

The last advertisements by Sam Aiken appeared in the *Statesman* in 1886. He had been very ill during the summer of 1884 and died in 1887 at the age of fifty-seven. Aiken was buried at Pioneer Cemetery in Boise City. After his death, Angeline was involved in many court cases regarding the settlement of his complex estate, which included lumber company and real estate investments, as well as the ranch.

After Sam died, Green Meadow Ranch was managed by renowned Idaho lawman Orlando "Rube" Robbins, who was a deputy U.S. Marshal for twenty-five years, Boise City Chief of Police, and Ada County Sheriff. He also served in the Idaho Legislature. Robbins had come to Idaho from the California gold fields. Among other jobs, he worked on John Hailey's stageline riding shotgun to prevent robberies. In Green Meadow, Robbins cleaned up Aiken's walnut grove to make a pleasant park for public picnics according to the *Statesman* (March 13, 1888).

Meanwhile Angeline lived in Boise
City. She had a delicate surgical
operation there in 1893, when three
doctors removed a twenty-eight-
pound ovarian tumor from her body
according to the local newspaper.
Evidently, she recovered from the
surgery and lived until 1915. She
died in Salt Lake City, Utah.

By the early twentieth century,
prominent cattleman John Gary
owned much of Green Meadow
Ranch.

Thomas H. & Catherine Cox Rutledge

Thomas (Hugh) Rutledge was born
in Alabama in 1837 and served as a
Confederate officer in the Civil War.
He commanded Company G of the
43rd Alabama Infantry before
mustering out as a First Lieutenant
at the end of the war. Catherine Cox
was also a southerner, born in
Missouri in 1853. She was the
daughter of Green Meadow
homesteaders Reuben and Anna
Cox.

Catherine married thirty-two-year-
old Hugh in Idaho in 1869 when she
was sixteen. They had eight
children: Annie, Ella, Mattie,
Josephine, Emma, John W., Walter
H., and Raymond. Emma and John
may have died as children.

Hugh settled 160 acres along the far
eastern edge of Green Meadow in
the 1860s and patented the farm in
1877. In 1870, his 120 acres of
improved land produced 250
bushels of spring wheat, forty
bushels of Indian corn, 200 bushels
of oats, 200 bushels of barley, and
fifteen bushels of potatoes.[43] At the
time, Rutledge had one milk cow. By
the end of the decade, he had
increased his butter production
substantially: his eight milk cows
produced 300 pounds of butter in
1879. He also owned nineteen
horses and forty-five head of beef
cattle.[44]

Green Meadow farmers were often in
town on business and Rutledge's
experience with a runaway horse
team in Boise was reported in the
Statesman (January 18, 1876). He
was in front of Julius Hager's
furniture store when his team of
horses took off with Hugh in
pursuit. He caught the horses at the
corner of Ninth Street by hanging on
to them and running the team into
Dry Creek homesteader James
Baldwin's old wagon, which was
parked near Baldwin's blacksmith
shop. Although the horse team
pulled Rutledge over the top of the
wagon before they stopped, he
sustained only a few bruises and his
escape was considered very
fortunate.

In addition to farming, Rutledge was
active in the community and in
1875, served on the Board of
Trustees of the Blagg School at the
southeastern end of Green Meadow.

Catherine died in the winter of 1885
at the age of thirty-two not long after
her son, Raymond, was born. After
her death, Hugh moved his family to
Meridian, Idaho, where he
continued to farm in the 1890s. By
the turn of the century, only
Raymond remained at home with
Hugh. Hugh died in 1923 at the age
of eighty-six. He was buried in Dry
Creek Cemetery next to Catherine.

Andrew J. Rutledge

Andrew Rutledge, born in Tennessee

around 1830, was the elder brother of Hugh Rutledge and seems to have arrived in Idaho with Hugh in the 1860s, probably after having served in the Confederate Army. By 1870, Andrew was farming eighty acres in Green Meadow near the mouth of Pierce Gulch. His thirty-five acres of improved land produced 150 bushels of spring wheat and fifty bushels of barley. Andrew owned a horse and four oxen.[45] He patented the property in 1879.

Andrew remained a single man, living with his brother's family into the twentieth century. In addition to his farming activities, he ran a saloon in Boise City in the 1890s. On January 1, 1896, the *Statesman* reported his arrest for selling liquor to minors.

Andrew was dangerously ill in 1898 according to the *Statesman* (March 14, 1898), but he survived into the new century. He died in 1907 and was buried in Dry Creek Cemetery.

The Farmworkers & Tradespeople

As in the Dry Creek Valley, few Green Meadow farmworkers from this era owned their own land. Most appear to have worked in the area for a short time before moving on to other opportunities. In addition to farmworkers, two cooks, Emile Blance and John Quinn, lived in Green Meadow by 1870.

The End of a Decade

By the end of the 1860s, Green Meadow, like Dry Creek, was well settled and improved. Resident landowners and their families ran most of the farms, with some owning multiple properties throughout the western Boise River Valley.

Most Green Meadow farmers engaged in a variety of civic activities including state and county governance. Their proximity to Boise City allowed for more interaction with the city and territory than Dry Creek farmers had.

The coming decade of the 1870s would bring technological advances in farm production, increasing crop diversity, and the controversial beginning of sheep ranching in Green Meadow.

Endnotes

1 John Hailey, *The History of Idaho* (Boise: Syms-York Company, Inc., 1910), 88.
2U.S. Geological Survey, 1867 Plat Map, T4N, R1E.
3 James H. Hawley, *History of Idaho Volume II* (Chicago: S.J. Clarke Publishing Company, 1920), 900.
4 Laurie L. Baker, City of Eagle, and Ronald J. Baker, *Images of America: Eagle* (Charleston, South Carolina: Arcadia Publishing, 2012), 9.
5Henry G. Langley, *Pacific Coast Business Directory for 1867* (San Francisco: H.G. Langley, 1867), 22.
6Idaho State Historical Society (ISHS), "Eagle Island Ditches" (Reference Series Number 507, 1974).
7IRS Tax Assessment Lists, 1862-1918.
8Hawley, *History of Idaho Volume III, 120.*
9Hawley, *History of Idaho Volume III, 123.*
10Ibid.
11Henry E. Prickett, *Reports of Cases Argued and Determined in the Supreme Court of Idaho Territory* (San Francisco: A.L. Bancroft and Company, 1882).
12Ada County Deeds Book III, 300.
13Ada County Deeds Book III, 781-782.
14*Illustrated History of the State of Idaho* (Chicago: The Lewis Publishing Company, 1899), 31.
15*Idaho Statesman*, November 23, 1876.
16Ada County Deeds Book 3, 527.
17Hawley, *History of Idaho Volume III,* 661.
18ISHS, "New Union Ditch Company Canal" (Reference Series Number 513, 1974).
19Ada County Officials 1865-1885.
20Hawley, *History of Idaho Volume III,* 834.
21Ibid., 837.
22Hawley, *History of Idaho Volume III, 837.*
23Ibid.
24Ada County Court Cases, 1890-1922.
25*Illustrated History of the State of Idaho,* 165.
26Ibid.
27Ibid., 166.
28French, *History of Idaho, Volume II,* 756.
29Ibid.
30Boise City Directory, 1891.
31IRS Tax Assessment Lists for Idaho Territory, 1865.
32U.S. Census, 1870 Agricultural Schedule.
33Ibid.
34*Idaho Statesman*, November 11, 1917.
35U.S. Census, 1870 Agricultural Schedule.
36Ibid.
37Ibid.
38U.S. Federal Census Mortality Schedule 1870, Ada County.
39Hawley, *History of Idaho Volume II,* 489.
40U.S. Census, 1870 Agricultural Schedule.
41Elliott, *History of Idaho Territory,* 255.
42U.S. Census, 1880 Statistics of Agriculture.
43U.S. Census, 1870 Agricultural Schedule.
44U.S. Census, 1880 Statistics of Agriculture.
45U.S. Census, 1870 Agricultural Schedule.

4 Diversity & Plenty: the 1870s

Technological improvements in farming like silos, deep-well drilling, and barbed wire changed the face of agriculture during the 1870s. The fencing of rangeland in the West gradually ended an era of unrestricted, open-range grazing. Although the number of farms in southwestern Idaho increased between 1867 and 1870, the demand for farm goods began to drop during the 1870s as the mining boom played out in the Boise Basin. However, farmers still had to pay high prices for their own necessities including farm implements. The bright spots during this economic downturn were fruit and livestock production, which continued to provide good income.

In 1870, most southwestern Idaho farms clustered in the Boise River Valley and its tributaries.[1] Ranching challenges included livestock disease, insects, floods, and heavy rain. Rains decimated the grain harvest in September of 1872 and severe hailstorms destroyed local grain and vegetables in July of 1875, according to reports in the *Statesman* (September 10, 1872; July 13, 1875). Insect invasions followed the harsh weather from 1874 to 1876 when grasshoppers plagued the valley and the West as a whole. The insect plague led to the establishment of the U.S. Entomological Commission in 1877 to work on grasshopper control.

Farm production remained diverse in Dry Creek and Green Meadow as farmers raised every kind of livestock and crops from fruit to hay. Several had orchards, primarily apple, in what the newspapers touted as a prime fruit-growing area. Farmers sold crops and other goods at Boise City. In 1875, hay went for $25 a ton, wool for twenty cents a pound, green apples for fifteen cents a pound, eggs for forty cents a dozen, onions for $3 per 100 pounds, potatoes for three cents a pound, oats and wheat for $3.00 per 100 pounds, dried peaches for twenty-two cents a pound, dried apples for twenty cents a pound, and bacon for twenty-five cents a pound.

Local farmers could purchase the goods they did not produce. These often included certain staples like flour at $8.00 a barrel, coffee at thirty-three to forty cents a pound, tea at seventy-five cents a pound, sugar at twenty-five cents a pound, gunshot at twenty-five cents a pound, salt at ten cents a pound, and rice at $7.50 a sack according to the *Statesman* (July 17, 1875).

By the end of the decade, most Dry

Creek and Green Meadow farmers grew at least barley, oats, and wheat. About half also grew potatoes, mainly in the Green Meadow area. Some raised an acre or two of "Indian corn." Only P.L. Schick and Robert M. Crawford in Dry Creek grew ten or more acres of corn in 1879.[2] Crawford and Thomas Kingsbury also had apple orchards in the valley. Godfrey Rhodes grew apples in Green Meadow.

Ranchers also bred saddle horses for sale to the U.S. Army and for the general market. Cattle, sheep and other livestock grazed freely in most places until the spring or fall roundup. In the spring of 1873, the *Statesman* reported that "China Sam" rounded up about 300 head of hogs on Dry Creek and corralled them on Willow Creek, where they could eat the camas plants along the creek. They were to remain there until fall, to be finished with grain before going to market.

Almost all of the farms raised cattle

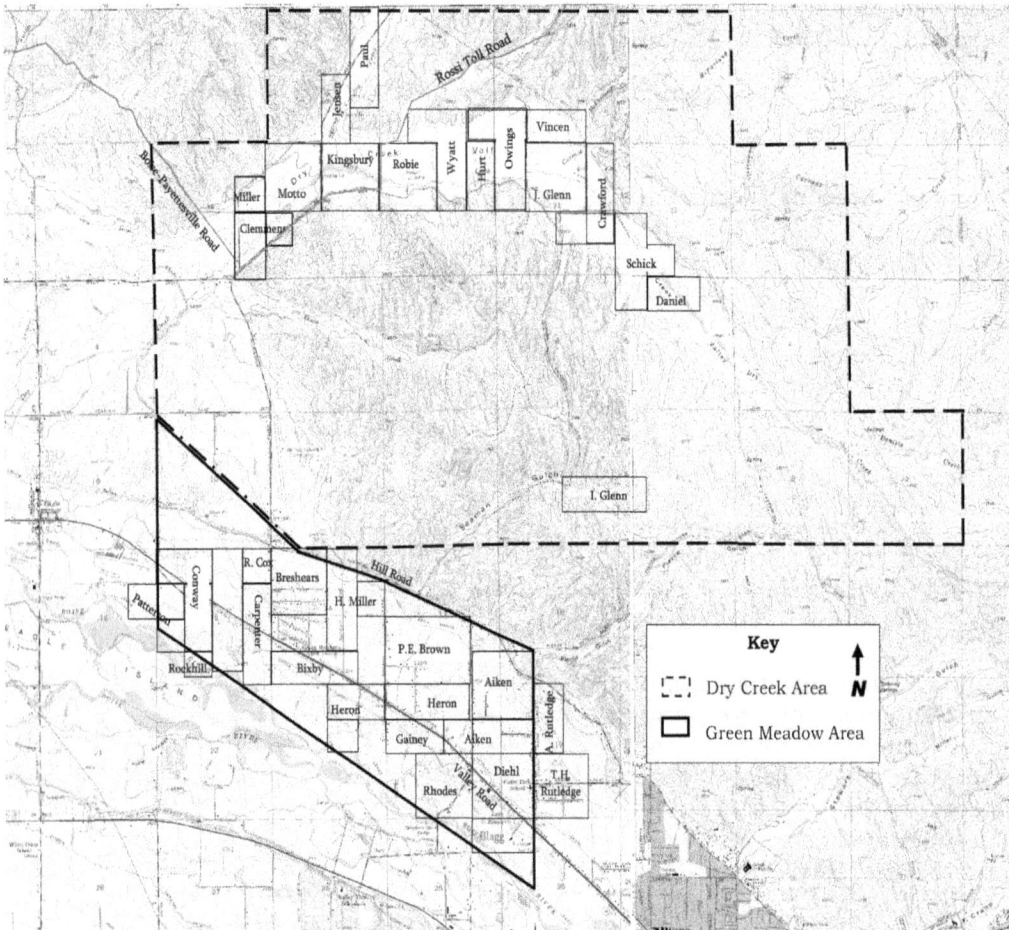

Dry Creek and Green Meadow homesteads, 1870s. *Sources: GLO Land Patent Records & Ada County Records.*

for meat and milk, along with chickens and swine. None had sheep in Dry Creek in the early 1870s. Green Meadow rancher Peter Brown, however, reported owning 1,500 sheep by the end of the decade.[3] As area ranchers began raising sheep, conflicts between sheepmen and cattlemen played out in the courts and in the local press. For example, farmers at the mouth of Dry Creek complained in the *Statesman* (February 22, 1873) that sheep were eating the grass off their ranch lands so they would not have summer pasturage for their cattle. However, Idaho cattle interests were so strong that in 1875 the Territorial Legislature passed a law prohibiting sheepherding within two miles of any human habitation or cattle range.[4]

Dry Creek Valley

Despite the ongoing challenges facing agricultural operations, the mid-1870s were arguably the heyday of the Dry Creek Valley. Homesteads thrived up and down the valley on some of the area's most prosperous farms. A number of prominent citizens of Boise City either had farms in the valley or took day trips there for recreation. Local newspapers regularly discussed Dry Creek commerce and activities. For example, the *Statesman* (September 26, 1874) reported that Idaho Governor Thomas W. Bennett and a bird-hunting party bagged ninety-three birds on Dry Creek in the fall of 1874. In June of 1877, seven Boise City families went to Dry Creek for an early summer day in the country. They took a ten-mile buggy ride

before breakfast, spent the day fishing for trout, and then had dinner along the creek according to the *Statesman* (June 12, 1877).

A number of freighters lived in the valley during this decade, reflecting the potential for income from transporting agricultural and other goods to and from Boise City, Washington, Oregon, Utah, and the Idaho mines. Some freighters were also landowners whose wives and children worked the farm while they were on the road.

Miners from Willow Creek explored the potential for mining deposits on Dry Creek. Homesteader Barrett Williams conducted a successful placer mining operation on the creek for several years. The *Statesman* (September 7, 1872) also reported on a group of miners who set out from Boise City to find the source of Dry Creek, presumably with lode mining in mind.

An old man prospecting on Dry Creek in 1879 reportedly struck an eight-foot-wide lead seam about ten feet down. The man may have been Willow Creek miner John Allen who said he struck an ore lode down about ten feet along Dry Creek at an undisclosed location. He brought the ore to town to have it assayed in 1879 according to the *Statesman* (September 16). Despite these efforts, there were no big strikes on Dry Creek, although a few valley homesteaders made small change mining their land claims along the creek.

Rossi's Shafer Creek Mill and other milling operations supported the construction needs of Dry Creek Valley farmers. Ranchers A.J. Wyatt,

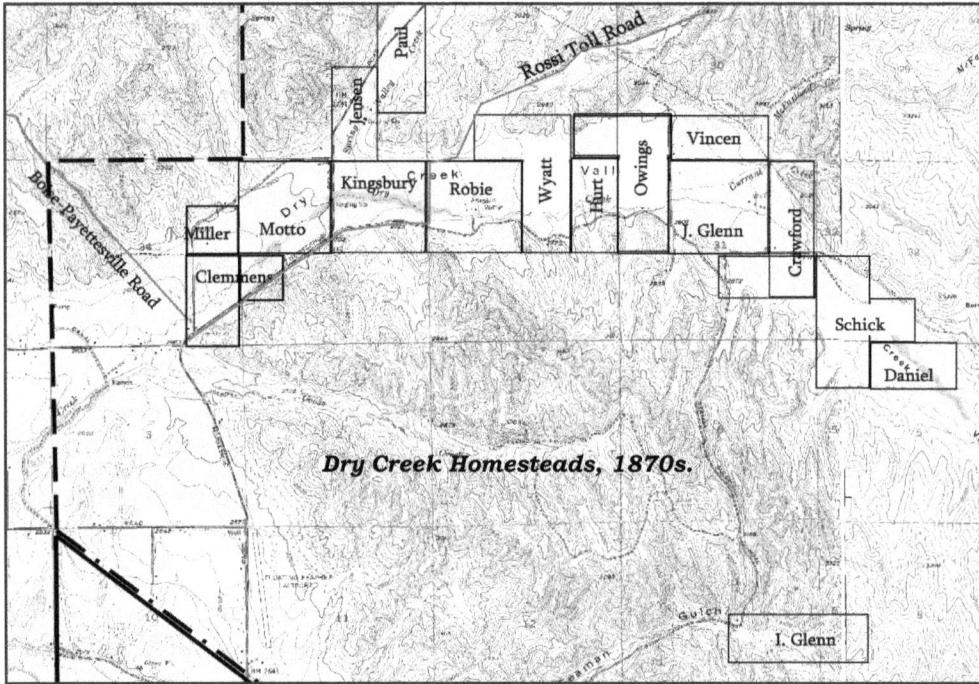

Dry Creek Homesteads, 1870s.

Thomas Kingsbury, Robert Crawford, John M. Glenn, William Daniel, William Francis, John Owings, and William M. Marlatt purchased lumber from Rossi's Mill. Kingsbury also hauled lumber directly from the Shafer Creek Mill for Owings, Glenn, and others in the valley.[5]

The first federal census of the Dry Creek Valley took place in July of 1870, recording about twenty-four households in the valley. The General Land Office (GLO) commissioned its second mapping to complete the eastern or upper Dry Creek Valley in 1874. Surveyor John B. David hired Harry Newland and William Lambing (chainmen) and William Herman (axeman) to assist him.[6]

Political views in the valley varied,

with vocal Democrats and Republicans in about equal numbers. Issues of the day included the controversy surrounding possible enactment of a federal income tax. Democrats generally opposed it and Republicans were generally in favor of it according to the *Statesman* (February 17, 1870). Elections took place in private homes and later in schoolhouses, with members of both parties in close supervision. The 1870 election for Ada County Sheriff led to some controversy in the Dry Creek Precinct. When Kingsbury and Jacob Motto cast votes in the election, the election judges rejected their ballots, saying the men were not legal voters according to a report in the *Statesman* (December 22, 1870). Although they clearly lived in the precinct, they may have been unregistered at the time.

In 1872, the *Statesman* (April 16, 1872) listed Ada County election officials in the Dry Creek Precinct as Wyatt, Schick, and another landowner, Neri Jack. Voting took place at Wyatt's house. In 1876, Kingsbury and David Clemmens were election judges for the Ada County Democrats' primary in the Dry Creek precinct and Clemmens was the one of the Dry Creek delegates to the state convention that year according to the *Statesman* (August 3 and 8, 1876).

As families settled in the valley, they built schools and hired teachers to educate their children. Schick built upper Dry Creek School on the Glenn homestead in 1879. Others built a school in the Brookside area where Dry Creek opened out onto the plain of the Boise River.

Even as homesteaders thrived during the early 1870s, the end of the decade brought major changes in the local economic situation. Ranch commerce came to halt in 1877 and 1878 with general Native American unrest in Idaho and the hostilities associated with the Bannock Indian War.[8] Many mining operations shut down as it appeared unsafe for small parties to prospect in the mountains. Histories of the

time describe stock raisers losing animals to theft and being unable to graze their herds on what they considered the best rangelands. Local conflicts interrupted stage and freight transportation as horses were stolen, stage drivers killed, and stage stations burned. Freighters lost livestock and several wagons loaded with merchandise burned.

A number of Dry Creek families left their ranches to stay in Boise City for a time until they felt safe enough to return to their remote properties. Some of the stories told by white children who lived in and near the Dry Creek Valley during this tense period conveyed their fear of encountering Indians. William F. Hartley, whose family lived in Stewart Gulch, told of an 1877 encounter in the foothills above Dry Creek. Hartley, then a boy of thirteen, was hunting for horses in the hills when he saw an Indian riding quickly down the road toward him. Young Hartley was frightened, but later realized that somebody was chasing the man, who had not even noticed him.[7]

The Landowners

Many of those who homesteaded the valley in the 1860s remained on their farms into the 1870s, taking advantage of the thriving rural economy in the early years of the decade. A few new farm families arrived from Green Meadow, Boise City, and other locations. The farm families first recorded in the valley during the 1870s are chronicled here from the eastern valley farms to the west.

---

[8] *The Bannock War of 1878 was the culmination of a number of issues including treaty violations and the destruction of central Idaho camas fields, an important food source for the Bannock people, by white settlers. Hostilities ensued as Bannock and Northern Paiute people attempted to drive white settlers from the area. The War ended in the fall of 1878 after U.S. Army involvement.*

David & Sarah Clemmens & Angelo Macklin

Green Meadow homesteader David Clemmens purchased Barrett Williams' ranch on Dry Creek in 1870 and continued to work in the freighting business between Boise City and Kelton, Utah. The Clemmens home was a way station on the stage line from Kelton to Umatilla, Oregon. At the Brookside way station were a saloon, dance hall, and brewery.[8]

David and Sarah's three younger children were born in the 1870s: Ida A., John W., and D.E. Their daughter Sabina died in 1871 at the age of seven and was buried in Dry Creek Cemetery.

A major tragedy struck the family in the autumn of 1877 when David Clemmens lost his life in an accident described in a newspaper clipping preserved in an old family Bible. On returning from a freight trip to Kelton, he camped at Desert Station on Rock Creek on the Overland Trail. A group of settlers moving west on the Overland Trail were camped nearby. Clemmens set out to visit their camp after dark. At some point, he decided return to his camp alone and fell to his death from a sixty- to eighty-foot-high cliff above the canyon. His body was recovered and returned to Dry Creek where he was buried in Dry Creek Cemetery.

Sarah was pregnant with her youngest child at the time of her husband's death. Their son, David E. (D.E.), was born after Clemmens died and was named for him. After David's death, Sarah remained in Dry Creek with her children

Catherine, James, Ada (Annie), Ida, John, and D.E. on the ranch she inherited.

Of the nine Clemmens children, only Ida and D.E. survived into the new century. Annie had married Enos Walling at age sixteen and died at nineteen while giving birth to her second child. James Clemmens drowned in the Snake River at Walter's Ferry in 1888 at age twenty-three. John died in 1894 at age eighteen. Catherine married Charles C. Smith and lived in Dry Creek until her death in 1900. Ida married James M. Potter in 1895 and lived in Dry Creek into the twentieth century.

In 1883, Sarah married Angelo Macklin, an Indiana farm laborer and Civil War veteran who received

Annie Clemmens and Enos Walling around the time of their marriage (Photo courtesy Vance Day).

a military pension because of a leg wound.[9] Macklin had enlisted in the Iowa 22nd Infantry Regiment in 1862 at the age of nineteen, and was discharged with wounds in 1865.[10] In 1895, federal authorities arrested him for forging signatures on a Civil War pension application, including the signatures of a doctor, a druggist, and a judge in support of his pension claim. The *Statesman* (August 24, 1895) reprinted the alleged affidavit of the druggist, complete with misspellings:

> I practis and sell drugs. I have bin in the drugs business for 9 years. I have subscribed for him and sold him lots of drugs, mostly for rumatism, but his main doctor was Dr. Smith, but he is dead. Now I have none him for 10 years, and I have none him when he couldent walk alone. I do this writing myself and aint interested in this clamence no shape whatever.

In 1900, Macklin resided at the Idaho Soldier's Home along the Valley Road between Green Meadow and Boise City. After Sarah died, he moved to Oklahoma to live with his son from a previous marriage. He died in 1916 and was buried in Oklahoma.

D.E., still a single man, was at the ranch with his mother Sarah until she died in the summer of 1906 and was buried in Dry Creek Cemetery near her children. After her death, D.E. married Margaret (Retta) Vincen, daughter of Dry Creek ranchers Halley and Maggie Hurt Vincen. D.E. died in 1958 and Retta in 1967.

D.E. & Retta Vincen Clemmens wedding portrait (Photo courtesy Sharon Ketchum).

John N. & Elizabeth Shoffner Howard

Elizabeth was born in Ohio in 1831. She apparently did not learn to read or write until late in life. She was married to John Shoffner (or Shoftner) and they had ten children, four of whom lived to see the new century: Ester A., Martha J., Simeon, and Moses M. Their daughter Ester married Green Meadow farmer Martin Cobb in 1873 before moving west.

John and Elizabeth seem to have

moved to Idaho late in the 1870s. They were farming at the mouth of the Dry Creek Valley near the Clemmens family when John died in February of 1880. Later that year, in November, Elizabeth married Andrew J. Howard at Dry Creek.

Elizabeth's grown sons Simeon and Moses also lived at the farm. Simeon was a freighter who got married the day after his mother remarried in 1880. By 1900, Elizabeth and Andrew had moved to California where Simeon lived.

Martha married James A. McGinnis (not to be confused with Dry Creek resident James J. McGinnis) in 1877 and eventually moved to Weiser.

William H. & Sarah Dawson Smith

William Smith was a farmer from Virginia born in 1837. His wife Sarah was born in Missouri in 1838. They married in 1862 and had nine children: Jonathan, John W., Benjamin A., Newman, George H., Samuel D., William, Orval O., and Bessie E. All were born in Kansas except Orval and Bessie who were born in Idaho.

The Smiths arrived in Idaho between 1876 and 1879. Sarah's father, Dawson Crews, lived with them in 1880. By 1900, the family had left Dry Creek and was farming in the White Cross Precinct southwest of Green Meadow.

Jacob C. & Rosa Gibbs Motto

Jacob Motto was born in 1851 in Virginia. He was a Civil War veteran who was a young boy when he served in the 18th Iowa Infantry from 1862 to 1865. After the war, he

moved west.

By 1870, Motto was boarding in Green Meadow with David and Sarah Clemmens. He homesteaded 160 acres at the mouth of the Dry Creek Valley and patented it in 1878. However, Motto appears not to have remained at the ranch for long and may have sold the land soon after patenting it.

After leaving Dry Creek, he moved to the Boise Basin to seek his fortune in mining. In 1886, he married twenty-year-old Rosa Gibbs, the daughter of a blacksmith in the mining town of Centerville. They had five children.

By 1895, Motto was receiving a Civil War pension as an invalid. He continued to live and mine in Boise County for the rest of his life. The *Statesman* (August 10, 1903) reported that Jacob Motto died in a mining accident at the Mineral Hill Mine at Placerville. He was buried in the Placerville cemetery. Rosa Motto continued receiving his Civil War pension until she remarried.[11]

Thomas & Elizabeth L. Ragon Morrison

Thomas Morrison was a farmer born in 1821 in North Carolina. Elizabeth Langston was born in 1836 in Tennessee. She first married Cleveland Ragon, with whom she had three children in the 1850s: Marion, Mary, and David M. By 1860, Elizabeth was married to Thomas Morrison, who was fourteen years her senior. Thomas and Elizabeth had seven children of their own: Flora A., John, Fannie W., Thomas C., Anna L., Nettie M., and Bettie. All were born in Missouri except for Bettie who was born in Idaho. Flora and John had died by 1870 and Thomas C. by 1880.

The Morrisons came to Idaho in 1877[12] and may have purchased the Jacob Motto place around 1878. By 1880, Elizabeth's older sons lived at the farm and worked as laborers. In the spring of 1888, Morrison reported a major hailstorm in the Dry Creek Valley. Hail fell to a depth of four inches, cutting the new leaves on the fruit trees at his ranch and the adjacent Macklin (Clemmens) and Lemp ranches. The Lemp ranch was referred to in a *Statesman* article (May 29, 1888) as the "old Kingsbury place."

Elizabeth died in 1887. After her death, Thomas lived with his daughter Nettie Potter's family. Thomas died in 1903 and was buried alongside his wife in Dry Creek Cemetery.

Jacob & Anna Marie Eskledsen Jensen

Jacob Jensen was a farmer and freighter who claimed land at the mouth of Spring Creek just north of Kingsbury's place. He was born in Denmark in 1827, and Anna Marie in 1830. They had nine children, seven of whom survived to adulthood. The three eldest were born in Denmark: Meta M. (Mary), E. Peter, and Annie. Caralena was born on the Overland Trail in the winter of 1864 as the family traveled west. She died shortly after birth and was buried along the trail. Mattie C. and Jacob Jr. (Jake) were born in Utah. Emma and Allen were born in Idaho after the family arrived in 1870.

At the time of the 1870 U.S. Census, the Jensens were just getting started on their eighty acres in Dry Creek. They had produced ten tons of hay on two acres of improved farmland. Their livestock consisted of two horses and a milk cow.

In 1875, Jacob hauled 2,600 pounds of household freight and two passengers to Kelton, Utah, in seven days. The *Statesman* (August 7, 1875) reported Jensen's trip as the quickest ever made to Kelton with a full load. Evidently, Jensen was anxious to get back to his ranch in time for the harvest.

He patented his Dry Creek land in 1881 and sold part of the property to W.M. Wiley in 1883.[13] He sold 109 acres to sheep rancher William Jones for $700 in 1891 and another forty acres for $945 in 1897 according to the *Statesman* (November 23).

Jacob and his son Allen continued to work the farm until the turn of the century. Allen competed in rodeo and regularly won competitions in Idaho and Oregon.[14] Jake married Alma Saxton in 1895 and lived at Green Meadow into the twentieth century. Mattie married Newton A. Morgan in 1899 and lived in Dry Creek. Jacob died in 1910 and Anna in 1930. Most Jensen family members were buried in Dry Creek Cemetery.

John A. & Anna Owings

John Owings was born in Indiana in 1837 and Anna in Iowa in 1840. They married in 1866 and probably came west on the Overland Trail after 1872. The Owings had six children while living in Iowa, Kansas, and Oregon. Five of them survived to adulthood: Sarah, Henry B., Laura, William O., and Alice B.

Around 1874, Owings homesteaded 126 acres in the Dry Creek Valley, including the east half of the old Andy Wiley homestead and some land to the north. He patented the homestead in 1879. In 1880, he and his family lived in the Green Meadow area. Evidently, he sold the Dry Creek farm shortly thereafter and had moved to Oregon by 1882.

In 1900, Owings was farming in Oregon with his adult children. By 1910, however, he was an inmate in the Oregon State Insane Asylum where he died in 1911.[15]

Jacob & Anny Bash

Jacob Bash was a freighter and farmer in the Dry Creek area. He and Anny were both from Germany, born in 1850 and 1858. They had three children in the late 1870s: Frank S., Clara B., and Anny. Frank was born in Colorado, but the younger children were born in Idaho, suggesting the family moved to the area from Colorado after 1876.

Bash lived near another freighter, Thomas West, who may have moved to Idaho from Colorado at the same time. Jacob also worked at the Shafer Creek Mill and farmed land next to Wyatt's, probably the former Owings ranch.

Halley & Margaret Hurt Vincen

Idaho histories write that Halley Vincen was born in Illinois in 1845 and came to Idaho in 1864. Mormon genealogical records say that the man known in Dry Creek as Halley Vincen was indeed born in Illinois in 1845 at the Mormon settlement of Nauvoo under the name of Silas M. Wood. He is said to have married two wives in Utah in 1865 before coming to Idaho.

In any case, the year 1870 found Vincen working as a laborer at Boise City, where he lived in a boarding house. Vincen eventually homesteaded in Dry Creek and married Margaret (Maggie) Hurt in 1873 at her parents' home. Maggie was the sister of Dry Creek farmers William and Bradford Hurt. She patented part of the Vincen homestead in her name in 1898.

Maggie and Halley had six children: Anna Belle, Charles H., R. William, Margaret (Retta), Frank L., and Alice P. Their daughter Anna Belle died in 1891 at the age of seventeen and was buried in Dry Creek Cemetery. Alice married Edward C. Smith in 1911. Smith eventually ranched at Stack Rock in the Dry Creek uplands. Alice died in 1940 and was also buried in Dry Creek Cemetery.

The early years of the twentieth century brought an ongoing feud between the Vincen boys and their mother's relatives, the Hurts. After a dispute over an election, an arrest warrant was issued for Halley Vincen who was accused of attempting to murder Bradford Hurt. The *Statesman* (December 5, 1900) reported that Vincen pulled a gun on Hurt at the Schick schoolhouse. Hurt allegedly hit Vincen's son while on the porch of the school, at which point Vincen pulled a gun to put a stop to the disagreement. The case was dismissed on the grounds of self-defense according to the *Statesman* (December 28, 1900).

In 1901, the Vincens were involved in another conflict with Bradford Hurt at Hurt's home in Dry Creek. The Vincen brothers allegedly fired six shots in the dispute, so Hurt secured a warrant for their arrest. According to Hurt, the brothers came to his place and tried to shoot his dog. When he protested, they tried to shoot at him and a bullet passed through his hat.

Halley and Maggie continued to live in Dry Creek well into the new century. Their twenty-three-year-old daughter Alice and seventy-four-year-old Patrick McFarland, who homesteaded the property adjoining theirs to the east, lived with them in 1910. A decade later, they lived with their son Frank in Dry Creek. Halley died in 1921 and Maggie died in 1939. Both were buried in Dry Creek Cemetery.

James M. & Elizabeth Brownlee Stewart

James Stewart was born in Ohio in 1831 of Irish parents. By 1860, he was mining at Gold Hill in Nebraska Territory. Elizabeth seems to have been born between 1842 and 1845 in Ireland, although she gave her birthplace variously as Ireland, Ohio, Wisconsin, and Connecticut. Elizabeth was listed as unable to write in the 1870 U.S. Census, but by 1880 was said to both read and write.

She and James married in Colorado in 1862. Their son Charles was born there. By 1865, they were in Idaho, where William B., Adelbert, George, and four other children were born. All of the Stewart children except Charles and George died by 1900. Both William and Adelbert died in

1875. When they died, William was ten and Adelbert was six years old.

James Stewart lived in the Boise Valley in 1866 and owned real estate valued at $150 by 1870. Eventually the Stewarts farmed in the Dry Creek Valley near the Vincen family. James and Elizabeth left Dry Creek during the early twentieth century and lived in the Union Precinct west of Dry Creek. James died after 1910 and Elizabeth after 1920, possibly in Oregon where her son George lived.

Phillip Paul

Phillip Paul was born at Hessen, Germany, in 1832. By 1870, he worked for and boarded at the Rossi/Robie ranch, but also homesteaded his own 160-acre property along the south part of Spring Creek near where it entered Dry Creek. His purchase of that property was finalized in 1874.

Paul worked for Alexander Rossi, taking his livestock to winter range, among other tasks. In 1873, he was paid $290 for the work, and $312 the following year.[16] The winter of 1873/1874 would be one to remember for Paul. In December, he froze his feet badly on the way out to Dry Creek from Boise City. The *Statesman* (January 3, 1874) reported that Dr. Ephraim Smith had to amputate all the toes on Paul's left foot, and he stayed in town to recover.

By 1880, Paul was living in a boarding house in Boise City near the residence of his longtime employer Alexander Rossi.

Charles & Phoebe Peck Hurt

Charles Hurt and Phoebe Peck were

both born in Virginia, he in 1826 and she in 1821. They married in 1854 and lived in Virginia at least until 1862. Sarah may have been married previously because her eldest daughter was born three years before she and Charles married. The Hurts had six children, five of whom survived: Sarah Anne, Margaret (Maggie), William, Bradford, and Mary Jane. All were born in Virginia.

The Hurt family came to Idaho in 1863, first settling in Green Meadow, ¼ mile west of where the Saxton Station of the Boise Interurban Line was later located. By 1880, Charles and Phoebe lived in the Dry Creek Valley on the old Wylie place between the Glenn and Wyatt homesteads. Charles also patented 160 acres in 1886 at the upper end of the Spring Creek Valley north of Dry Creek.

Hurt was an active Democrat, serving as the delegate from the Spring Valley/Tollgate precinct to the Democrats' state convention in 1882 according to the *Statesman* (September 12).

His son Bradford married Bessie A. Gilbert in 1877. She was the daughter of John and Betsey Gilbert who farmed along the Hill Road near Pierce Gulch. William married Ellen Cox in 1881, and Mary Jane married James M. Cox in 1886. Maggie married Halley Vincen and lived out her life in the Dry Creek Valley.

Charles Hurt died at his home on Dry Creek in March of 1898 at the age of seventy-two. After his death, Phoebe lived with her son Bradford and his family. She died in 1909

and was buried in Dry Creek Cemetery alongside her husband.

William & Ellen Cox Hurt

Virginian William Hurt was born in 1857, the son of Charles and Phoebe Hurt. Ellen Cox, a daughter of Green Meadow farmers Reuben and Anna Cox, was born in 1865 in Idaho. William and Ellen married in 1881. They had eight children, seven of whom survived: Claud, Viola, Lester, Cuddy, Leona, Carl, and Earl L. Lulu died in 1896 at the age of thirteen and was buried in Dry Creek Cemetery.

William had half of his father's farm, while his brother Bradford had the other half. In 1881, the *Statesman* (December 10) reported that several Dry Creek homesteads sold at auction for back taxes, including William Hurt's. His farm seems to have been purchased by Jake Jensen. Later, in 1894, William patented eighty acres at the north end of Spring Valley. He must have continued living in Dry Creek because his civic activities included serving as clerk of the Dry Creek School District in the early 1900s.

Around 1910, the Hurt family moved to Boise City. William worked at Thomas Healy's sawmill with his sons Lester and Cuddy for a time. By 1920, he was back on the land farming with his sons Lester and Earl. In their later years, William and Ellen lived at Boise City with their daughter Leona Brown who was a nurse. They both died in 1940 and were buried in Dry Creek Cemetery.

Claud Hurt remained in the Dry Creek Valley for many years, patenting an eighty-acre ranch in the foothills south of Kingsbury's place in 1914. Claud died in 1970 while living at Caldwell, Idaho. He was buried in Dry Creek Cemetery.

Bradford & Bessie Gilbert Hurt

Bradford (Brad) Hurt was William's older brother, born in Virginia in 1856. His family lived next door to William and Ellen. Bessie was born about 1859 in Utah. She and Brad married in 1877. They had two daughters, Ida B. and Ada M. In June of 1880 when the U.S. Census was taken, Bessie and her one-year-old daughter Ida were staying with her parents John and Betsey Gilbert at their farm between Green Meadow and Boise City.

In addition to farming, Brad mined on Willow Creek with his father Charles. The Hurt mines included the Birthday, Old Man, Gray Eagle, and Silver Leaf claims. Their mines were mentioned in a claims location case before the Idaho Supreme Court in which Dry Creek homesteader William B. Francis testified.[17] This was one of many mining-related court cases to which Brad was a party well into the twentieth century. He was no stranger to the local courts, his apparently hot-temper leading to ongoing disputes with both family and neighbors. Hurt's numerous lawsuits included cases against his brother William and his neighbor Halley Vincen.

At the turn of the century, Brad and Bessie were still living in Dry Creek just west of the Glenn ranch with their daughter, Ada, and Brad's mother, Phoebe. Ralph Vincen also boarded in their household.

Brad and Bessie left Dry Creek after

1905 to mine at Pearl, Idaho. Bessie died in 1925. Brad remained at Pearl with Ida and her husband. He died in 1935. Both were buried in Dry Creek Cemetery.

William Daniel

William Daniel was an unmarried miner born in England in 1828. He moved to Dry Creek sometime after 1870 and purchased seventy-eight acres along Dry Creek just southeast of Schick's place in 1876. He lived in the "first house below [the] crossing" of Dry Creek.[18] At that time, the Dry Creek crossing was on P.L. Schick's ranch. By 1880, Daniel was living at Rocky Bar in Alturas County and Schick had acquired his property.

Isaac Y. & Ellen Bishop Glenn

Ellen Bishop was born in Illinois in 1836. She was first married in Iowa around 1861 and had four children there: Alfred, Henry, Nettie Jane, and Jesse. Her husband seems to have died by 1870. She married Isaac Glenn in 1872 in Idaho. Isaac, born in Tennessee in 1829, was the brother of Dry Creek settler John M Glenn. Isaac had previously been married to Selina Johnson and had ten children. Selina died in Oregon in 1870.

Isaac and Ellen settled on 120 acres in the hills above Bogart (Seaman) Gulch where they lived until Isaac died of consumption in the summer of 1879.[19] The next year, Ellen married Charles Masters on July 4. She patented the Dry Creek ranch in 1881.

By 1900, Masters had died and Ellen was living in Boise City with her daughter Nettie's family. She later moved to Bruneau, Idaho, where she died in 1913.

Thomas & Louisa Custer Mathers Healy

Canadian Thomas Healy was born in 1844 and moved to Pennsylvania with his parents as a young man. He worked in the lumber industry in Michigan, Kentucky, Colorado, Arizona, and Nevada, and spent three years mining in Nevada before settling at Silver City, Idaho, in 1873.[20]

Healy worked for Driscoll, Posey & Shea, timbering contractors for the mines, until 1875 when the Bank of California failed. The bank had heavily invested in the mines and when it failed, hundreds of miners were left without their earnings or their jobs. Healy moved on to the mines at Atlanta, Idaho, where he stayed until those mines shut down in 1879.

Healy also worked for Rossi & Lambing in the mid 1870s[21] and bought Rossi's toll road and tollgate above the Dry Creek Valley in the 1880s. GLO records show that Healy patented land around the tollgate in Boise County in 1886 and in 1893. With his partner Amos T. Bennett, he bought Rossi's Shafer Creek sawmill and conducted a substantial lumber business until a fire burned the operation, causing the loss of 275,000 feet of lumber.[22]

In 1880, he and seventeen other men boarded together and worked in the sawmill. Healy advertised matched flooring, siding, ceiling and rustic lumber, shingles, laths, pickets, and molding for sale from the "old Rossi mill" on Shafer Creek.

He was willing to take hay and grain in trade for lumber, according to his advertisements in the *Statesman* (1888-1889).

Healy and Louisa Mathers married in 1884. Louisa and her first husband Thomas Mathers had one child, Manaphee. Louisa and Healy are not known to have had children. By 1900, the Healys lived at Pearl, Idaho, where he had a farm. Six men boarded with them, mostly miners. Healy continued his ownership and management of the toll road until 1909 when he moved to Boise City to run a sawmill.

After Louisa's death in 1910, Thomas partnered with his close friend D.E. Clemmens at Clemmens' Dry Creek ranch. Healy lived with the Clemmens family for the rest of his life. He died at the ranch in March of 1925 and was buried in Morris Hill Cemetery.

The Farmworkers & Tradespeople

By the end of the decade, at least nineteen farmworkers and laborers lived in the Dry Creek Valley and nearby foothills. Also living in the valley during the 1870s were freighters, schoolteachers, saddlers, a carpenter, a printer, and a lumberman, as well as miners and cattle dealers. One woman listed her occupation as musician.

In the northern foothills above the valley were tollgate tenders, lumber workers, and a smattering of miners, along with housekeepers and cooks in the boarding houses.

Thomas W. & Louisa J. West

Thomas West was a freighter born in Ohio in 1828. Louisa was born in

1833. Their five children were James W., Frances C., Richard, Martha J., and Thomas W. Jr. All were born in Illinois or Colorado in the 1860s and 1870s. The West family seems to have moved to Idaho between 1875 and 1880.

In the fall of 1880, a wagon ran over Thomas Sr.'s hand and badly broke it. He retained some use of the hand, except for the little finger, according to a *Statesman* report (November 13, 1880). By 1900, Thomas Sr. and his three sons were mining in Custer County, Idaho. His daughter Frances married and lived at Boise City with her mother Louisa.

Thomas & Margaret McGauley

Thomas and Margaret were both born in Ireland around 1835. Their first two children, Delia and Anna, were born in Pennsylvania in 1856 and 1860. By 1865, they lived in Colorado where their youngest child, William, was born.

In 1870, Thomas was a farmworker living near two other Irish families in the valley. Neither Thomas nor Margaret could read or write, so historical records spell their name in a variety of ways, making them difficult to track in printed records.

John & Catherine Heren

John Heren was a farmworker in the valley in 1870. He and Catherine lived next door to James and Rosa Heren. John and James may have been brothers.

John and Catherine were born in Ireland, he in 1843 and she in 1840. Their daughters, Margaret and Delia were born in New York after 1865. Their youngest daughter Mary, born

in Utah Territory, was only one month old when the census was taken on July 13, 1870, suggesting they had just arrived in Idaho. Neither John nor Catherine was literate.

Like most farmworkers who did not own land, the Herens seemed to have stayed in Idaho only briefly. By 1871, they were back in Utah, then in Colorado, and by 1880 lived in California.

James & Rosa Heren

James Heren, born in Ireland about 1837, was a farmworker in Dry Creek in 1870. He and Rosa, born in Ireland about 1847, had five children, all born in New York after 1862: Irma, Henry, Margaret, John, and Patrick. Since their youngest child was born in 1869, it is likely that they came to the valley in 1870, probably with the family of John and Catherine Heren around June of 1870. Neither James nor Rosa was able to read or write, making it difficult to track them in the historical record.

William M. & Esther Coffin Grow

William Grow was a farm manager born in Pennsylvania in 1842. Esther was born in Indiana in 1849. Grow made the trek west in 1851 with a group of Mormon pioneers. Esther and William married in Utah in 1865 and had nine children: Mary A. William N., James A., David H., Jesse, Horace I., Cyrus L., Charles, and Effie.

The Grows lived in Oregon before moving to Idaho in the 1860s. In Dry Creek, they farmed 160 acres of the Robie Ranch when the land was valued at $7,000. The operation included five horses, thirty-six mules, four milk cows, 117 beef

cattle, and five swine. One hundred acres of improved farmland produced 100 bushels of rye, 900 bushels of barley, 100 bushels of potatoes, 150 tons of hay, and 150 pounds of butter.

Grow seems to have worked only briefly in the Dry Creek Valley before settling in eastern Idaho. A 1928 article in a Pennsylvania newspaper, *The Morning Herald*, (March 30), reported that eighty-five-year-old Grow had walked from his home in Idaho Falls, Idaho, to Ogden, Utah, (180 miles) to attend "an old folks celebration" that unfortunately had been cancelled. William died in 1932 at Ammon, Idaho.

Dry Creek Farmworkers, 1870

Farmworker	Boarded with
William G. Grow	Robie Ranch
Reuben L. Brown	Barrett Williams
James Chism	Barrett Williams
Thomas Wilson	Barrett Williams
George Deitz	Barrett Williams
George Nightingale	Barrett Williams
Thomas, Richard, Henry & William Williams*	Barrett Williams
William F. & Thomas J. Kingsbury*	Thomas Kingsbury
Williston G. Osborn	A.H. Robie
John Sink	A.H. Robie
Phillip Paul*	A.H. Robie
Alexander Montoya	A.H. Robie
James McChung	A.H. Robie
Frank Newhall	A.J. Wyatt
Andrew J. Regan	A.J. Wyatt
Charles Kelley	Neri Jack
Thomas & William Glenn*	John M. Glenn
James Smith*	John M. Glenn
John Johnson	Robert M. Crawford
Edward G. Lewis	Phillip L. Schick
Pierson S. Patten	Self
James K. Ford	Self
Thomas McGonley	Self
James Heren	Self
John Heren	Self

*Later landowner or landowner's son
Source: 1870 U.S. Census*

Green Meadow

Green Meadow was planted in crops as far as the eye could see in the 1870s. From a vantage point on the Hill Road looking toward Green Meadow, about two miles from Boise City, one could see a vast area of fields and green grain spreading to the horizon according to the *Statesman* (May 4, 1876). To the west of Sam Aiken's Green Meadow ranch, sagebrush still covered the land near the foothills, as most of the farms lay close to the Boise River along the Valley Road, one half mile or further from the foothills. The same article also remarked on the local importance of timber culture in Green Meadow, where Lombardy poplar twigs were planted about eight feet apart with hardwood trees between them. The plan was to harvest the poplar for firewood in a few years after its early growth protected the young hardwood trees.

In the late 1870s, new lands in Green Meadow opened to irrigated farming with the construction of the Dry Creek Canal. The canal route, surveyed in early 1879 by Alexander Rossi and others, had among its promoters and builders John Hailey and John Patterson, both of whom had farms in the area. Initially, the canal irrigated 1,425 acres north of the Boise River.[23]

On its west end, Green Meadow merged into the settlement that became the town of Eagle, an area with a reputation for violence in the late 1860s and early 1870s. The Junction House at the homestead of Hamilton Maxon along the Overland Trail was often mentioned as the locus of the violence. The 1870s began with the capture of a thief who had stolen four horses from the Junction House the previous fall according to the *Statesman* (January 6, 1870).

The *Statesman* (August 5, 1871) also reported that nine men had been shot in the Junction House vicinity by 1871, and suggested that it should be called "Bloody Run." In one case, there was a shootout over a share cropping agreement between two farmers. Green Meadow homesteaders Henry Conway, Felix Johnson, and John Roberts testified at the trial.

In addition to farming and mining, many Green Meadow men belonged to fraternal organizations, especially the Masons. In 1872, the *Statesman* (February 20, 1872) announced the organization of Green Meadow Lodge (No. 17 IOGT) at the Whitson home. Officers included William Gainey, Sam Aiken, and William Rash. The Lodge was the center of local temperance activities for some years.

Thomas H. (Hugh) Rutledge and John B. Pierce, Sr. represented the Green Meadow Precinct at the Ada County Democrats' 1874 convention according to the *Statesman* (October 3). In 1876, Reuben Cox, William Davidson, and Rutledge served as election judges for Green Meadow in the Ada County primary. David Heron and Seth Bixby were also election officials in the 1870s.

Green Meadow farmers met at Blagg's school in 1874 to organize a Grange Society with James N. Whitson as the first secretary and David Heron as the first chairman of the organization. Interestingly, the 1870 U.S. Census (perhaps in error) listed Whitson as being unable to write.

Ada County Commissioners declared a school district at Green Meadow in 1872 according to the *Statesman* (April 16). The Cox School served the western end of Green Meadow, while the Blagg School taught students at the southeastern end of Green Meadow on the way to Boise City. Rutledge, John Pierce, and Heron served as Board members for the Blagg School.

Local entertainment included balls and dances, lectures, sleigh rides, and horse races, among other activities. In January of 1876, several Green Meadow and Dry Creek young people attended an all-night ball and supper at a local hot springs. They included Ruby and John Rash, Frederick Kingsbury, and young James Baldwin. In 1877, the *Statesman* (September 13) reported that the Harmen & Taylor Troupe entertained at Green Meadow Hall, followed by a dance for all.

The Landowners

Most of those who had first homesteaded in Green Meadow remained on their farms into the 1870s. Some new farm families arrived from Boise City and other locations, and adult children of the first homesteaders set up operations of their own. The farm families first known in Green Meadow during the 1870s are described here approximately as their farms lay, from west to southeast along the

Valley Road toward Boise City.

John Robert & Ruby Rash Carpenter & Mary Stierman Carpenter

John Robert Carpenter, known as Johnny, was the son of Green Meadow pioneers John and Mary Carpenter. He was born in New York in 1846 and headed west with his father in 1859. They ended up at Idaho City in 1863. With his father ill that year, Johnny earned $800 for the family by hauling logs and shingles to Idaho City.[24]

Johnny married Ruby Rash, daughter of Green Meadow farmers William and Mary Rash, in 1876. They had three children: Frank, George, and Mary. George and Mary were twins, but George died at birth.

After his parents returned to Pennsylvania in 1876, Johnny took over the family ranch. He also worked as a stage driver for the Northwestern Stage Company and as a freighter, gaining renown as one of the top stage drivers in the area. He was said to have driven the largest single load of stage passengers at one time (twenty-two) on a run to Silver City. He served as a scout and messenger in the Bannock Indian War of 1878.

Johnny and Ruby divorced in the 1880s. In 1882, he moved to the Wood River area where he worked supervising stage routes for John Hailey. Carpenter later returned to Ada County and helped found the town of Eagle.[25] He married Mary Stierman in 1891. Johnny and Mary had six children: John Robert, Anna, Maymie, William W., Henry L., and Leona D.

*John R. Carpenter
(Hawley 1920 Vol III).*

Johnny was honored in August of 1897 as a pioneer in a parade of more than 130 early settlers through downtown Boise City. The group was photographed and the honorees autographed an album. Carpenter died in 1936 and was buried in Pioneer Cemetery.

Thomas H.B. & Nancy Potter Breshears

Thomas H.B. Breshears was born in Missouri in 1844 and fought for the Union in the Civil War in the 14th Regiment, Missouri State Militia Cavalry.[26] Nancy was born in Kentucky in 1850. The Breshears married after the war in 1866 and lived with the Potter family in Missouri. They came to Idaho in 1877,[27] first living at Rocky Bar in Elmore County.

Nancy gave birth to at least thirteen children, five of whom lived to see the new century. Mary F., John F.,

Joseph H., and Thomas C. were born in the 1860s and 1870s in Missouri. James A., Reuben N., and Minnie A. were born in Idaho. Mary died when she was a year old and James died of "brain fever" in the spring of 1880 at the age of three.[28] There were also four unnamed infants who died.

Nancy's younger brother, David S. Potter, lived with them as a teenager. He later married Nettie Morrison, the daughter of Dry Creek homesteaders Thomas and Elizabeth Morrison. Potter patented a homestead in the Dry Creek foothills in 1910.

In the late 1870s, Breshears homesteaded eighty acres in the Green Meadow area along the Hill Road east of Cox's place. He patented the land in 1883. Breshears seems to have had financial problems in the early 1900s. Ada County sold part of his land for back taxes in 1900 according to a report in the *Statesman* (May 29). More of the Breshears homestead sold for back taxes in 1902 for $56.84 according to the *Statesman* (May 26, 1902).

Thomas received income in the form of a Civil War invalid's pension beginning in 1903, but appears not to have overcome his financial difficulties. His brother-in-law, David Potter, sued him for debts in 1907. Thomas H.B. died in 1916 and was buried in Dry Creek Cemetery. After his death, Nancy received a Civil War widow's pension. She died in 1931.

Joseph Breshears married Anna Saxton, daughter of Green Meadow farmers Hiram and Diantha Saxton and farmed at Green Meadow. Minnie married Ernest Eytchison and lived at Green Meadow, as well. John did not marry and remained with his parents until his death in 1929.

Henry & Regina Miller

Henry was born in Switzerland in 1814 and Regina (Rachel) in 1823. Their children Henry, Jr., Pauline, Augustus, and John F. were born in Germany. By 1858, they were in Utah where Julius C., Abraham, and Isaac were born. The family moved to Idaho between 1863 and 1866 and had an eighth child, Louise M. (Mary). Miller and his family first lived at Ruby City where he was a shopkeeper in 1866. They later settled 160 acres in Green Meadow east of Breshears' and patented the farm in 1879. Miller's son Abraham worked the farm with him.

Henry Miller died in early 1895 and was buried in Dry Creek Cemetery. After Henry's death, Julius took over the farm and lived there well into the twentieth century. Mary married Cloyce Marlatt, the son of Dry Creek farmers William J. and Clarinda Marlatt, in 1884. At the turn of the century, Abraham was working as a farm laborer and boarding with the

*Thomas H.B., Minnie, and Nancy Breshears
(Photo courtesy Michael Harris)*

widow Caroline Brown at Green Meadow. John and his family also farmed in the area.

Reuben & Anna Napier Cox

Tennesseean Reuben Cox was born in 1820 and Kentuckian Anna Napier in 1822. Anna could not read or write according to U.S. Census records. Reuben and Anna married in Missouri in 1840 and had fourteen children, including an unnamed set of twins who died in infancy: Riley, Martha, Henry, Mary, Savannah, Lawrence, Catherine, Emily, Sarah, Anderson M, James M., and Ellen. All were born in Missouri except Ellen who was born in Idaho Territory in 1865. Emily and Sarah had both died in 1857 when they were one and two years old. Lawrence probably died in the 1860s.

Unlike his neighbor Thomas Breshears who was a Union man, Reuben Cox's eldest son Riley fought for the Confederate Army in the Civil War and may have been a prisoner of war for a time.

The Cox family headed west in 1863 or 1864. Reuben was living in Ada County in late 1865 when he was mentioned in the *Statesman* (December 5). He worked in the retail liquor trade at Boise City according to the U.S. Tax Assessment List for 1867. The Cox daughters Martha and Savannah were both married in Idaho in 1866. Mary married in 1867 and died a few weeks later at the age of

nineteen. Catherine married T. Hugh Rutledge and settled at Green Meadow.

By 1870, the Coxes farmed land valued at $2,000 in rural Ada County. He claimed a homestead of forty acres in Green Meadow along the Hill Road at the junction of the road to Dry Creek and Willow Creek, and patented it in 1879. John Patterson sold him 137 additional acres of improved farmland with dwellings and outbuildings for $2,300 in 1876 according to the *Statesman* (January 13). This farm, located about six miles from Boise City, was considered to be one of the "best improved places in the valley."

Elliott's 1884 *History of Idaho Territory* mentions that eight

Reuben Cox farm (Elliott 1884).

members of the Cox family fell ill with "typho-malaria fever" one autumn early in the 1880s as the result of a trip to the mountains.[29] The Coxes continued to farm their land in the early 1880s with two of their children, James M. and Ellen, still living at home. Ellen married Dry Creek farmer William Hurt in 1881 at her parents' home. James Cox married Mary Jane Hurt in 1886.

Like most of the southerners in the area, Reuben was an active Democrat and a delegate to the state convention. He also served as an election judge in the 1870s and 1880s. The Cox schoolhouse, where civic activities and local meetings took place, was a regular polling place. In the fall of 1891, the

Baptists of southern Idaho and eastern Oregon held their annual meeting there according to the *Statesman* (September 20, 1891).

In the spring of 1887, the *Statesman* (March 19) reported that "Uncle" Reuben Cox had been ill all winter and had sold his ranch to his neighbor Hiram Saxton for $5,000. By the time of Cox's death in 1894, the family was living at Caldwell, Idaho. He was buried in Canyon Hill Cemetery. Riley, Savannah, Anderson, James, and Ellen survived into the new century. Anna Cox had outlived nine of her fourteen children when she died in 1906.

In the 1890s, the Cox Ranch was a stop on the Beal Stage Line that ran from Boise City to Horseshoe Bend,

Anderson & Mary Elizabeth Cox
(Idaho State Historical Society #72-158-4)

along old Horseshoe Bend Road. A route from the Cox Ranch to Willow Creek was added in 1897 according to the *Statesman* (February 18, 1897).

The Farmworkers & Tradespeople

By the end of the 1870s, eleven farmworkers lived at Green Meadow. Several were relatives of landowners or later became landowners themselves. Also living in Green Meadow during those years were a blacksmith, a stonemason, a saddler, and a cooper.

The End of a Decade

As the 1870s ended, the local farm economy was much weaker than it had been at the beginning of the decade. About half as many farmworkers lived in Green Meadow and Dry Creek by the end of the 1870s, compared to the heyday of the early 1870s. The Boise Basin mines were playing out and the initial mining boom had ended. Agriculture was becoming less profitable and some of the Dry Creek Valley and Green Meadow farmers fell on hard times, setting the stage for the consolidation of ranches in Dry Creek and the subdivision of ranches in Green Meadow in the coming decades.

Green Meadow Farmworkers, 1870

Farmworker	Boarded with
Eugene D. Whipple	Samuel Aiken
Sackfield Dyre	Samuel Aiken
Robert Aiken*	Samuel Aiken
Thomas J. Sconce	Samuel Aiken
James C. Hudson	Samuel Aiken
Patrick Carroll	Samuel Aiken
Joseph Chamberlain	Jacob Diehl
John W. Rash*	William A. Rash
James Hoy	William A. Rash
Thomas Roberts	David Heron
Edward Morriss	David Heron
Robert T. Noble	David Heron
Gilbert L. Bixby*	Seth Bixby
Jackson Read	Seth Bixby
Jacob Clemmens*	D. Clemmens
Jacob Motto*	D. Clemmens
John Robert Carpenter*	John Carpenter
Orlando Cunningham	John Carpenter
Henry Dickman*	John Carpenter
George Welch	Felix Johnson
Dennis McCarty	Felix Johnson
Frank Bowen	Henry Conway
Patrick Gildy	John Patterson

Source: 1870 U.S. Census
*Later landowner or landowner's relative

Endnotes

[1] Carlos A. Schwantes, *The Pacific Northwest: An Interpretive History* (Lincoln: University of Nebraska Press, 1996), 241.

[2] U.S. Census 1880 Agricultural Schedule.

[3] U.S. Census 1880 Agricultural Schedule.

[4] Idaho Revised Codes 1908 § 6872.

[5] Rossi & Lambing 1873-1876, Idaho State Historical Society [ISHS] Archives.

[6] U.S. Geological Survey, Surveyor's Notes, October 1874, 582.

[7] James H. Hawley, *History of Idaho Volume IV* (Chicago: S.J. Clarke Publishing Company, 1920), 652.

[8] Hawley, *History of Idaho Volume III*, 661.

[9] List of Pensioners January 1, 1883, Idaho Territory Ada County.

[10] Roster and Record of Iowa Soldiers in the War of Rebellion.

[11] Civil War Pension Index, 1861-1934.

[12] Hawley, *History of Idaho Volume III*, 655.

[13] Ada County Deeds, January 8, 1883, Book 9, 415.

[14] Hawley, *History of Idaho Volume III*, 509.

[15] Oregon Death Index 1903-1998.

[16] Rossi & Lambing 1873-1876.

[17] Orville E. Jackson, *Idaho Mining Rights Revised and Enlarged* (Boise: Jackson, 1906), 39.

[18] Rossi & Lambing 1873-1876.

[19] Federal Mortality Schedule 1880.

[20] Hawley, *History of Idaho Volume III*, 123.

[21] Rossi & Lambing 1873-1976.

[22] Hawley, *History of Idaho Volume III*, 123.

[23] ISHS, "New Dry Creek Ditch Company" (Reference Series 529, 1974).

[24] Hawley, *History of Idaho Volume III*, 124.

[25] Ibid.

[26] National Park Service (NPS), "Civil War Soldiers & Sailors" (2005), www.itd.nps.gov/cwss.

[27] Hawley, *History of Idaho Volume III*, 654.

[28] Federal Mortality Schedules (1880).

[29] Wallace W. Elliott, *History of Idaho Territory* (San Francisco: Wallace W. Elliott & Co., 1884), 259.

5 The Railroad Arrives: the 1880s

Settlement of Idaho by emigrants moving west on the Overland Trail was still underway during the 1880s. The *Idaho Statesman* (July 22, 1880) reported on emigrant wagons passing through Boise City that summer from Missouri, Kansas, and Iowa—all bound for Washington Territory. Some folks stayed in Idaho, but most ended their trip in Oregon or Washington, backtracking to settle in Idaho later on.

However, change was on the horizon. A new silver and lead mining boom and completion of the railroad through Idaho Territory set the stage for the economy of the 1880s. The railroad brought new markets for Idaho goods, as well as new people and new ideas. Idaho's population more than doubled during this decade.[1] Boise City's School District established Idaho's first high school in 1881 and a few farm families from the Dry Creek Valley moved to town to take advantage of the enhanced educational opportunities.

Area agricultural production was still somewhat varied, although not as much as in the past. Most farmers in Dry Creek and Green Meadow grew potatoes, barley, oats, wheat, and fruit. A few grew corn.

All had cattle and poultry, some raised horses, but only one rancher produced sheep at the beginning of the decade.[2]

Dry Creek Valley

By 1880, the Dry Creek Valley had established itself as a prime horse-producing area. Among the ranchers who raised large numbers of horses on the lush valley grasslands were Elizabeth Glenn (fifty-six horses), Robert M. Crawford (fifty horses), and Phillip L. Schick (thirty-four horses).[3] Robie Ranch, near the mouth of the Dry Creek Valley, advertised livestock grazing for ten cents a night per head for those stopping along the road to the Boise Basin. They also sold baled hay for a penny a pound according to the *Statesman* (October 12, 1880).

However, the agricultural prosperity of the 1870s was waning in Dry Creek. Some of the farmers there, and in Spring Creek to the north, struggled economically. In 1881, the *Statesman* (December 10) reported that several Dry Creek homesteads were sold for back taxes, including those belonging to Robert M. Crawford and William Hurt.

Throughout the valley, the size of ranches increased as small farmers sold out to livestock producers who consolidated large spreads consisting of several of the original homesteads. At the beginning of the decade, Dry Creek reportedly only had nine farms,[4] but this may have counted only those at the mouth of Dry Creek that were involved in local irrigation efforts. The 1880 U.S. Census actually recorded fourteen farmer/landowners living in the Dry Creek Valley. A few others owned land in the valley but did not live there.

The General Land Office (GLO) embarked on its second major land survey of the valley in 1880. Surveyor Allen M. Thompson was assisted by O.A. Moore and O.R. Robinson (chainmen), and C.E. Robinson (axeman) in May of that year. It was also time to repair local infrastructure that had seen fifteen to twenty years of use. In 1888, the *Statesman* (May 25, 1888) reported that the bridge over Dry Creek had crumbled and collapsed as a band of horses crossed it. Inspection revealed that the bridge timbers were in an advanced state of decay.

Conflicts among cattlemen and sheepmen continued into the 1880s as sheep ranching took on regional importance. Some local ranchers published a notice in the *Statesman* (January 13, 1880) requesting that sheep owners keep their sheep three miles away from the settlements on Dry Creek. The request was signed by Dry Creek farmers Charles Hurt, John M. Glenn, George W. Williams, A.J. Wyatt, Thomas Glenn, John A. Owings, Jacob H. Bash, W. Kelly, Thomas Morrison, Thomas Kingsbury, and others. Ever-increasing numbers of sheep were said to be "devouring" the Dry Creek

hills according to the *Statesman* (February 19, 1881).

Adding to the economic problems of this decade, thousands of cattle died during the frigid winters of 1885 to 1888, including the "Big Die Up" during the winter of 1886 through 1887.[5] The severe winter of 1888 broke water pipes in Boise City and froze hundreds of "nuisance" jackrabbits in Ada County according to the *Statesman* (January 15-17, 1888). When the cattle died, sheep owners moved in to serve the market for meat and wool at profitable prices. Sheep could also feed on more marginal rangeland than cattle and required less water.[6] The effects of winter livestock deaths were compounded by "unprecedented drouth" on Dry Creek in 1889. Livestock were unable to easily access water and the grain crops were stunted according to a *Statesman* report (August 30, 1889).

News of the Valley

Newspaper reports from the Dry Creek Valley in the 1880s covered everything from human-interest stories to political and business announcements, providing a sometimes-detailed insight into day-to-day life. In the early 1880s, an army lieutenant from the Boise Barracks experimented with burning limestone found on Dry Creek to see if it would meet the needs of the military. The limestone met the test and a large quantity was hauled to the Boise Barracks for burning according to the *Statesman* (April 26, 1881).

The year 1882 began with a *Statesman* report (January 17) of

John Watkins and a man named Scotty watching cattle out on Dry Creek when their dog jumped a lynx about ½ mile above "Whiskey Johnson's place." That spring, local Seventh Day Adventists held a week-long series of meetings at the Clemmens place at the mouth of the valley, declaring that the Second Coming would take place in nine years according to a *Statesman* report (April 27, 1882).

Late summer and fall brought the election season along with the harvest. Among the election officials in the Dry Creek precinct were A.J. Wyatt, P.L. Schick, and E. James Smith. The 1882 polling place was "Kingsbury's schoolhouse" according to the *Statesman* (July 1882). Election officials in the Spring Valley precinct north of Dry Creek were Thomas Healy, Harry Warburton, and Charles Hurt, with polling taking place at Rossi's tollgate.

With the heavy work of the fall harvest complete, winter festivities often included rounds of parties and weddings. Rancher William Jones and his wife held a dance at their home in November of 1889. A large number of "well known and influential" people were present according to the *Statesman* (November 15, 1889).

The December 29, 1883 *Statesman* featured a story on Christmas in Dry Creek, where the reporter found twenty "thrifty and prosperous farms" with "substantial buildings and good fences." The writer spent Christmas at the Morrison ranch with the Morrison and Kingsbury families. The women decorated pine and fir trees from the foothills and the festive atmosphere extended to include many guests.

The Landowners

By 1880, many of the original Dry Creek homesteaders of the 1860s had moved away. The Clemmens, Kingsbury, Wyatt, Smith, Glenn, and Schick families were still in the valley at the beginning of the decade. Those who left were replaced by a number of new families whose names first appear in the Dry Creek Valley records of the 1880s. Since all of the farmland on the valley floor had long since been claimed, folks now began homesteading the dry foothills at the edge of the valley with varying success.

Families whose names are first associated with the valley in the 1880s are described here from the western farms on the flats between the Dry Creek Valley and Green Meadow, to the eastern or upper valley. Homesteads on the Dry Creek flats, where the creek flows out of the valley onto the Boise River plain first appear in the records during this period.

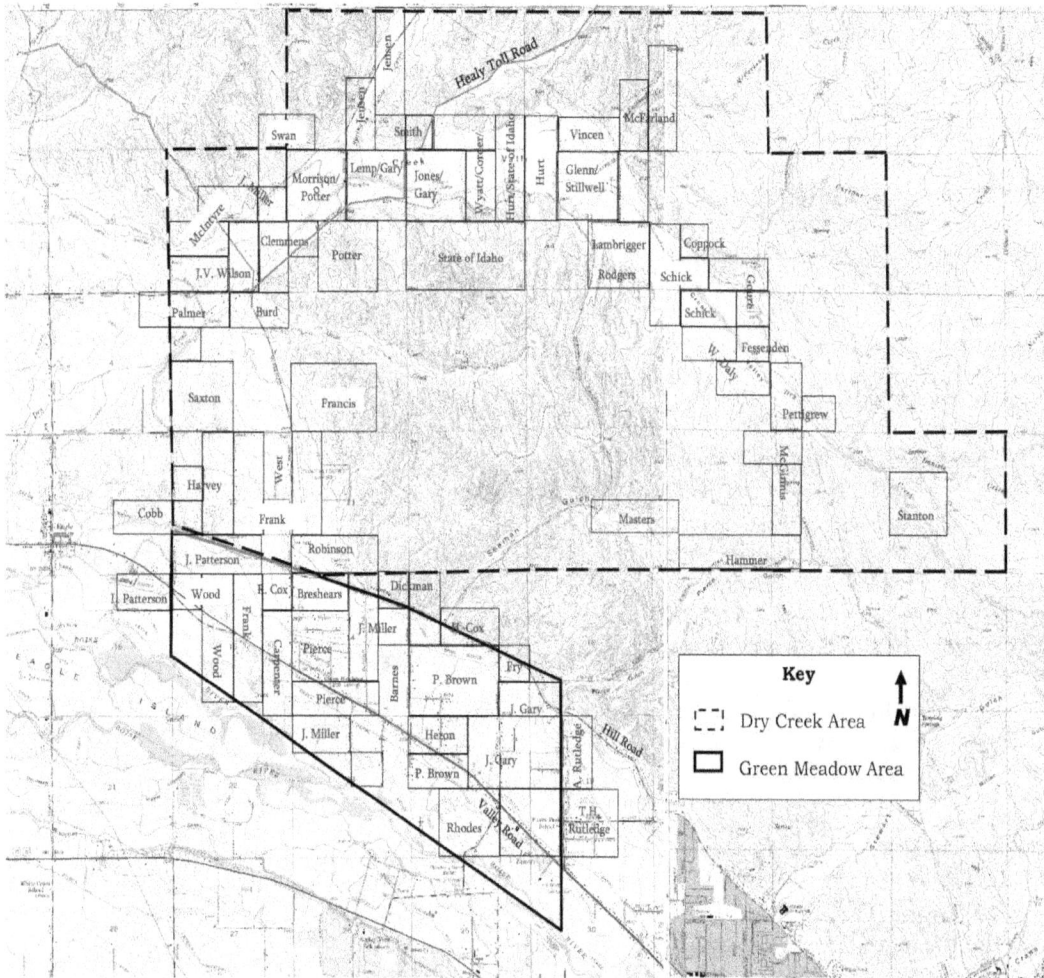

Dry Creek and Green Meadow farms, 1880s and 1890s. *Sources: GLO Land Patent Records & Ada County Records.*

Martin S. & Ester Shoffner Cobb

Martin Cobb was born in Indiana in 1844. Ester, born in Michigan in 1851, was the daughter of Dry Creek homesteader Elizabeth Shoffner. Martin and Ester married in Kansas in 1873. Their first two children, Ella A. and Bert E. were born in Kansas.

By 1880, the Cobb family was in Idaho where Etta E., Minnie J., and Melvin H. were born. They lived near Samuel Aiken in Green Meadow where Martin worked as a farm laborer before he bought his own place. In 1889, Cobb patented a 120-acre farm near Eagle. The Cobb family farmed there for at least a decade.

By 1920, the Cobbs were living separately. Martin was in Boise City

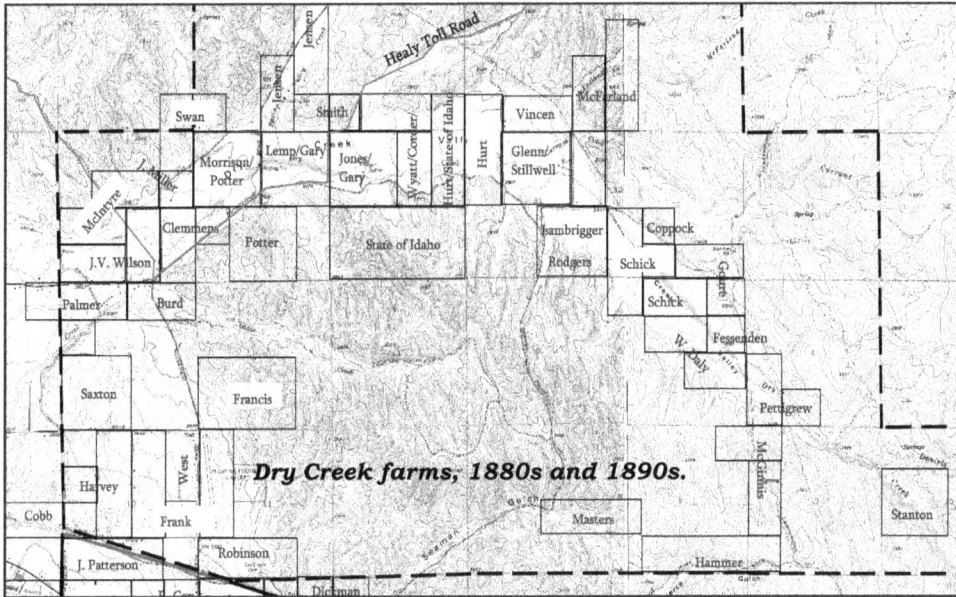

Dry Creek farms, 1880s and 1890s.

with his son Bert's family, while Ester was in Caldwell with Melvin. Martin died in 1922 and Ester in 1929.

Hiram G. & Diantha Wilson Saxton

Union soldier Hiram Saxton was born in New York in 1834, but was living in Michigan by the time he was a teenager. He enlisted in the Union Army in Michigan in 1861 and mustered out in 1865 in Tennessee. After the Civil War, he and Diantha married in Michigan in 1866. The Saxton's had ten children: Lena R., Anna V., Albert C., Alma M., Frances H. (Frankie), Charles D., Leonard L., Lillie M., William W., and George H. All were born in Michigan except George who was born in Idaho.

The Saxtons came to Idaho in 1882.[7] Hiram claimed 160 acres on

the plains between Green Meadow and the Dry Creek Valley in 1889. He patented the ranch in 1894.

Hiram and Diantha seem to have had a stormy relationship that was very public. The *Statesman* (April 7, 1898) reported that she had him arrested on a charge of insanity because he thought she was trying to take all of his property. The case went to trial and several physicians testified as to his sanity. The court found Hiram to be sane and chastised Diantha for bringing a family dispute to court. In the end, Hiram promised his wife that he would go home and be a "good and faithful husband." The Saxtons remained together until they died.

The Saxton's daughter Frankie married Cyrenius Randall and lived at Green Meadow for a time before moving to Washington County. Anna married Joe Breshears in 1893 and lived at Green Meadow. Hiram remained at the ranch until he died in 1916. After his death, Diantha lived with her unmarried son Leonard until she died in 1921. Hiram and Diantha were buried at Dry Creek Cemetery with Baptist funerals.

Phillip S. Palmer

Phillip Palmer was the son of Amanda Wilson, whose ranch lay just to the north of his at the mouth of the Dry Creek

Hiram & Diantha Saxton family circa 1903
(Photo courtesy Michele Randall).

Valley. Palmer was born in Oregon in 1865 and moved to Idaho with his mother sometime before 1870.

Palmer patented 158 acres along Dry Creek in 1891. He may have sold his land shortly thereafter, probably to his stepfather, John V. Wilson. Palmer taught school in the area in 1891 according to the *Statesman* (October 30, 1891). He died in California in 1896 at the age of thirty-one. Palmer may not have married.

John V. & Amanda M. Palmer Wilson

John Vance Wilson was born on a farm in Indiana in 1843. Amanda was born in 1847 in Illinois and had been married in Oregon in 1862 to Ephraim Palmer. The Palmers had two children, both born in Oregon: Dillie P. and Phillip S. Dillie lived for only a month. Amanda and Ephraim were no longer married after 1865. Ephraim died in Oregon in 1880.

John V. arrived in Idaho in 1864, mining in the Boise Basin for two

years.[8] He and Amanda married in 1869 at Boise City. The Wilsons had seven children: Harriet A. (Hattie), John M.A., Thomas R., Ella Mae, Elizabeth, Mary L., and Pearl A. The children later recalled times during the Bannock Indian Wars of the late 1870s when their mother hid them for fear of Indian attacks in the Boise area.[9]

John V. first acquired property along the Valley Road about two and a half miles west of Boise City and southeast of Green Meadow. There he had 120 acres in grain and hay according to the *Statesman* (May 17, 1877). In the early years of the twentieth century, Wilson sold about seventy acres of this farm, which was subdivided into small residential parcels as Boise City expanded to the northwest. He acquired property at the confluence of Dry Creek and Goose Creek, just west of the Williams/Clemmens place during the 1880s. There he sowed ten acres in white spring wheat—reportedly the earliest seeding of the year in 1889. The thirty acres of fall wheat sowed in November were up and growing in February according to the *Statesman* (February 27, 1889). Wilson patented his 160-acre Dry Creek farm in 1893.

In the summer of 1892, Wilson was shot in the arm and pistol whipped by Dudley Hedden in downtown Boise City. According to reports in the *Statesman* (August 9 and 10, 1892), the two men had several arguments about irrigation water over the course of the year. That day, they met at the saloon of Green Meadow rancher Andrew Rutledge. The argument started inside and culminated in a shootout outside when the men left the building.

The bullet fractured Wilson's humerus (upper arm). At first, the doctor thought his arm might require amputation, but it subsequently healed. Hedden was charged with assault with a deadly weapon and a jury, including Dry Creek homesteader William Marlatt, was selected for the trial. After a short trial and deliberation, Hedden was found not guilty.

John V. Wilson's civic activities included serving as the Ada County District 10 Roadwork Overseer according to the *Statesman* (April 20, 1899). He was among those honored as a Boise City pioneer in the 1897 parade of more than 130 early settlers through downtown Boise City.

John V. and Amanda's daughter Hattie married Dry Creek farmer George Nibler in 1896. Part of the Wilson homestead later belonged to Nibler.[10] After their daughter Ella Mae died in 1899, her three children

Earl, Pearl, and Vance Shortridge lived with their grandparents at the ranch. Amanda Wilson died in 1910 and John V. moved to the Soldiers Home in Boise City. He died in 1919. They were both buried in Morris Hill Cemetery.

Joseph C. & Mary Newbanks McIntyre

Joseph McIntyre was a stonemason and carpenter born in Canada in 1862. He came to the U.S. at the age of ten. Mary Newbanks was born in Missouri in 1869. Joseph and Mary married in 1886. They had six children, five of whom survived to adulthood: Joseph E., George W., Claude E., James E., and Mary E.

The McIntyres patented 160 acres on Dry Creek near the Wilsons in 1893, but lived in Boise City by 1900. Most of the McIntyre children moved to California in the early twentieth century. Joseph died in Boise in 1949. After his death, Mary moved to California to live with her children. She died in 1950.

Christopher H. & Belinda Hagan Frank

Well-known rancher Christopher Frank was born in Germany in 1839 and immigrated from Germany with his parents in 1845 when he was six years old. Belinda was born in Pennsylvania in 1844. She married Christopher in 1865 and they had seven children born in Pennsylvania and Iowa: James R., Charles B., Burt A., Edward W., Elizabeth J., Belinda Jane, and Willard H. Burt and Edward died as children.

Christopher worked as a grocer in Iowa before the family moved to Idaho sometime after 1884. He homesteaded land along the Farmers Union Canal between the Dry Creek Valley and Green Meadow, south of today's Floating Feather Road. Frank patented 160 acres in 1889.

The Franks were a popular family in the area and were known for their integrity and kindness. In 1886, the *Statesman* (October 30, 1886) reported on a surprise party held for them by their neighbors when they planned to move back to Iowa temporarily.

By 1889, they had returned to Idaho where they lived out their lives. In 1902, the local newspaper mentioned Christopher as a political supporter of William E. Borah.

Belinda died in 1912 at Green Meadow and was buried in Dry Creek Cemetery. Christopher remained at the ranch where he died in 1915. Their son Willard and his family took over the ranch after his parents died and lived there into the 1920s.

John Lemp

Around 1884, Thomas Kingsbury sold his Dry Creek homestead to John Lemp, a prosperous and well-known Boise City businessman and one of the largest beer producers in the region. Lemp also served as mayor of Boise City in the mid-1870s. Lemp had immigrated from Germany in 1852. He followed the gold rush west to Colorado and the Boise Basin, ending up in Boise City in 1863.

Along with his brewery, he owned several saloons in Boise City and built a number of buildings in the downtown area, among a wide range of other business interests. The details of Lemp's life in Boise City are widely described in many local and state histories.

Lemp appears to have sold his Dry Creek ranch to John S. Gary around 1888. He is not known to have lived in the Dry Creek Valley.

John S. Gary & Ora A. Gary

John Gary was born in Indiana in 1865 and was living in Idaho with his younger sister, Ora, by 1890. The local newspaper referred to him as a "well-known sheep man" who owned a ranch in the Dry Creek Valley while living in Boise City. Gary acquired the old Wyatt and Kingsbury homesteads in the 1880s and sold them to William Jones in 1890.

Gary operated a number of successful sheep ranches into the early years of the twentieth century. In 1899, he bought a full rail car of salt for his large livestock operation. He shipped out a "spring clip" of 200,000 pounds of wool in what was described as a very active wool market by the *Statesman* (May 10, 1901). A buyer from Boston purchased his clip. In addition to sheep production, Gary also owned Sam Aiken's old Green Meadow Ranch, which was run by John's brother Adrian.

Unlike most Dry Creek ranchers, John and his sister Ora were regularly mentioned in the newspaper as part of Boise City's elite social circle. He purchased a home in Boise in 1898 for $4,500.

John Gary appears not to have married. He died in 1919 and was buried in Morris Hill Cemetery.

William M. & Jennie Emerick Jones

William Jones was a prominent sheepman from Montana who acquired a huge spread on Dry Creek comprising several of the original homesteads at the mouth of the valley. Jones was born in Wales in 1850 and emigrated to the U.S. at the age of twelve. William and Jennie married in 1882 in Montana and had four sons: DeForest W., R. Earl, and Otto M. (all born in Montana), and Delbert E., born in Idaho.

The Jones family moved to Dry Creek in 1886. Between 1888 and 1890, the *Statesman* reported that William bought part of the old Robie Ranch from Mary C. Robie, the daughter of A.H. and Martha Robie, for $2,000 (February 7, 1888), the rest of the ranch from Martha Robie and her husband Hank Vaughan (October 5, 1888), and the old Wyatt homestead from John Gary (March 9, 1890).

The Jones family lived at the ranch for a few years before moving to Boise City in 1892 so their children could be educated in the city schools.[11] Sons Earl and Otto later attended the Staunton, Virginia, Military Academy and Washington State College at Pullman. Otto became a noted outdoor writer and photographer who was appointed Idaho's Fish and Game warden in 1919.

In 1897, when William Jones was Deputy Sheep Inspector for Ada County he testified in an important court case regarding the moving of a band of sheep infected with scab, a contagious disease caused by mites feeding on the sheep's skin. John Gary also testified in the case. That same year, Jones sold his wool clip of 250,000 to 300,000 pounds for 10.5 cents a pound according to the *Statesman* (July 14, 1897), earning around $31,000.

Jones grew 1,200 tons of hay in 1901 on the Robie part of the ranch where a warm water spring flowed seventy-five inches continuously according to the *Statesman* (April 20, 1902). He operated the ranch until 1902 when he sold his 503-acre spread to two Oregon stockmen for $42,500. The new owners planned to raise shorthorn cattle and sheep. The purchase included 5,200 head of sheep. At the time, the *Statesman* (April 20, 1902) considered the Jones ranch to be one of the finest in Idaho, with a $3,000 lambing shed among other improvements. The ranch was fenced with "American coyote tight fence."

William died in Boise at the age of sixty and was buried in Morris Hill Cemetery. Jennie died in Seattle, Washington, in 1913.

Charles C. & Kate Clemmens Smith

Charles Smith was the son of Dry Creek farmers E. James and Alice Glenn Smith. In 1880, twenty-year-old Charles was living at the Robie Ranch south of his parents' place. That year, he and teenager John Clemmens went up Spring Creek north of the Smith and Robie ranches in May with some schoolgirls (probably including Kate Clemmens) to "pick flowers." A couple of miles up the creek, his dog attacked an animal, that they

Mayor Charles C. Smith
(City of Caldwell, Idaho)

thought was a lynx, in the brush. On approaching the fray, they discovered their dog fighting with an animal several times larger than itself. Smith, a large young man at 200 pounds, went after the cat with a willow stick. Eventually he and the other young folks killed it with rocks. After skinning the cat and taking it back home, it was determined that they had bested a large cougar according to the *Statesman* (May 27, 1880).

Charles married Kate Clemmens in 1881 at Dry Creek. They had two children: B. Mabel and E. Clyde. Kate died in the spring of 1900 and was buried in Dry Creek Cemetery. After her death, Charles moved to Pearl, Idaho, with his children. He married Pernetta Stephenson in 1902.

Charles eventually moved to Caldwell, Idaho, where he had a

harness shop and was active in local civic affairs. He served a mayor of Caldwell in 1906 and 1907. Charles died at Caldwell in 1910. He was remembered in the *Caldwell Daily News* (November 4, 1910) as a big man with a pleasant smile.

Mabel Smith and Orien Fisher were married in 1906 and lived at Green Meadow. Son Clyde returned to Dry Creek to ranch near Stack Rock in the early twentieth century. In 1930, his Dry Creek household included his seventy-five-year-old neighbor, Margaret (Retta) Vincen.

James C. & Louisa Ingram Corder

James Corder was born in Missouri in 1849 and Louisa Ingram in Georgia in 1849. They married in 1870 and had one son, John M., in Kansas before moving west to Idaho sometime in the 1870s. By 1880, Corder was working as a laborer in rural Ada County. He was apparently working in Dry Creek in 1881 when the *Statesman* (July 21) reported that he was found guilty of assaulting two men from the Fisher family in a dispute over a trespassing cow. Corder was sentenced to pay $57.

In 1886, Corder purchased the ranch originally homesteaded by A.J. Wyatt, but appears not to have stayed for long. By 1900, he was single and living in Oregon. He later remarried and moved to Arizona.

Charles T. & Cyrene Peebler Glenn

Charles Glenn, the eldest son of John and Elizabeth Glenn, was born in Indiana in 1834. He married and lived in Iowa and Kansas until the early 1880s. In 1884, he purchased his parents' Dry Creek ranch from his mother and brought his wife and children from Iowa to Dry Creek.[12]

Charles and Cyrene had eight children, all of whom were born in Iowa in the 1850s and 1860s: James M., William H., Mary Jane, John E., Elizabeth A. (Lizzie), Lydia (May), Samuel P., and Ada E. At least two of the Glenn children lived in Dry Creek after they married.

May married Samuel W. Stillwell in 1890 and lived on the Glenn family farm where they remained until the early 1900s. Samuel married Effie Berridge in 1898 and farmed near the mouth of the Dry Creek Valley.

Charles and Cyrene continued farming in Dry Creek as the century changed. Lizzie and her father Charles both died in 1900. Cyrene died in 1906. All were buried in Dry Creek Cemetery.

John W. & Iona Stillwell Case

One of Dry Creek's gentleman farmers, John W. Case, owned the Glenn/Stillwell ranch in the 1880s, but did not live there. He was born in Canada in 1850 and worked as a laborer at Slater Creek, Idaho, in 1880. Iona Stillwell, the sister of Dry Creek farmer Samuel W. Stillwell, was born in Missouri in 1860.

Iona and John married at Boise City in the winter of 1883 in a fancy ceremony described in detail in the *Statesman* (December 11, 1883). Cream-colored Spanish lace trimmed the bride's dress. She wore white kid gloves and slippers. John and Iona's wedding gifts included glassware, a clock, a

silver service, candlesticks, and a floor lamp. After the wedding, they lived in the Bledsoe Mansion on Grove Street in Boise City. The Cases had two children, John D. and Lucy M., and settled into society life in Boise.

Their family activities were regularly mentioned in the *Statesman* beginning when their children were very young. Once during an illness, three-year-old Lucy was taken to the hot springs in Ketchum, Idaho. The springs were thought to have curative effects and she regained her health according to the *Statesman* (September 19, 1888). Another illness was reported in 1892 when she had a "putrid sore throat."

Lucy went on to display the skills of

John W. Case
(Photo courtesy Rebecca Farley).

a proper young lady of means, including attending the University of Idaho, joining the Philharmonic Society in 1902 and performing for the Idaho University Club in 1906 when she was twenty-one. After college she married newspaper reporter Noel B. Rawls in a 1908 Boise wedding described in detail in the *Statesman.*

Case was not only a ranch owner, but also a merchant. His business interests included ownership of a dry goods store and the Western Hotel in Boise City in the 1880s. Case sold his store in 1888, but continued living in Boise until his early death in 1892 at the age of thirty-eight. He was buried in Dry Creek Cemetery.

After John's death, Iona remained in Boise with her children. She married F.W. January in 1893. By 1900, January was living in Alaska and Iona ran the Palatine Boarding House in Boise City. She died in 1927 and was buried at Morris Hill Cemetery.

William P. Coppock

William Coppock was born on an Ohio farm around 1857. He lived there until at least 1880 before moving west to Idaho. In 1886, Coppock purchased forty acres, consisting mostly of hillside, in the Dry Creek Valley. His property was just north of the Schick place and eventually became part of Schick's ranch.

By 1910, Coppock had sold out and was mining in the Grant's Pass, Oregon, area. He eventually returned to Ohio where he died in 1927. Coppock is not known to have married.

Ansel L. & Annie Hammer Goure

Like most Dry Creek homesteaders, Ansel Goure was a man of multiple talents. He was born in Wisconsin around 1854, the son of a French father and American mother. His travels took him to Iowa, Colorado, and New Mexico where he met his future wife.

Annie Hammer was born in Kansas in 1866, the daughter of William and Elizabeth Hammer who later homesteaded near Pierce Gulch. The Goures married in 1884 in New Mexico and came to Idaho between 1885 and 1888. They had three children: Arthur, Nellie, and Sidney.

Goure homesteaded 120 acres of dry hillside east of the Schick place. He also worked as a freighter, transporting vegetables and fruits to the Boise Basin mining communities, and opened a meat market in Boise City with his father-in-law in 1892 according to an advertisement in the *Statesman* (November 9, 1892).

One day March of 1897, Goure headed to Lemp's ranch at the mouth of the Dry Creek Valley to buy hay. On the way back home, he stopped at Jake Jensen's place on Spring Creek for dinner. Goure never made it home from Jensen's, however. The next day a group of children on their way to Dry Creek School found him dead in a field, apparently of a heart attack. The children told rancher James Glenn who notified the coroner at Boise City.

Goure was buried in Dry Creek Cemetery. He was forty-two. The

Statesman (March 31, 1897) reported that:

> He was a man apparently in the best of health, strong and well-built, weighing in the neighborhood of 200 pounds. There were no marks of violence on the body, and no cause is known for his death other than apoplexy or heart disease.

The next year, the *Statesman* (November 16, 1898) noted that Annie had sold part of her homestead to Schick for $150. The homestead was patented in 1899 after Ansel died. At first, Annie and her children moved to Pearl but by 1910, they lived in Boise City with Annie's father. At that time, the U.S. Census reported that Nellie was a schoolteacher and Arthur was unemployed. Sidney had moved away to California.

James J. & Matilda Smith Pettigrew

James Pettigrew was born in 1855 in New York of Irish parents. After moving west, he worked as a teamster in Colorado where he boarded with Matilda Smith. Smith was three years older than he and had two young sons, William and James, who were both born in Missouri like their mother.

Pettigrew and Smith apparently moved to Idaho in the early 1880s. Their infant daughter Nettie died at Dry Creek in 1883 at the age of four months according to a report in the *Statesman* (July 10, 1883). In later years, Pettigrew said that he and Matilda had been married in 1889. Their second daughter, Lettie M. (Maude), was born in 1890.

GLO records show that Pettigrew patented eighty acres in 1890 in far eastern Dry Creek, where the valley begins to narrow, and another forty acres in the foothills north of the valley in 1904.

The *Statesman* (March 14, 1899) reported that Pettigrew filed a lawsuit against his neighbor, Charles Stanton, to recover possession of nineteen head of cattle that he had turned over to Stanton to keep until September of that year, providing he took good care of them. In the suit, Pettigrew claimed that the cattle were not properly cared for and he wanted them back.

One of the larger social events of the valley took place in 1897 when the Pettigrews hosted a wedding reported in the *Statesman* (November 5, 1897) at their home. Charles Ball, of the community of Thurman Mills, and Mary E. Miller celebrated their wedding with a dinner hosted by the bride's parents and Matilda Pettigrew. Dry Creek guests at the celebration included Mary Schick, Jesse, William, and Mary Helm, and May Smith among many others.

Matilda died in 1899 and was buried at Dry Creek Cemetery. After her death, James remained in Dry Creek with his nine-year-old-daughter. He remarried in 1906 and was living in Colorado by 1910 with his new wife, his daughter Maude, and a two-year-old daughter Elsie.

Maude eventually returned to Dry Creek. She married Fred Lavelett in 1916 and they ran the Pettigrew ranch for a time. By 1920, they lived in Colorado, but owned the Dry Creek ranch, at least into the late 1930s.[13]

Charles A. & Mary Daly Stanton

Charles Stanton was born in Michigan in 1862 and Mary Daly was born in Missouri in 1866, the daughter of Dry Creek ranchers William and Margaret Daly. Charles and Mary had four children: John W., Maggie E., Albert, and James W. The Stantons homesteaded 160 acres in the foothills at the far eastern end of the Dry Creek Valley at the mouth of Daniels Creek.

Stanton was active in local civic affairs. He served as superintendent of the Ada County Poor Farm northwest of Boise City in 1892 and on the Dry Creek School Board along with Al Lambrigger and Samuel P. Glenn in 1902 according to the *Statesman* (July 13).

Mary died in 1904, the same year as Charles patented their homestead. Stanton remarried in 1908 and raised another family in the Caldwell area. He died in 1922. Charles and Mary were both buried in Dry Creek Cemetery.

William B. & Elizabeth Gum Hammer

William and Elizabeth were both born in 1835, he in Pennsylvania and she in Virginia. They married in 1864 and had six children, four of whom survived: Leslie L., Annie, Eva J., and Willie. The Hammers came to Idaho in the late 1880s, probably with the Goure family.

William was a carpenter and farmer who owned a 160-acre farm in the foothills between Dry Creek and Pierce Gulch. In 1900, he lived there with his son Leslie who was a miner. At the time of the U.S. Census, the Hammer's grandson, Sydney, was visiting them from Pearl. Hammer patented his land in 1904.

Elizabeth died in 1902 and William moved to town to live with his daughter Annie and her family in Boise City. He died in 1911. Both William and Elizabeth were buried in Dry Creek Cemetery.

George B. & Ella Forney Fisher

The patriarch of Dry Creek's largest family, George Fisher, was born in Ohio in 1849. Ella Forney was born in 1856 in Iowa. They married in Iowa in 1874 when Ella was seventeen. Their fifteen children were: Ada, Emma S., Eva J., Ida L., Orien B., William E., Theodore H. (Ted), Lula E., George C. (Cal), Maude E., Blanche E., Bryan Lloyd, Ina L., Lena G., and Earl C. The first seven children were born in Iowa between 1875 and 1885. One child was born in Kansas in 1887, and the rest were born in Idaho from 1890 to 1904. Ada died as a two-year-old and Eva was a year old when she died in Iowa. Ida died at age eighteen in Idaho. All the remaining siblings lived long lives, well into the twentieth century, and were prominent in the Eagle community.

The Fishers moved to Dry Creek from Iowa in 1889.[14] They made the westward trip with two "poor" horses and a wagon. In Wyoming, one of the horses became ill, so they borrowed an old mule from another member of the wagon train in order to complete their trip.[15]

George was reportedly a poor man who was so busy earning money to feed his many children that he did not acquire any land, the measure of a family's wealth. When the

Fishers had to collect firewood, it was a major effort that required borrowing all the equipment from their neighbors.[16]

Although they were not well off financially, the family was well respected in the community and very active in civic affairs. Ella regularly served as election registrar for the Dry Creek precinct and Emma Fisher was certified as a second grade teacher in Dry Creek in 1897 according to the *Statesman* (May 28, 1897). She married Samuel Swan that that same year, but kept their marriage secret since schoolteachers were required to be single.

William E. attended "Lower" Dry Creek School and married Clara Aiken in 1906. Clara was the daughter of Eagle founders Thomas and Mary Jane Conway Aiken. William and Clara lived in Dry Creek for a time before homesteading on the Black Canyon irrigation project in Canyon County. Orien, Cal, Ted, Blanche, Bryan, Maude, Earl, and Lulu all married and raised their families in Dry Creek and Green Meadow in the early twentieth century. Ina and Lena left the valley after they married.

George and Ella lived and worked in Dry Creek or Green Meadow for the rest of their lives. George died in 1909 and Ella in 1937. They were both buried in Dry Creek Cemetery along with most of their children.

William E. Fisher & Clara Aiken Fisher (Hawley 1920, Vol. III)

William B. & Margaret Crawford Daly

William Daly was born in 1839 in Missouri and served in the Civil War in the Missouri Infantry. He may have been injured during the war as he was declared an invalid in 1892 and received a Civil War pension.

He and Margaret Crawford (born in 1845 in Iowa) married in 1863 and had four or five children before moving west. Mary A., Robert, Thomas W., and Lucy were all born in Missouri. The family lived briefly in Kansas where Charles M. was born, and then headed west to Oregon in 1878 or 1879. Another child, Ernest J., was born in Oregon before they moved to Idaho. He died in 1892 at the age of thirteen. In Idaho, the Dalys had two more children: James L., and Dora Belle.

The Dalys lived in eastern Dry Creek in the 1880s near the old Baldwin/Daniel homestead. William patented 160 acres south of the

Daniel homestead in 1889. In 1902, he purchased additional property in the upper valley from Julia A. Miller for $50 according to the *Statesman* (April 12, 1902). That same year, he petitioned Ada County to establish a new road district (District 16) to include his property in eastern Dry Creek. He was appointed overseer for the new district and was paid $200 for that position according to the *Statesman* (July 18, 1902).

The Marlatt family acquired most of the Daly ranch through marriage in the late nineteenth and early twentieth century. Lucy married William M. Marlatt in 1897 and they lived at the Daly ranch in Dry Creek. Mary married Charles Stanton and lived in far eastern Dry Creek.

James L. and Charles Daly married Daisy and Marie McGinnis whose mother had a ranch southeast of the Daly place along Cartwright Road. James patented 160 acres in the foothills above upper Dry Creek in the early twentieth century. Charles evidently struggled with mental illness and the *Statesman* reported that he was being returned to the state asylum at Blackfoot, Idaho, where he died after experiencing a "second attack of insanity" in August of 1919.

By 1920, William and Margaret Daly lived at Boise City with the family of their son James. William died in 1928 and Margaret died in 1930. They were both buried in Dry Creek Cemetery.

Andrew J. Fessenden

Andrew Fessenden was born in Illinois in 1832. By 1880, he was mining in the eastern Dry Creek Valley. He claimed forty acres abutting the Daly and Pettigrew ranches on upper Dry Creek in 1884. Daly, Pettigrew, and others witnessed the claim. The Fessenden claim, patented in 1888, later became part of the Daly ranch.

William J. & Clarinda Marlatt

William J. Marlatt was born in 1832 in Illinois and lived in the Midwest until after 1870. He and Clarinda had two children in Indiana, Cloyce B. and James, before heading west to Oregon around 1866. Five more children were born in Oregon between 1867 and 1879: Olive, Ida, Grover, William M., and Burton. Clarinda died in the fall of 1880 of typhoid fever.[17] Young William M. later farmed in Dry Creek to the south of the Schick place.

After Clarinda's death, William J. was left with seven children ranging in age from one to eighteen. For a while, he farmed in Boise County above Dry Creek near the Shafer Creek sawmill and toll road. An African American cook, Simeon White, lived with his family. Nearby was the boarding house of the sawmill workers and the owner, Thomas Healy.

By 1900, William J. was living in Washington County, Idaho, with his daughter Olive and her family. He died in 1913 in Nez Perce County, Idaho.

The Tollgate & Sawmill Workers

Seventeen men shared a boarding house with Thomas Healy at the Healy Tollgate and Sawmill above the Dry Creek Valley in 1880. They were: Rufus Bridges, James Hagood, Frank Braley, Edwin F. Wood, Thomas J. Holland, Peter A. Farrett,

John J. Lawton, Jesse A. Helm, Amos T. Bennett, John Berryhill, Daniel Blair, Jacob H. Bash, Joseph and James Nibler, Harry M. Warburton, Sheridan Anderson, and George W. Titus.

Bridges was the sawmill clerk and Ridder the charcoal burner. The others labored in the mill. In addition to working at the mill, Jacob Bash was a freighter whose family lived in the Dry Creek Valley. Jesse Helm's nephew, also named Jesse A. Helm, eventually homesteaded in the valley, patenting his claim in 1917.

One woman, Sophia Young, lived at the mill in 1880. The U.S. Census reported that she headed a household including her twenty-seven-year-old son Nathaniel who was disabled by a broken back, her nineteen-year-old son Daniel, and her brother Charles Myers. Also boarding with the Young family in 1880 was Patrick McFarland who later homesteaded land in the Dry Creek Valley along McFarland Creek.

The Farmworkers & Tradespeople

At least twenty farmworkers lived in the Dry Creek area in 1880. Other tradespeople gave their occupation as printer, saddler, musician, schoolteacher, butcher, or freighter.

Dry Creek Farmworkers & Laborers, 1880

Farmworker	Boarded with:
John Masters	Ellen Glenn
Charles Hulbrish	Self
Joseph True	Self
Edward Randall	Self
Andrew Henderson	Self
William Johnson	Self
Joseph Rill	Self
Adam Jones	Thomas W. West
Horatio Hills	Self
Harry Gray	Self
Charles C. Smith*	Edward Smith
Adam Jones	Jacob Bash
John Miller*	Thomas Kingsbury
John Moore	Thomas Kingsbury
Marion Regan*	Thomas Morrison
David Regan*	Thomas Morrison
Hiram Miller	Charles Hurt
William Hurt*	Charles Hurt
Milton S. Duff	Self

*Later landowner or landowner relative
Source: U.S. Census 1880

Green Meadow

As land in the Dry Creek Valley consolidated into ever-larger ranches, Green Meadow farms were subdivided into smaller farms and even residential lots. Some of the original settlers subdivided their farms along the Valley Road and new families, not all farmers, moved into the area on these smaller parcels. As a result, the population of Green Meadow grew more quickly than Dry Creek during this era.

Nevertheless, there remained many open fields between residences along the Valley Road and the Hill Road. A wagon ride west on the Hill Road from Boise City to Dry Creek in the early 1880s first passed the farms of John F. Miller, Bob Newby, John Gilbert, the old Peck place at the mouth of Stewart Gulch, the Rutledge place, and Green Meadow Ranch.

In 1882, the *Statesman* (August 12) reported that a young woman, Lizzie Adams, was found dead in the sagebrush on the Valley Road from the effects of laudanum. She was buried somewhere in the Green Meadow Precinct, probably at Dry Creek Cemetery.

Green Meadow farmers remained active in community affairs throughout the decade. The *Statesman* (January 6, 1881) reported that Andrew Rutledge and Reuben Cox were among those selected to serve as Ada County Grand Jurors that year. John B. Wood, D.O. Stevenson, and John Patterson were election judges in the precinct in 1889 according to the *Statesman* (August 18).

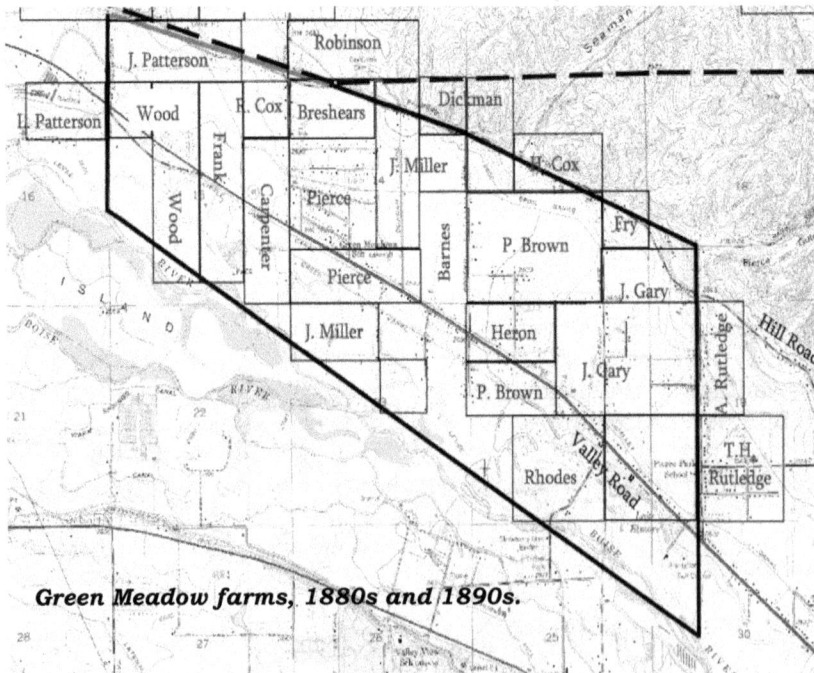

Green Meadow farms, 1880s and 1890s.

The Landowners

Some of the Dry Creek homesteaders of earlier decades, like Andrew Wylie and John Owings, now lived closer to town at Green Meadow while continuing to farm in Dry Creek. They joined many of the original Green Meadow farm families who were still in the area. These included the Cox, Patterson, Conway, Breshears, Brown, Rhodes, Aiken, and Heron families. Historical records also list a few new farm-owning families in Green Meadow in the 1880s. These new families are described here from northwest to southeast along the Valley Road toward Boise City.

John B. & Nancy Conway Wood

Long-time Green Meadow resident Nancy Conway married her third husband, John B. Wood, in December of 1882. Wood was a laborer, born in Tennessee about 1850. John and Nancy lived at the Conway ranch in Green Meadow, which John came to own as her husband. He patented eighty acres on both sides of the Dry Creek Canal northeast of the original Conway farm in 1895, and also owned the old Rockhill and Patterson homesteads. Wood's holdings were bounded on the west by Edgewood Lane, now in the town of Eagle. In 1901, his was reportedly the most valuable farm in the area at $15,500 according to the *Statesman* (August 10, 1901).

John died at Green Meadow in 1905 at age fifty-five. Nancy died in 1915 at age seventy-two. Her son William remained in Green Meadow at least into the 1930s.

Harmon & Sarah Simpson Cox

Harmon and Sarah Cox were both born in Iowa, he in 1837 and she in 1854. By 1870, sixteen-year-old Sarah and her twelve-year-old sister Alice boarded in the home of Frank and Hester Davis at Boise City. Harmon and Sarah married in 1872 when she was eighteen. She and Harmon had eight children, seven of whom lived to adulthood: Mary B., Alice J., Cyrus R., Bessie D., Susan, Alta B., and Alpha B. Cyrus died at the age of seventeen.

The Coxes lived in Cassia County, Idaho, for awhile during the late 1870s before returning to Ada County to farm. Harmon Cox patented an 80-acre ranch on the Farmer's Union Canal at the mouth of Seaman Gulch in 1888. By 1900, he had sold the ranch and was living in Meridian, Idaho. He died in 1922 and Sarah died in 1932. Both were buried at Morris Hill Cemetery.

Robert T. & Mary Barnes

Robert Barnes and his family came to Idaho sometime after 1874. He was born in 1844 in Missouri. Mary was from Wisconsin, born in 1851. The Barnes family's first two children, Sharlotta and Ada, were born in Missouri. A third child, Mary, was born in Idaho.

Barnes was working as a laborer in Green Meadow in 1880—probably for Peter Brown the farmer who lived next door. Barnes became a landowner in 1885 when he patented an eighty-acre farm just west of Brown's along the Valley Road.

In 1900, the *Statesman* (May 29) listed Barnes' farm for sale by Ada

County for back taxes. By that time, Mary had died. After losing his land, Robert worked as a farm laborer in Nampa and lived in a boarding house.

John H. & Gladys C. Smith Hall

John and Gladys Hall were born in 1860 and 1865, he in Arkansas and she in Iowa. John headed west, first to the mines of Colorado and then to Idaho in 1881. The last part of his journey, from southeastern to southwestern Idaho was on foot.[18]

John and Gladys married at Boise City in 1886 and bought a farm in Green Meadow, near the Breshears and Carpenter families, that had been known as the "Willis Place." The Halls had three children. A daughter died in infancy. A daughter and son survived: Grace C. and Fay Waldo.

Hall bought his sagebrush-covered forty-acre property along the road to

John H. Hall
(Hawley 1920 Vol III).

Eagle in 1894. He cleared the land and brought it under cultivation, growing prunes on eleven acres and hay and grain on the rest.[19] The Halls farmed there into the twentieth century. In 1914, John was also involved in a store in Eagle that became Diehl & Mace.

After World War I and John's death in 1919, his son Fay took over the farm and ran it until he died in 1926 at the age of thirty-one. He was buried near his parents in the cemetery at Star, Idaho. Meanwhile, Grace was a teacher in Eagle schools. She married and lived in Green Meadow into the late twentieth century.

Henry & Paulina Miller Dickman

Henry Dickman came to Idaho by way of Montana and Oregon, having lived in Oregon for six or seven years.[20] He was born in Ohio in 1844 of German parents. Paulina was a native of Switzerland, born in 1846. They married in 1868 and had at least six children born in Montana, Oregon, and Idaho: Louisa T., Henry Jr., Rosella, Frank, Oliver O., and Earl R. Louisa may have died as a child. The Dickman children attended Green Meadow School, but Henry Jr. left at age twelve to work in the fields with his father.[21]

Over the years, the family moved back and forth between Oregon and Idaho. In 1880, Dickman was mining in Oregon. The family returned to Idaho around 1884 and settled 120 acres on the Hill Road at the mouth of Seaman Gulch. They patented the property in 1890 and sold it shortly thereafter. Dickman then claimed another 160 acres under the Timber Culture Act. He farmed and raised stock there for about fifteen years.[22] After he sold this second property, he retired and moved to Nampa.

Like many area farmers, Dickman was often in court resolving disputes with his neighbors. In 1888, he was sued by his neighbor to the south, Peter Brown, who claimed that certain items on a note between the two had not been credited to Brown according a *Statesman* report (September 18).

Paulina died in 1909 and Henry in 1916. Both were buried at Nampa, Idaho.

Adrian J. & Patience A. O'Dell Gary

John Gary's older brother Adrian was born in Indiana in 1860. Patience (Alice) O'Dell was born in Michigan in 1862. They married in Nebraska in 1884 and had four children there. Two of the children survived, aptly named Alpha and Omega. Adrian farmed Sam Aiken's old Green Meadow Ranch between the Farmers Union Canal and the Valley Road along what was later called Gary Lane.

In 1904, Alice was involved in a tragic accident with a friend and her child. It was reported in the *Statesman* (October 7, 1904) that Mrs. Henry K. Fritchman and her eighteen-month-old son were riding with Alice in her buggy at the Gary ranch. After riding through a gate, Alice got out to close the gate. The horse spooked and threw Fritchman and her child out of the buggy, impaling the child on a nail

protruding from a nearby fence. The nail pierced the base of the child's skull and he died instantly.

The Garys divorced by 1910 and lived separately at Boise. Adrian ran a feed yard and Alice worked as a practical nurse in private homes. Alice married William Derig in 1927 and lived in Canyon County. The Gary's daughter Alpha married C. Otis Brown the son of Green Meadow pioneers Peter and Caroline Brown, whose farm lay just across the Valley Road from the Gary's. Adrian died in 1941 at Weiser, Idaho.

George W. & Mary Robinson Fry

George Fry was a farmer from Iowa, born in 1855. Mary was born in Iowa in 1860. The Frys married in 1880. They were living in Idaho when their first child was born in 1882. Three of their four children survived past infancy: Otto, Azel (died at age six), and Russell.

George claimed forty acres between Pierce Gulch and Seaman Gulch that he patented in 1884. Around that time, they left Green Meadow and returned to Iowa to live for a while, probably having sold the property.

By 1891, they were back in Idaho, where Azel and Russell were born. After their return, the Frys lived in the Union Precinct west of Dry Creek. George died in 1937 and was buried in Star Cemetery.

Julius C. & Barbara C. Miller

Julius Miller was born in Utah in 1858, the middle son of local farmers Henry and Regina (Rachel) Miller. By 1880, he was mining gold in Oregon, where he married Barbara in 1881. Barbara was born in Illinois in 1861. The Millers had their first child, Fred J., in Oregon. By 1884, they were farming in Idaho where five more children were born: Lulu B., Jesse T., Charles H., Grover A., and Marie.

The Millers were very active in civic affairs. Julius served as Superintendent of the Ada County Poor Farm in 1889 and 1890, and as a County Road Overseer in 1899. In 1902, he ran for a seat on the Green Meadow school board, losing to local farmer and teacher Mathew Duncan by five votes. He also served as a delegate to the Ada County Democrats' convention. Barbara was an election registrar in the Green Meadow Precinct.

After his father died in 1895, Julius took over the Miller ranch, which included land on the north shore of the Boise River south of the old Bixby place. A 1905 map shows a school on their property next to the river.[23] The teacher, John C. Breshears, boarded with them in 1900. They also owned the 160-acre ranch patented by Henry Miller in 1879 along what later became Duncan Lane. Julius died in the winter of 1930 and was buried in Dry Creek Cemetery.

John B. & Catherine Pryor Pierce

John B. Pierce was born in Kentucky in 1827, and later lived in Illinois and Missouri. He headed west for Oregon in 1850 and mined in the California gold fields. Pierce then followed the gold to Idaho, first to the Boise Basin in 1862, working a successful claim there, and then

John B. Pierce
(Idaho State Historical
Society #111A14).

on to Silver City in Owyhee County. While there, Pierce was elected to the Idaho legislature several times.[24] He would later also serve as a director of the Idaho Insane Asylum in the 1880s.

Catherine Pryor was born in Scotland in 1833. She immigrated from Scotland in the late 1850s. Her son, Edward M., was born in 1859. John and Catherine married around 1865 and had five children, four of whom survived: Margaret, John, Jr., Alice Jane (Jennie), and Thomas S.J.

Eventually the Pierce family ended up in Ada County, leasing farms east of Green Meadow before purchasing their own 280-acre farm along the Valley Road in Green Meadow.[25] Their children attended Blagg's school and Cox's school in Green Meadow. John, Jr. recalled playing with Indian children in the sagebrush, but also seeking safety

110

at Fort Boise during the Bannock Wars.[26]

John B. died in early 1888 and was buried in Dry Creek Cemetery. John, Jr. took over the farm after his father. He married Bertha Wiggins in 1897 and they had five children. Jennie married Mathew Duncan and lived at Green Meadow near her parents. Duncan taught at the Cox (Green Meadow) School on what was later Duncan Lane. Catherine died in 1917.

Thomas A. & Sarah A. Farmer Mann

Farmer Thomas Mann was born in Rhode Island in 1812. He lived in Ohio and then Iowa for much of his life. Thomas was unable to read or write. He married his first wife, Maria, in 1835 and they had at least six children. After her death in 1869, Mann married Lucy Chandler

in Iowa in 1870 and they combined households. By 1880, he lived in Idaho and identified himself as divorced. Interestingly, Lucy, who remained in Iowa, referred to herself as a widow.

Mann had a farm in Green Meadow near Pierce's. He married New Yorker Sarah Farmer in Idaho when he was seventy years old. Mann died in 1888 after being kicked by a horse. He was buried in Dry Creek Cemetery. Sarah died in 1890.

The Farmworkers & Tradespeople

At least fifteen farm laborers lived in the Green Meadow area in 1880. Also in the area were a blacksmith, a miner, and a farmer from Portugal.

Green Meadow Farmworkers & Laborers, 1880

Farmworker	Boarded with:
Andrew J. Rutledge*	Thomas H. Rutledge
Thomas N. Eldridge	Thomas H. Rutledge
Samuel H. Burris	Thomas Mann
John Carter	David Heron
William Smith	Nancy Conway
Robert B. Reed	John V. Wilson
Martin S. Cobb*	Self
Robert P. Barnes*	Self
William R. Farmer	Self
Josiah Sites	Self
Jacob Philipps	Self
John Masters	Ellen Glenn
Abraham Miller*	Henry Miller
John Thomas	Reuben Cox
John Hughes, Jr.	John Hughes, Sr.

*Later landowner or landowner's relative
Source: U.S. Census 1880

Endnotes

[1] Carlos A. Schwantes, *The Pacific Northwest: An Interpretive History* (Lincoln: University of Nebraska Press, 1996), 226.
[2] 1880 U.S. Census, Statistics of Agriculture.
[3] Ibid.
[4] Idaho State Historical Society (ISHS), "Ada County" (Reference Series Number 30, 1964).
[5] John J. Hasko, "Cattle v. Sheep: The Idaho Experience," *The Crit* 3, no. 2 (Summer 2010), 79-103, www.thecritui.com.
[6] Ibid.
[7] James H. Hawley, *History of Idaho Volume III* (Chicago: S.J. Clarke Publishing Company, 1920), 837.
[8] Wallace W. Elliott, *History of Idaho Territory* (San Francisco: Wallace W. Elliott & Co., 1884), 266.
[9] Hawley, *History of Idaho Volume III*, 685.
[10] Ibid.
[11] Ibid., 486.
[12] Ibid., 652.
[13] Charles F. Metsker, *Metsker's Atlas of Ada County* (1938).
[14] Hawley, *History of Idaho Volume III*, 792.
[15] Ibid., 797.
[16] Ibid.
[17] Federal Mortality Schedule 1880.
[18] Hawley, *History of Idaho Volume III*, 504.
[19] Ibid.
[20] Ibid., 162.
[21] Ibid.
[22] Ibid.
[23] J.E. Dunbar and J.M. Hollister, "Map Showing Approximately All the Agricultural Lands in Ada County, Idaho" (1904).
[24] Hawley, *History of Idaho Volume III*, 678.
[25] Ibid., 679.
[26] Ibid.

6 A New State: the 1890s

On July 3, 1890, Idaho became the forty-third state in the U.S. A huge Fourth of July celebration took place at Boise City that year. The *Idaho Statesman* (July 3-4, 1890) described a "Grand Parade" in the morning and a "Magnificent Spectacular Parade" in the evening. Young ladies represented the goddesses of Liberty, Peace, and Plenty, as well as Boise City and the State of Idaho in the parades. Between the two parades were a free lunch provided by Boise City, games at the fairgrounds, fireworks, and a baseball game (Pocatello vs. Boise). In the evening, the Governor's Guards hosted a Grand Ball at the armory.

Along with the exuberance of statehood, the 1890s brought severe economic troubles. A populist movement swept the western states, including Idaho, giving voice to grievances associated with economic distress. A Populist Party formed in 1892 with proposals for unlimited silver coinage (favored by mining and farming interests) as a solution to economic depression. Free silver was opposed by eastern bankers and insurance companies in favor of the gold standard. At the same time, organized labor was on the rise among miners and railroad workers.

Widespread bankruptcies signaled the depression of 1893 to 1894.

Green Meadow and Dry Creek ranchers, both men and women, continued their activity in local politics with meetings often held in schools. In 1896, a gathering of Republicans at Dry Creek School, reported in the *Statesman* (October 23, 1896), was addressed by three speakers on the topics of a national tariff and other national and local issues. Locals decorated the school with flags and evergreens surrounding a portrait of presidential candidate William McKinley. The Boise Mandolin Club provided music for the event.

The 1896 election judges in Green Meadow were Christopher H. Frank and Julius Miller, with Gardner P. Harvey serving as election clerk at Pierce School. Charles Hurt and P.L. Schick judged the election in Dry Creek that year, with William B. Hammer as election clerk at Dry Creek School. In November, Schick reported twenty-six votes cast in the Dry Creek Precinct according to the *Statesman* (November 3, 1896). Frank and Mathew Duncan were election judges at Cox School in 1900, with Miller serving as election clerk. Forrest E. See and Patrick McFarland judged the 1900 election at Dry Creek School and Charles Stanton served as clerk.

Women were also election officials and political party functionaries. For example, Louisa Patterson (Green Meadow) and Mary Schick (Dry Creek) served on the Ada County Republican Central Committee in 1898.

As the end of the century neared, Boise celebrated the pioneer settlers who had arrived before 1867 with a parade downtown. Nearly 140 old timers walked in the parade ending with a group photograph in front of City Hall. Among the pioneers on parade were Dry Creek and Green Meadow landowners P.L. Schick, Barrett Williams, William B. Francis, John Lemp, John V. Wilson, John

R. Carpenter, and David Heron, according to the *Statesman* (October 17, 1897).

Some of the sons of the early settlers were mobilized in 1898 to serve in the Spanish American War. In spring of that year, Company H of Idaho's First Regiment formed at Boise City. The Company included young men from Green Meadow and Dry Creek farm families including Privates Fred W. Diehl, George Jensen, Edward E. Smith, and Charles B. Frank.

By the end of the nineteenth century, agriculture was increasingly mechanized and commercialized in Idaho. In 1890, forty to fifty labor-hours were required to produce 100 bushels of

Dry Creek and Green Meadow farms, circa 1905. *Sources: Dunbar & Hollister 1905; GLO Land Patent Records.*

wheat on five acres with a gangplow, seeder, harrow, binder, thresher, wagons, and horses. Farmers produced corn at a rate of thirty-five to forty labor-hours per 100 bushels on two and a half acres with a two-bottom gangplow, disk and peg-tooth harrow, and two-row planter. Meanwhile, in dairying, cream separators made the production of butter and milk more efficient, increasing returns for area farmers.

Idaho permitted irrigation districts to organize, build, and own irrigation canals and ditches under state law beginning in 1891.[1] This offered a new farming opportunity that encouraged settlers to homestead lands on the flats between the Dry Creek Valley and Green Meadow to take advantage of irrigation water from the northwestward extension of the Farmer's Union Canal.

Families who settled north of the canal are described here as part of the Dry Creek area. Those who settled south of the canal are considered to be part of the Green Meadow community, although movement between the two areas was always fluid and continuous.

Boise-area pioneer portrait in 1899 included: 10. John V. Wilson, 11. Barrett Williams, 27. P.L. Schick, 86. John Lemp, 96. Andrew S. Yaryan, 112. Mrs. Grace (Godfrey) Rhodes, 124. Mrs. Sarah Baldwin Bowers, 128. Mrs. Nancy Conway (John B.) Wood, & 132. David Heron (Idaho State Historical Society #1846).

Dry Creek Valley

As is often the case during hard times, mining efforts picked up on Dry Creek during the depression of the 1890s. One day of ground sluicing reportedly produced a little more than an ounce of gold for Fred and George Wheeler and Henry McCoy in 1893. A few months later, Harry Clyne retrieved an ounce of gold worth $15 from a seventeen-hour run with two men and a double rocker on Dry Creek.[2]

Corn crops were the latest agricultural success in the valley. Dry Creek farmer Budd Clark showed off his tall stalks with foot-long ears of yellow corn at the Columbian Commission at Boise City in 1892. Clark had grown four acres of corn with some stalks as tall as thirteen feet according to the *Statesman* (December 9, 1892). His irrigated hillside field featured seeds planted in ridges between furrows so as not to drown the young plants.

Out in Dry Creek, the Jullion brothers' purchase of a steam thresher in 1900 was a matter of much interest in the local newspaper. The Jullions threshed 76,000 bushels of grain in forty-one days for seventy-six Ada County farmers as reported in the *Statesman* (September 25, 1901).

As ever, success in farming and ranching was subject to the vagaries of the weather. For example, in 1897, upper Dry Creek had water only in the early part of the year, sufficient to irrigate just one crop of hay for livestock.[3]

Sheep production finally came to the forefront in the Dry Creek Valley during the later years of the nineteenth century. Some of the livestock holdings were so large that ranchers like William Jones and John Gary sometimes purchased a rail car full of salt for their stock according to various newspaper accounts in the late 1890s. Many of the ranchers owned sheep that grazed part of the year in Boise County to the north.

Jones was reportedly the most successful Dry Creek sheep rancher at the time. In 1897, he reported to the *Statesman* (November 27) that numerous coyotes in Dry Creek were entering his sheep corral to take his young lambs. He had already trapped twenty coyotes and shot many more.

As Deputy Sheep Inspector for Ada County, Jones was involved in a number of sheep-related disputes. In an 1897 court case reported in the *Statesman* (November 25), sheepman John McMillan was charged by Dry Creek rancher Charles Brown with moving a herd of scab-infected sheep without a permit. The preferred treatment for scab was dipping sheep in insecticides. Although Jones had not given McMillan a permit to move the infected sheep, he had told him that the quickest way to take care of the problem was to get the herd to the dipping works as soon as possible. McMillan proceeded to do so (although without a permit), so he was acquitted of the charges.

In 1901, Ada County commissioners learned that a number of local sheep growers failed to report production of more than 169,000 pounds of wool worth about $10,000 to the

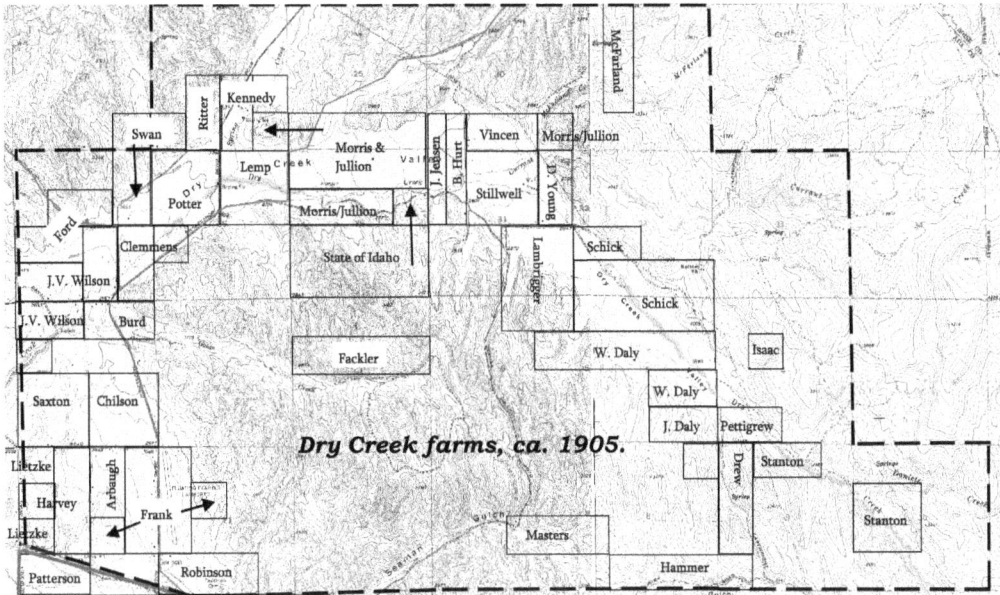

Dry Creek farms, ca. 1905.

County Assessor.[4] Several sheepmen were subpoenaed, including Dry Creek ranchers James Pettigrew (3,150 pounds unreported) and William Jones (22,000 pounds unreported). The *Statesman* (August 10, 1901) noted that the three Dry Creek ranchers who owned property valued at more than $5,000 in 1901 were all sheep ranchers:

John S. Gary	$11,788
William Jones	$23,355
P.L. Schick	$ 6,209

By the end of the decade, the U.S. Census recorded 130 people living in the Dry Creek Precinct.[5]

News of the Valley

Newspaper accounts from this decade provided sometimes detailed insight into the health and welfare of valley residents. Ailments that were uncommon in the late twentieth century were still reported in the late nineteenth century in Dry Creek. Typhoid and malaria were present seasonally. The newspaper reported two typhoid deaths in Dry Creek in the fall of 1891. D.E. Clemmens and Samuel Stillwell also had typhoid at some point, but both survived. Mrs. James D. Daly contracted malaria and was taken to a sanatorium according to the *Statesman* (August 14, 1901).

Other illnesses were still common more than a century later. Stillwell's infant son Walter came down with "membranous croup" in the winter of 1893 and was not expected to live. He did pull through, however, and survived to the age of ninety. In 1892, Julia Miller of Dry Creek died of spotted fever, a tick-borne illness like Rocky Mountain spotted fever.

And finally, an important new technology arrived in the valley with the new century. The Independent Telephone Company announced plans in the *Statesman* (February

28, 1900) to install a telephone line out to Dry Creek.

The Landowners

As the nineteenth century ended, the original homesteaders in the Dry Creek Valley were growing old. Their children or grandchildren now ran the family farms or owned their own farms nearby. Most of the old folks moved to town when they retired, some selling their ranches. In 1897, a 109-acre ranch in Dry Creek was offered for $2,800 in the *Statesman* (April 23). Someone also wanted to trade a $3,000 home on Warm Springs Avenue in Boise City for a ranch with water rights in Dry Creek (May 4, 1897).

Of the Dry Creek Valley homesteaders from the 1860s, only the Clemmens, Miller, Glenn, and Schick families remained by the 1890s.

Much less is known about valley residents from public records during this decade than in earlier years because the 1890 U.S. Census for Idaho was among those lost in a fire in Washington D.C. in the 1920s. Nevertheless, newspapers and other historical sources provide some information about those who lived there during the decade. These are the farm families whose names are first associated with the valley during the 1890s.

Alexander E. & Margaret L. Mencer

Farmer Alexander (Alex) Mencer was born in 1847 in Pennsylvania and Margaret Lemantine in 1859 in Missouri. They married in 1877 and had six children in Idaho, four of whom survived: Joseph, Edwin, John M., and Charles. Alex could not read or write.

In 1880, Alex, Margaret, and their eldest son Joseph boarded with a farmer in rural Ada County. Alex was a laborer and his wife a servant for that family. By 1900, the Mencers owned land in Dry Creek. Their son Edwin was a teamster who remained in Dry Creek after he married. Sons Joseph and Charles homesteaded in the hills west of Spring Creek in the early twentieth century.

Alex died in 1909 and Margaret in 1938. Both were buried in Dry Creek Cemetery, as were other members of their family.

Budd R. & Lydia Heath Clark

Budd Clark was born in New York in 1841. He was wounded in the Civil War while serving in the Iowa Infantry. After the war, he returned to Iowa where he married Lydia in 1867. Lydia, born in 1843, was from Canada. The Clarks had five children, two of whom were born in Iowa (Albert and Alberta). They seem to have also lived in Kansas before coming to Idaho sometime in the 1880s. By 1892, they were farming in Dry Creek. It is unclear whether they owned the land they farmed.

Budd applied for a Civil War Pension in the 1890s. Lydia continued to receive it as a widow after his death in 1899. He was buried in the Fort Boise Military Cemetery. By 1900, Lydia and her children were farming in Canyon County. She died that year at the age of fifty-seven.

Gardner P. & Martha Bennett Harvey

Gardner Harvey and Martha Bennett were both born in Kentucky, he in 1849 and she in 1848. They married there in 1871 and had three children, two of whom survived: a daughter, Montrie, and son, Leslie. In 1893, Montrie married Frank E. Heron, the son of Green Meadow farmers David E. and Fidelia Heron.

The Harveys settled on the flats between Dry Creek and Green Meadow in the 1890s when the land there became accessible to irrigation. In 1898, they patented 160 acres between Floating Feather Road and the Farmer's Union Canal where they farmed with their son Leslie. Staying with them in 1900 was their three-year-old granddaughter, Ethel Heron and thirteen-year-old David K. Heron.

By 1910, the Harveys had left Green Meadow and were living elsewhere in Ada County. Martha died in 1913 and Gardner in 1939. Both were buried in Dry Creek Cemetery.

Martin M. & Eliza Chase Suisted Burd

Pennsylvania farmer Martin Burd was born around 1833 of German parents. He married Louisa E. Moore in Missouri in 1873. She died the next year. By the early 1880s, Martin was in Utah where he married Eliza Suisted in 1885. Eliza, born in Utah in 1856, had been married to a New Zealand man, Carl Suisted. They had two daughters, Mary and Elizabeth.

Two years after Carl's death in 1882, Eliza married Martin Burd.

Eliza and Martin had four children, all born in Utah in the 1880s and 1890s: Eli M., Iliff C., May, and Lula. Lula died as an infant. Eliza died in 1895 at the age of thirty-nine. Martin remained in Dry Creek with his mother-in-law, Elizabeth Chase and his children.

In the 1890s, Burd claimed seventy-nine acres where Goose Creek enters Dry Creek. He patented the land in 1903. Iliff patented 161 adjacent acres on Goose Creek in 1923 and married Norma Mason at Len Dobsen's place that same year.

Within a few years, Burd family members developed an unsavory reputation for encounters with the law. The *Statesman* (April 15, 1899) reported that in 1899 Martin, with his revolver drawn, tried to prevent the annual spring cleaning of the Farmer's Union Canal where it crossed his land. The next year, in a fit of road rage along the Hill Road, he drew his revolver on some freighters whose wagons he attempted to pass (October 25, 1900).

By the early twentieth century, the Burd ranch was "headquarters for a gang of marauders" according to the *Statesman* (February 3, 1911). Martin and Iliff were convicted of the theft of tools from an Eagle ranch and sentenced to sixty days in the county jail in early 1911. Iliff was later convicted of stealing sheep from a Dry Creek ranch and served a term in the Idaho penitentiary. Martin was tried and acquitted of charges in a burglary of a Goose Creek ranch while the owners were away at a Christmas dance. He allegedly stole a number of small articles including a fountain pen and shaving set according to reports in the *Statesman* (April 23, 1911).

Iliff, Eli, and May eventually moved to California. Martin remained in the Dry Creek area until he died in 1916 of kidney disease at the age of eighty-five. He was buried in Dry Creek Cemetery.

George & Harriet Wilson Nibler

George Nibler was born in Minnesota in 1860 of German parents who headed west to Oregon when he was a child. The family moved to Idaho in the early 1870s. Initially, George and his brothers worked as miners in the Wood River region.[6] In 1896, Nibler married Harriet (Hattie) Wilson, daughter of Green Meadow homesteaders John V. and Amanda Wilson. George and Hattie had four children: Gladys F., George E., Crawford W., and Victor L.

Nibler farmed and raised stock on 120 acres along Dry Creek about a mile from the Brookside School, on part of John V. Wilson's old homestead. Later, his son, George E., had a cattle range at the head of Dry Creek.[7]

During some years, the Niblers lived at the farm and in other years, they lived in Boise City. They were in town in 1900 when George worked as a day laborer. A decade later, they were back living at the farm. In the early twentieth century, they settled in the Collister area near the Soldiers' Home.

Their daughter Gladys taught school on upper Dry Creek during the 1910s and eventually worked for the University of Washington. George

lived to the age of ninety-three and died in 1953. Hattie died in 1959. They were both buried in Morris Hill Cemetery.

Charles B. Frank

Charles Frank, the son of Christopher and Belinda Frank, was born in Pennsylvania in 1868. When he was in his early twenties, he claimed 160 acres just west of his father's land along the edge of the foothills where Floating Feather Airfield[9] was later located. He patented the land in 1894 and owned it into the twentieth century, although his father probably farmed it. Charles also claimed 160 acres west of the Harvey family in 1898 under the Desert Land Act, after providing irrigation to the parcel.

That same year, Charles enlisted in the U.S. Army to serve in the Spanish American War. At that time, he gave his occupation as blacksmith. He was still in the military at Fort Myers, Virginia, in 1903.[8]

Charles seems not to have spent much time in Idaho after his military service. He worked as a real estate agent in Florida in the 1920s and in the 1930s was in Alaska with his brother James mining for gold. He died in Florida in 1935.

---

[9] *Floating Feather Airfield was a small airfield with three unpaved runways developed between 1937 and 1943. The airport burned during World War II when a bomber crashed there according to Paul Freeman's internet history "Abandoned and Little Known Airfields: Southwestern Idaho," 2010.*

Edward K. & Annie Van Winkle Lewis

Farm worker Edward Lewis was born in Illinois in 1863. Annie Van Winkle was born in Indiana in 1865. They married at Boise City in 1885 and had five children: Sadie D., Mary E., Nathan A., Olive J., and James O. All of the children were born in Illinois after the family had moved to Idaho. Perhaps Annie returned home to her parents whenever a child was due to be born.

Fire destroyed the Lewis home on Dry Creek in 1891 while the family was asleep inside. The *Statesman* (November 1, 1891) described it as a nicely furnished five-room house, with the loss estimated at $4,000. No one was injured but the family escaped with only the clothing they carried as they fled.

The family left Dry Creek by 1900 and lived in northern Idaho.

Joseph & Jeanne (Jane) Gavroy Jullion

The Jullion family came to the U.S. from France in 1883. Joseph was born in 1836 and Jane in 1839. Their six children were born in France: Ernest, John, Emile, Celia, Alfred, and Matilda. They lived in South Dakota before moving to Idaho around 1896.

By 1900, Jullion and a partner owned a good deal of land in the Dry Creek Valley, including the old Rossi/Robie, Wyatt, Ross, and Smith homesteads. The family also owned large acreages to the west of Dry Creek along the westward route of the Farmer's Union Canal. Joseph operated his ranches with the help of his sons, who also owned some of the land. Ernest Jullion served as secretary of the twenty-five mile long Farmer's Union Ditch Company in 1900, when the canal irrigated about 2,000 acres of farmland.[9]

The *Statesman* (October 30) reported that Jeanne died in 1901 of blood poisoning and Joseph died of unknown causes in 1914. Both were buried in Morris Hill Cemetery.

Samuel W. & Lydia Glenn Stillwell

Samuel (Sam) Stillwell was a farmer from Kansas who was born in 1866. He came to Idaho some time after 1880. Lydia (May) was the daughter of Dry Creek farmer Charles Glenn. She was born in Kansas in 1871. The Stillwells had two sons, Walter P. and Charles L., in the 1890s.

They initially farmed in Dry Creek where Sam operated the ranch owned by his sister and brother-in-law, Iona Stillwell Case and John W. Case. Sam lived with his family next door to May's parents. He raised grain, potatoes, and a farm garden, mostly without irrigation water according to a newspaper report. Sam also had a contract to deliver the U.S. Mail between Boise City and Pearl, Idaho, beginning in 1896, according to the *Statesman* (June 16, 1896).

Stillwell eventually purchased the old Glenn ranch. After running the ranch in Dry Creek, he began improving a new ranch for himself closer to Green Meadow near the Christopher Frank place. By 1910, the Stillwells lived in the Green Meadow area where they remained into the mid-twentieth century.

Their son Walter married Maude Fisher, daughter of Dry Creek ranchers George and Ella Fisher. Charlie married Mary E. Conway, daughter of William H. Conway and Frances Breshears Conway of Green Meadow. May died in 1941 and Sam in 1942 of Bright's disease (diabetes). The Stillwells and their sons were buried in Dry Creek Cemetery.

Patrick & Mary C. Stephens McFarland

Patrick McFarland was born in Ireland around 1835. His parents brought him to the U.S. as an infant. He lived in Pennsylvania before moving west in the 1860s. McFarland settled land mostly in the Dry Creek foothills near what is now McFarland Creek, a small tributary flowing into Dry Creek from the north. McFarland may have become interested in the valley when he worked as an axeman on the 1868 USGS survey of Dry Creek. However, he was not listed in the U.S. Census for Dry Creek until the year 1900.

In the 1880s, McFarland worked as a laborer at the Shafer Creek sawmill and tollgate north of the valley. He married Mrs. Mary C. Stephens in 1890 at Boise City and they lived in Dry Creek. McFarland patented eighty acres in 1898 and an additional 120 acres in 1908.

Both Patrick and Mary were active in civic affairs, serving as election officials in Dry Creek during the late nineteenth and early twentieth century. After a lifetime in the U.S., McFarland finally filed a declaration of intent to become a citizen in 1902.[10] By 1910, an elderly McFarland lived with his neighbors the Vincen family.

Samuel P. & Effie Berridge Glenn

Samuel (Sam) Glenn was the youngest son of Charles and Cyrene Glenn and the brother of May Stillwell. He was the third generation of the Glenn family to farm the Dry Creek Valley. He and Effie, born in Michigan in 1879, married in 1898 and lived at Dry Creek where he was clerk of the Dry Creek School District during the early years of the twentieth century.[11] Sam and Effie had seven children, all but the youngest were born at Dry Creek: Earl H., Mable, Ethel, Elbert E., Frank T., George N., and Roy C.

In 1897, Sam and Effie Glenn's smokehouse and storehouse on Dry Creek reportedly burned and everything was lost—a value of about $300 according to the *Statesman* (June 9, 1897).

Sam Glenn patented 160 acres in the Dry Creek foothills up at the end of McFarland Creek in 1911. He died in 1932 and Effie died in 1960. Both were buried in Morris Hill

Cemetery.

Alphonse J. & Flora Hough Lambrigger

Alphonse (Al) Lambrigger owned the old Crawford homestead in the 1890s. He was a farmer from Illinois, born in 1861. Flora was born in Illinois in 1859. They married in 1885 and had seven children: Bonnie, Ella, Hallie L., Jean M., Roxie I., Theodosia M., and Alphonse (Wesley).[12] The children attended Dry Creek School at least through 1908.[13] Al served as clerk of the Dry Creek School District for a time in the early 1900s.

By 1905, the Lambriggers owned 240 acres in the Dry Creek Valley and nearby foothills and lived in a brick house along Dry Creek Road north of the Schick house. The land was purchased in the names of Flora and her daughter Theodosia. Flora also purchased a number of residential lots in Boise City over the years.

Hallie Lambrigger died in 1909 at the age of nineteen and was buried in Dry Creek Cemetery. Shortly thereafter, the whole family left Dry Creek and moved to Los Angeles to live with their daughter Bonnie and her husband. Al died in 1929 and was buried in Dry Creek Cemetery near his daughter Hallie.

James J. & Melvina Pritchett Rodgers

James Rodgers was born in Illinois in 1863, and Melvina in Missouri in 1868. They married in 1884 in Missouri. James and Melvina had seven children: Azaleon (Azie), Charles S., Henry H., Mark W., and Adai E., all born in Missouri. The Rodgers family moved to Idaho in late 1891. There they had two more children: James F. and Clara L. Mark died at nine months of age and Adai at the age of two. The rest of the children lived well into the twentieth century.

Rodgers patented a 160-acre homestead in the foothills west of Schick's place and south of the Crawford homestead in 1902. It was part of the old William B. Francis homestead. By 1905, they had sold the ranch to the Lambriggers and moved to rural Canyon County.

James died in 1938 and Melvina in 1937. Both were buried in Dry Creek Cemetery.

Forrest W. & Clara Schick See

Clara Schick, the daughter of Dry Creek homesteaders P.L. and Mary Schick, married Forrest See in January of 1892. They had one son, Merl E., in December of that year. The See family lived at the Schick ranch with Clara's parents. Forrest and Clara worked the ranch for a decade before Schick died. In 1900, See listed his occupation as sheep man.

Forrest was the subject of a sex scandal in 1900 that was reported in detail in the *Statesman* (August and October). At the time, Dry Creek resident James W. Gibson had filed for divorce, accusing his wife Jennie of adultery with two local men: Forrest See and Daniel Drake. The Gibsons lived in a house owned by See, probably at the Schick ranch. The house stood on a well-traveled road that See frequented while tending irrigation ditches. See had been seen alone in the house with Jennie on several occasions.

However, the judge ruled that See had a right to be there as the landlord of the property.

Drake, also charged with being at the house, testified that he had intercourse with Jennie. However, the judge did not believe his testimony and did not have it entered into evidence. The judge also did not believe the other witnesses who testified that Jennie told them she committed adultery. Instead the judge awarded a divorce to Jennie Gibson, whom he called a woman of good reputation, on the grounds of cruelty to her, and ordered her husband to pay her $50 in damages.

After P.L. Schick died in 1902, his farm passed to Clara and her mother, and in 1910 to Clara and Forrest. It was valued at $2,196 that year.[14]

When Forrest died of diabetes in

Forrest See in front of his house
(Dry Creek Historical Society).

1922, Clara bought a house in Boise City where she lived with her son Merl who was divorced at the time. Clara died in 1960 and was buried near her husband at Morris Hill Cemetery.

James W. & Jennie Ireland Gibson

James Gibson was born in Montana in 1866 and moved to Idaho from Colorado in the late 1880s. He and Mrs. Jennie Ireland married at Boise City in 1895. After their divorce in 1900, James left Dry Creek and farmed in other parts of rural Ada County. He remarried in 1911.

Newton A. & Martha Jensen Morgan

Newton Morgan was a farm manager born in 1859 in Missouri. He and Martha (Mattie) Jensen married in 1899 at Dry Creek. Mattie was the daughter of Dry Creek homesteader Jacob Jensen. She was born in Utah in 1868. The Morgans had two daughters: Mabel M. and Viola M., both born in Dry Creek.

The 1900 U.S. Census reported that Morgan headed a household of farmworkers who lived near his wife's family in Dry Creek. The household included five farm laborers and a Chinese cook. By 1910, the Morgan family had left Dry Creek and lived elsewhere in Ada County.

Samuel W. & Emma Fisher Swan

Samuel (Sam) Swan was a farmer from Kentucky, born in 1860. He and Emma Fisher, born in 1876, married in 1897. Emma was one of the fifteen children of Dry Creek farmers George and Ella Fisher. She taught at the Dry Creek School according to the *Statesman* (December 19, 1897). Sam and Emma had six children, five of whom survived: Charles, Edna, Theodore M., Walter S., John M., and Jesse W.

The Swans farmed 160 acres, mostly foothills, east of the old Motto place. In 1902, Sam was embroiled in a complex legal case involving several tons of hay grown by Dry Creek sharecropper Charles Brown for George Fry. Brown and Fry sold the very same hay to two different buyers, including Swan, according to a *Statesman* report (December 12, 1902). The case was decided in Swan's favor and he retained ownership of the hay.

The Swans left Dry Creek after 1905 and farmed at Kuna, Idaho. By 1920, he was no longer living with the family. He and Emma had divorced by 1930.

David S. & Nettie Morrison Potter

David Potter was born in Missouri in 1866 and arrived in Idaho in 1877 with the Breshears family. His sister Nancy was married to Green Meadow farmer Thomas H.B. Breshears. Nettie, born in 1874, was the daughter of Dry Creek farmers Thomas and Elizabeth Morrison, for whom David worked. David and Nettie married in Dry Creek in 1896. They had four children, all born in Dry Creek. Three of them survived to adulthood: Marion E., Raymond S., and Morrison S.

Potter purchased Thomas Morrison's 160-acre farm, the old

Motto place, in 1897 and later homesteaded an additional 160 acres adjoining that.[15] GLO records show that he patented the land in the foothills south of Kingsbury's in 1910.

David and Nettie farmed in Dry Creek until the 1920s when they moved to California with their youngest son Morrison. Nettie died in 1948 and David in 1953. Potter family members are buried in Dry Creek Cemetery.

Charles R. & Sarah Pope Brown

Sharecropper Charles Brown was born in 1849 in New York. Sarah (Sallie) was born in 1860 in Tennessee. She had two children from a previous marriage to John B. Pope: Albert L. and Dora S.

Charles and Sallie married in 1884 and had six children of their own. Five were born in Colorado: Charles (Ches), Robert, Ella A., William D., and John. Another daughter, Elizabeth (Lizzie), was born in Utah in 1894, indicating that the Browns arrived in Idaho sometime after 1894. Charles Brown worked a farm at the mouth of Dry Creek near the Clemmens and Potter places.

According to reports in the *Statesman* (July 28, 1899), the Brown family appears to have had serious problems. Ches and Rob Brown ran away from home in June of 1897. In 1899, Charles was charged with raping and impregnating his seventeen-year-old stepdaughter Dora. The issue came to public attention when Dora was sent to town with Rob to sell some chickens. They spent the day in town and later Dora told her stepbrother she was going to a concert at the Columbia Theater.

After sleeping with the wagon and horse at the stable that night, Rob was unable to find her the next morning and reported it to the police. The next day the police found her wandering in downtown Boise City and noticing that she was pregnant, took her to a local home where she told her story to the woman who took her in. Dora said that beginning in January of that year, Brown had forced her to submit to him and threatened to kill her if she told anyone. The pregnancy evidently was not successful as Dora was recorded in the 1900 U.S. Census as not having had any children.

By 1900, neither Dora nor Albert lived with the Browns. Ches had also moved away. Dora married Michael O'Brien, who was eighteen years older than she, in 1900. They rented a house in Green Meadow near Heron's farm, where Michael worked in an orchard.

James J. & Elizabeth H. Garrett McGinnis

Elizabeth Hamm, was born in 1852 in Kentucky. She married in 1867 at the age of fifteen and had five children with farm laborer J.W.L. Garrett before moving to Idaho in the 1880s. Her youngest son, Benton (Ben) Garrett, born in Kentucky in 1881, later lived with her in Dry Creek. James J. McGinnis, born in New York in 1849, was mining at Idaho City by 1867. He claimed land in Dry Creek in 1888. He and Elizabeth Garrett married around 1890 and had two daughters, Marie A. and Daisy O., in 1891 and 1892.

The McGinnis family was hit hard by the depression of the early 1890s. James suffered a breakdown and went to live at the Soldiers' Home northwest of Boise City, leaving Elizabeth at the ranch to fend for herself and her three children. In May of 1895, the *Statesman* reported that she made the trip into Boise with her two young daughters to beg for food. Elizabeth was described as a "pale, hollow-cheeked woman with care and suffering depicted on every line of her countenance..." She said that her neighbors in Dry Creek could not or would not help her, "we are starving and I was forced to come to the city for assistance."[16]

The Ada County Commissioners recommended that she take her children to the Poor Farm near Boise, but Elizabeth declared that she would rather starve than go to the Poor Farm. They gave her a few provisions and she returned to Dry Creek:

> *She started for home late in the evening in a dilapidated cart—a dry goods box set on two wheels —drawn by a half-starved horse.*[17]

James returned home later that year and died in the spring of 1896 at Dry Creek. He was buried at their ranch, his name carved into a piece of granite from the nearby foothills. Unlike most Dry Creek residents, Elizabeth, it seems, did not have the money to bury him in a cemetery.

She remained in Dry Creek with her children and married Theodore Drew in 1900. She patented 160 acres in upper Dry Creek along Cartwright Road in 1904. She and

Theodore appear not to have been married long because by 1910 Elizabeth was using the name McGinnis again. She patented an additional eighty acres in Dry Creek in 1919.

Her daughters Daisy and Marie married brothers from a nearby ranch family, Charles and James Daly. Elizabeth and her son Ben continued living in Dry Creek until her death in 1927. She was buried in Morris Hill Cemetery.

Ben seems not to have married. He patented property at the edge of Pierce Gulch, where Cartwright Road enters the Gulch, in 1921. After his mother's death, he continued living in Dry Creek with a housekeeper and her daughter. Ben died in 1964 and was buried in Morris Hill Cemetery.

William M. & Lucy Daly Marlatt

William M. Marlatt was born in 1874 in Oregon, the son of William J. and Clarinda Marlatt. He married Lucy Daly, the daughter of Dry Creek farmers William and Margaret Daly, in 1897. William and Lucy had

Dry Creek Farm Laborers, 1900

Farmworker	Boarded with:
Benton Garrett*	Eliz. McGinnis
Charles Daly*	William Daly
Ralph Vincen*	Bradford Hurt
Charles Vincen*	Halley Vincen
Allen Jensen*	Jacob Jensen
George F. Hart	Newton Morgan
Arthur J. Lang	Newton Morgan
Solomon A. Little	Newton Morgan
Ren E. Brown	Newton Morgan
Roy Lukert	Newton Morgan
Oscar Townsend	Ruben Ross

*Later landowner or landowner relative
Source: U.S. Census 1900

seven children: twins Charles and William M. Jr., Jesse, Agnes, James, Edward, and Lucy S.

In the summer of 1900, William M., Sr. was working as a miner in Elmore County and staying at a boarding house while Lucy remained in Dry Creek with their three young sons Charles, William M. Jr., and Jesse. Living nearby were Lucy's parents and three of her siblings.

By 1910, the Marlatts had left Dry Creek and farmed elsewhere in Ada County. They returned to Dry Creek to live at Stack Rock in the 1920s with their daughter Lucy who was born in 1915. Their older sons worked with them at the ranch. The family remained in the area well into the twentieth century. By that time, the Marlatts owned the original Daly homestead in the foothills at the far eastern end of Dry Creek.

William M., Sr. died in 1967. He and several of his sons were buried in Dry Creek Cemetery.

The Farmworkers & Tradespeople

By 1900, most of the owner-operated farms in the valley were worked by family members of the landowner. An exception to this was the old Robie Ranch, which was a very large operation run by a manager, Newton Morgan, who supervised a crew of five farmworkers and their Chinese cook, Wing See. Also living in the valley area were miners, a teamster, a lumberman, and a carpenter. Schoolteachers lived in the valley seasonally, although they were not often present during the summer census taking.

Green Meadow

The 1890s was a decade of growth in Boise City as it expanded northwestward toward the Green Meadow area. Some of the Green Meadow farms were subdivided into smaller residential parcels and the area became more densely populated. In 1890, the Green Meadow Precinct had 253 residents, nearly double that of Dry Creek.[18] Still, farms dominated the landscape and cattle moved from field to field down the local roads.

Several controversial cattle theft trials relating to Green Meadow farmers took place in 1896 and 1897. The *Statesman* (March 4, 1896) reported that John Pierce Jr. and Edgar Ferris were charged with cattle theft. Specifically, they were accused of stealing several bull calves owned by George Williams and J.F. Connaughton. The calves were found mixed in with a herd of a dozen or so cattle Ferris and Pierce were moving from one pasture to another. The herd included cattle belonging to Pierce, Thomas Aiken, and Martin Cobb. The trials received extensive coverage in the local press in part because the defendants were represented by noted lawyer and later Idaho Senator William E. Borah, and prosecuted by renowned lawyer James H. Hawley.

Local farmers testified on both sides of the case according to the *Statesman* (March 1896-April 1897). Most had seen the cattle moving along the open roadways. A number of them testified that the bull calves were not among those driven by Ferris and Pierce. One rancher noted that Pierce's fences were down in several places and cattle could enter and leave the pasture at will, suggesting that the calves in question may have wandered into the herd on their own.

The jury found Ferris not guilty in his first trial. However, they did not seem to take their duty seriously, as they were heard cheering and singing during their deliberations. Both the public and the judge expressed outrage at this seeming lack of propriety, and the jury in Ferris' second trial (for theft of the second calf) found him guilty of grand larceny using the *same* evidence as in the first case. Pierce was tried next with evidence from the Ferris case, but he was found *not* guilty. Ferris's lawyers later appealed his second case to the Idaho Supreme Court, which reversed the conviction for cattle theft.[19]

As ever, farmers were subject to the forces of nature. Those in eastern Green Meadow were flooded in May of 1897 when river water overflowed the Dry Creek Ditch. Ranches owned by Godfrey Rhodes, Caroline Brown, Roy Heron, John Pierce, and Harmon Saxon were flooded and the head gate of the ditch washed out, according to the *Statesman* (May 8 and 9, 1897).

Green Meadow's rural openness with accessibility to Boise lent itself to large social and religious gatherings. In 1895, the Christian churches of Star and Boise City held a large picnic service in Sam Aiken's old walnut grove. More than 500 people brought their picnic dinners

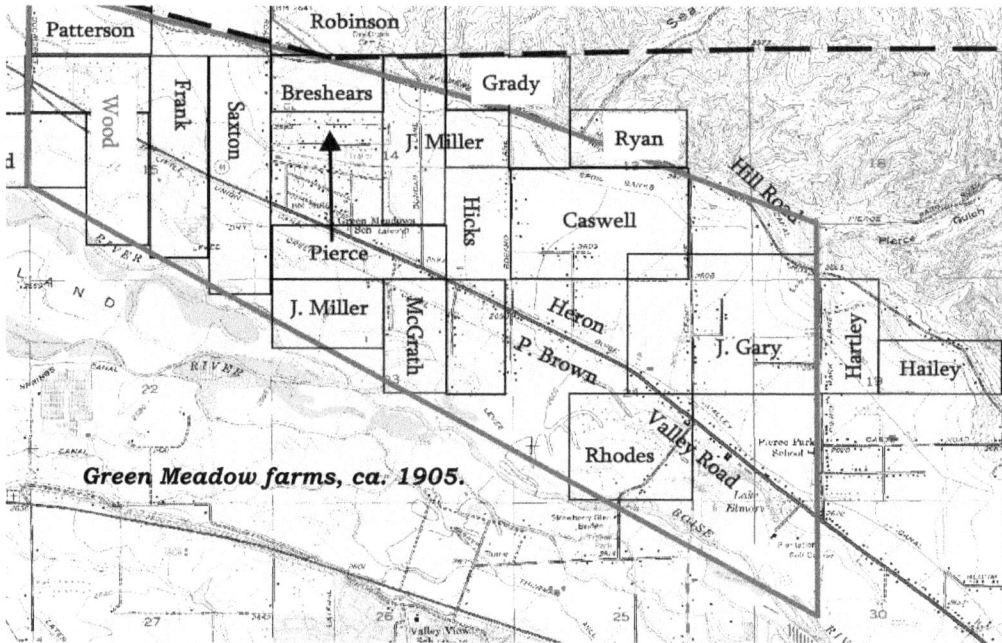

Green Meadow farms, ca. 1905.

to the gathering on that summer day according to the *Statesman* (July 16). Social and cultural events also regularly took place at the schools. For example, farmers David Potter, Jacob Bash, John Breshears, and Edward Frank were among the members of the Green Meadow Literary Society when it met at Cox School in January of 1893.

Even as farming persisted in the area, Boise City gradually extended to encompass Green Meadow. The City chartered a street railway company in 1890 and service began a year later. In 1905, lines connected Boise with Green Meadow and beyond. The Boise and Interurban Railway approached Caldwell in 1906 along the Valley Road through Green Meadow, Eagle, Star, and Middleton.[20] There were trolley facilities at Pierce Park on the old Blagg ranch and small waystations every mile or two along the route.

In 1900, the Green Meadow Census Precinct extended from the Ada County Poor Farm and the Soldiers' Home on the Valley Road near Boise City, nearly to the town of Eagle. The U.S. Census recorded 253 people in Green Meadow in 1900.

The Landowners

Some of the early Green Meadow settlers and their descendants still lived in the area in 1900. Pioneers Thomas H.B. and Nancy Breshears were in Green Meadow, as were John W. and Lucy Patterson and John B. and Nancy Wood. Caroline Brown lived next door to her parents, Joseph and Mary Sexton. Godfrey and Emma Rhodes also remained in Green Meadow. Some new farm families moved in, cultivating smaller parcels as the area grew in population. Absentee owners who rented out the land to small farmers now owned a number of the farms.

Because of the loss of the 1890 U.S. Census, there is much less information about those who lived in Green Meadow in 1890 than in earlier decades. Newspapers and other historical sources such as GLO records offer some insight into the 1890s. The 1900 U.S. Census and land ownership maps of the era show some new farm owners and renters in the area.

William C. & Mary McKissick Ferrell

William Ferrell was born in Kentucky in 1871 and Mary in Iowa in 1876. They married at Boise City in 1895 and had seven children: Ethel, Edith, Edna, Walter, Esther, Elsie, and Henry.

Ferrell rented a farm in Green Meadow for a time around the turn of the nineteenth century before moving to Rupert, Idaho, in the early twentieth century, presumably to take advantage of farming on one of the large, new irrigation projects there.

The Ferrell family eventually came back to southwestern Idaho. Most of the Ferrell children farmed in Canyon County. Mary died at Weiser in 1941 and William died in Canyon County in 1953.

Thomas R. & Louisa McGrath

Both Thomas and Louisa McGrath were born in Ohio, he in 1845 and she in 1849. They married in Ohio in 1869 and had ten children: John H., Sarah F., Charles B., Albert O., Ellie O., George L., Flora, Ida, Ralph, and Lizzie E. Ida died as an infant.

By the 1880s, the McGraths were in Kansas and then in Idaho. They seem to have moved to Green Meadow between 1890 and 1894, and farmed rented land. Their sons George and Ralph farmed there well into the twentieth century. Charles farmed on the north shore of the Boise River east of Julius Miller at the old Burmester homestead.

Louisa died in 1917 and was buried in Dry Creek Cemetery along with a number of her children and their spouses. Thomas died in 1933.

Andrew J. & Ellen Crosby Baker Robinson

Andrew Robinson was born in 1856 in Tennessee. Ellen Crosby was born in Oregon in 1862. In 1879, when she was seventeen, she married Jesse M. Baker at Boise City. They had a son, Jesse M., Jr. before Jesse, Sr. died in 1888. Ellen married Andrew Robinson in 1890. Their daughter Fay C. was born in Arizona in 1892.

By 1900, they had returned to Idaho and lived between Dry Creek and Green Meadow just north of the Breshears place along the Farmer's Union Canal. Their 160 acres, patented in 1902, surrounded Dry Creek Cemetery.

The Robinsons had divorced by 1930 and Andrew lived at the Soldiers' Home in Boise City. He died there in 1933.

Alfred C. Fouts

Alfred Fouts was born in Missouri in 1874. His parents Samuel E. and Sophia Fouts lived in Boise City by 1900. After the death of his father in

June of 1900, his mother Sophia and brother Perry lived with him at the farm he owned near Christopher Frank's place in Green Meadow.

Fouts married during the twentieth century and by 1910 lived in Owyhee County. He died at Boise in 1946 and was buried in Cassia County.

Mathew E. & Alice J. Pierce Duncan

Teacher and civic activist Mathew Duncan was born in Arkansas in 1867 to a Confederate Civil War veteran who could neither read nor write. Mathew, however, was educated. He seems to have moved west to Idaho in the late 1880s. Alice (Jennie) Pierce was born at Silver City in 1870, the daughter of John B. and Catherine Pierce. Mathew and Jennie married in 1891 and had five children: Garland P., Mathew E., Jr., John I., Catherine N. (Kate), and Lila.

The Duncan family farmed rented land on the Pierce farm (the old Clemmens and Bixby homesteads) well into the twentieth century. Their presence in the area is memorialized by today's Duncan Lane.

Mathew was a teacher at Cox School in the early 1890s. The *Statesman* (March 23, 1890) reported that he "closed a very successful term" at the school, which had fifty-two students in 1891.[21] In 1892, Duncan was appointed superintendent of the Ada County Poor Farm northwest of Boise City, replacing Dry Creek rancher Charles A. Stanton. Duncan was an active Democrat.

Jennie died in 1924 and was buried in Morris Hill Cemetery. After her death, Mathew moved to Gooding, Idaho, to live with his daughter Kate. He died in 1934 and was buried in Morris Hill Cemetery.

William M. & Harriet E. Van Ormer Huckba

Farmer William Huckba was born in Missouri in 1863. Harriet (Lizzie) was born in Illinois in 1869. Both had moved west to Oregon by the time they were married around 1886. They had two children before arriving in Idaho in the early 1890s: Minnie May and Dora B. Dora lived only a year. In Idaho, ten more children were born: Hugh T., Daisy, Letitia C., Nellie E., Frances E., Georgia L., William F., Effie L., Allen, and Franklin.

In 1894, William Huckba came before a justice of the peace along with a group of other men accused of assaulting some Japanese men. According to a *Statesman* report (November 22, 1894), the group had gone to the home of the Japanese men at Mora Station to gamble. A dispute over money arose between the two groups and Huckba's group beat up the others.

The Huckbas and their children farmed in Green Meadow well into the twentieth century. William died in 1929 and Harriet in 1938. Both were buried in Dry Creek Cemetery.

John F. & Julia Entsminger Sacks

Civil War veteran John Sacks was born in Ohio in 1843. Julia was born in West Virginia in 1855. John served in the 5th West Virginia Cavalry and later participated in the

William & Harriet Huckba family in 1900. Children (largest to smallest) are Minnie, Hugh, Daisy, Nellie, Letitia & Frances (baby) (Idaho State Historical Society #1876B).

Boise Grand Army of the Republic (GAR) according to the *Statesman* (June 19, 1897). John and Julia married in 1876 and had seven children before moving to Idaho at the end of the nineteenth century: Isaac H., Tessie, Carl F., Roy J., Julia Dollie, Earnest D., and Gilbert J.

The Sacks family arrived in Idaho

sometime after 1894, claiming forty acres in the foothills at the mouth of Pierce Gulch above the Farmer's Union Canal. In the summer of 1897, their youngest son Gilbert drowned in the canal at the age of three. He was buried in Dry Creek Cemetery.

By 1910, John and Julia were living in Washington State while the Sacks brothers farmed the Green Meadow property.

Clinton F. & Lottie C. Hartley

Clinton (Clint) Hartley was born in Missouri in 1862 and traveled west with his parents on the Overland Trail in 1864. After his father died in 1871, his mother married William Dobson and they ranched in the Stewart Gulch area where Clint was raised with five siblings. In later years, Clint recalled some hair-raising experiences growing up in the Dry Creek foothills.

While driving cows out to pasture as a boy, he came face to face with a convict who had escaped from the Idaho penitentiary. At that time, prisoners were marked by shaving one half of their heads, leaving the hair long on the other half. The convict claimed to be armed and threatened to kill Clint if the boy did not cut his hair. Clint used an old pocketknife to do the job. The convict promised to give Clint a watch and other belongings, but was apprehended before he had a chance to make good on his promise.[22]

Clint and Lottie married in 1897. They farmed in the Green Meadow area along Hill Road on the old Andrew Rutledge place. The Hartleys did not have children. Clint died in 1916 and was buried in Morris Hill Cemetery.

Green Meadow Farm Laborers, 1900

Farmworker	Boarded with:
Charles Petty	William H. Conway
Jesse H. McPike	Self
George McGrath*	Thomas McGrath
A.J. Robinson*	Self
George E. Hodgdon	Hiram G. Saxton
Cyrenius Randall	Self
John Dunn	Self
Miller L. Joiner	John B. Wood
Daniel K. Gordon	Thomas Breshears
Frank Denton	William B. Huckba
John Week	Adrian J. Gary
Henry S. Earll*	John P. Gilbert
Abraham Miller*	Caroline Brown

Source: U.S. Census 1900
*Later landowner or landowner relative

The Farmworkers & Tradespeople

In addition to farm laborers, Green Meadow was home to a sheepherder, several schoolteachers, and an engineer.

The End of a Century

By the end of the nineteenth century, Boise City had grown to the northwest along the Valley Road to meet the Green Meadow community. During the 1890s, the population of Green Meadow more than doubled from 256 in 1890 to 582 in 1900.[23] Some farmers sold their land, subdividing it into residential parcels. Others continued to farm on smaller parcels. These parcels, too, were eventually subdivided as Green Meadow became part of Boise City in the twentieth century.

The Dry Creek Valley, however, continued as a rural community. The population remained steady during the decade, with 130 residents in 1890 and 127 residents in 1900.[24] The small homesteads of 160 acres or less had consolidated over the years into larger operations that relied more on ranging livestock for their economic survival than on growing a variety of food crops. This ranching lifestyle continued in the valley throughout the twentieth century.

Claudia Druss

Endnotes

1 James H. Hawley, *History of Idaho Volume I* (Chicago: S.J. Clarke Publishing Company, 1920), 441.

2 *Idaho Statesman* (December 17, 1893 and February 7, 1894).

3 Waldemar Lindgren, "Description of the Boise Quadrangle" (1897).

4 *Idaho Statesman* (August 7, 1901).

5 U.S. Census Office, *Report on Population of the United States at the Eleventh Census: 1890, Part I.* (Washington D.C.: Government Printing Office, 1895), 99.

6 Hawley, *History of Idaho Volume III*, 684-685.

7 Ibid.

8 Post Return of Fort Myer, Virginia, February 1903.

9 *Idaho Statesman* (May 7, 1900).

10 ISHS Archives Naturalization Index.

11 Schick-Ostolasa Farmstead Archives.

12 J.E. Dunbar and J.M. Hollister, "Map Showing Approximately All the Agricultural Lands in Ada County, Idaho" (1904).

13 Schick-Ostolasa Farmstead Archives.

14 R.L. Polk, Boise City and Ada County Directory 1909-1910, Vol. VI.

15 Ibid.

16 Quoted in the *Idaho Statesman* (May 25, 1895).

17 *Idaho Statesman*, "Sad Case of Poverty" (May 25,1895).

18 U.S. Census Office (1890), 99.

19 *The Pacific Reporter* Volume 51 (1898).

20 Idaho State Historical Society (ISHS), "Boise Valley Electric Railroads" (Reference Series Number 220, 1982).

21 *Idaho Statesman* October 24,1891.

22 Hawley, *History of Idaho Volume III*, 652.

23 Twelfth Census of the United States, Census Bulletin No. 18 (Washington D.C.: November 28, 1900), 3.

24 Ibid.

7 The End of an Era

More than fifty families looking to own land and put down agricultural roots in a new place laid the ground work for the communities of Dry Creek and Green Meadow in the 1860s. Although their beginnings were similar, the paths of their development diverged over the decades. Dry Creek's rural landscape evolved from small farmer landowners growing diverse crops for local consumption, to large ranch operations with resident managers and a focus on growing livestock for shipment elsewhere.

Green Meadow moved toward smaller farms and residential areas, a wider variety of tradespeople and producers, and increased connections with a less rural environment. The homesteads of western Green Meadow gradually became part of the Eagle community and those in the east, part of Boise City. Dry Creek would remain rural for another century and more.

Despite the changes in land use, Dry Creek and Green Meadow were bound to each other by the ties of family, marriage, and shared values. The homesteaders sometimes moved back and forth, living in both Dry Creek and Green Meadow as their family and economic needs dictated.

In both communities, families decreased in size as the decades passed, and more children survived to adulthood.

In addition to providing for their families, homesteaders in both places dedicated significant time to making their communities a better place. Many were active in local politics, schools, lodges, and granges. Literacy and education increased as opportunities for local schooling improved. Self-improvement efforts also included literary societies and temperance and church activities.

Marriage, Divorce & Childbirth

Marriages among Dry Creek and Green Meadow families cemented social bonds and added stability to the communities. Men and women formed important work partnerships where the unique sets of skills each provided were necessary to run the farm.

The first homesteaders often married spouses from distant places whom they met during the great westward migration. Their children, however, nearly always married into nearby farm families. In both generations, there were girls who married as young as age thirteen or fourteen, but most married between the ages of sixteen and nineteen. Men were generally in their late twenties or early thirties when they married.

Despite the important role of marriage in these agricultural communities, divorce was not unheard of. Remarriage of both the husbands and the wives quickly followed divorce in most cases. At least ten of the homesteader couples are known to have divorced during the nineteenth century—a few divorced more than once. Some also seem to have left families back east or in other states and may have married in Idaho without having divorced their first spouses. The death of a spouse was also followed by remarriage almost immediately— an economic necessity in an agricultural setting.

Life expectancy among children in Idaho Territory was good. Only

Reported Divorces, Dry Creek & Green Meadow

Married Couple	*Divorce Year*
James & Sarah Baldwin	1872
Henry & Nancy Conway	1873
Peter & Catherine Brown	1882
James & Louisa Corder	1880s
Johnny & Ruby Carpenter	1880s
Henry & Louisa Vaughn	1880s
Anneas & Phoeba Wyatt	1885
John & Louisa Patterson	1890s
James & Emma Baldwin	1898
James & Jennie Gibson	1900
Adrian & Alice Gary	ca. 1905

Childbirth Rates, Dry Creek & Green Meadow

Women born before 1850

1-5 children	13 families	32% of all families
6-10 children	25 families	61% of all families
11+ children	2 families	4% of all families
Unknown	1 family	3% of all families
All children reached adulthood (age 18)*	13 families	32% of all families

Women born from 1850 to 1880

1-5 children	14 families	52% of all families
6-10 children	10 families	37% of all families
11+ children	3 families	11% of all families
Unknown	-	-
All children reached adulthood (age 18)*	13 families	48% of all families

Based on 1900 U.S. Census data. Information may be less accurate for the children of women who died before 1900.

Sources: U.S. Census data; family histories.

about five percent of the children born there in 1880 died before reaching the age of one year, compared to eleven percent in the U.S. as a whole.[1] Among the forty Dry Creek and Green Meadow farmwomen who were born before 1850, most gave birth to between six and ten children. At least 247 children were born to these women. Some additional births may have been unreported when the infant died at birth. Among the recorded births, an estimated 203 children (82 percent) survived to adulthood.

The twenty-seven younger farm women, born between 1850 and 1880, generally had fewer children than the older group. Families became slightly smaller in this generation and more children survived. Of the 153 known births to these women, an estimated 133 children (87%) survived to adulthood.

Education

Although most of the Dry Creek and Green Meadow settlers were farmers, laborers, and tradesmen,

they were generally literate. The exceptions were primarily among recent immigrants from Ireland. All those who were illiterate were born in the 1840s and earlier, more often women than men.

Children from farm families generally attended school through the eighth grade unless they were needed to work on the family farm at a younger age. Some families who owned ranches in Dry Creek either lived in Boise City or moved there explicitly so that their children could attend what they considered the better schools.

Ada County had twelve school districts in 1866, but none seems to have included Dry Creek. Dry Creek children were not reported in the U.S. Census as having attended school in 1869/1870 unless they had just arrived from out of the area. In Green Meadow, at least five children attended school in 1869/1870: Lerah and Subina Clemmens and John, Sarah, and Ruby Rash, possibly at the nearby Blagg School.

Green Meadow School circa 1913 (Monahan 1914).

By the 1870s, with families well settled in the area, new schools were built and teachers hired. Local farm families often cooperatively built these rural schools. Then, Ada County funded the operation and supplies. Teachers were expected to remain unmarried and to board with farm families

Brookside School 1917 (Idaho State Historical Society #74-22-3a).

during the school session.

The Ada County Commissioners declared a school district at Green Meadow in 1872 according to the *Idaho Statesman* (April 16). Cox School was established at the western end of Green Meadow; Green Meadow School was centrally located on the old Bixby homestead; and the Blagg School served students at the southeastern end of Green Meadow on the way to Boise City. P.L. Schick built upper Dry Creek School in 1879 and another school was built in the Brookside area where Dry Creek opened out onto the plain of the Boise River.

Boise City's school district established Idaho's first high school in 1881 and a few farm families from Dry Creek and Green Meadow moved to town to take advantage of the expanded educational opportunities.

Dry Creek School

P.L. Schick built Dry Creek School on land at the edge of the Glenn

homestead. John Glenn evidently donated the property to the Dry Creek School District on the condition that no dances be held there, presumably for religious reasons. Decades later, in 1902, the *Statesman* (July 3) reported that when the District wanted to improve the school, the Glenn family informed them that they had forfeited the right to use the property due to years of holding dances for young people there. The issue was apparently resolved, however, because the school continued in use into the 1950s.

Based on limited documentation preserved at the Schick-Ostolasa Farmstead, it appears that Dry Creek School District received funding on a quarterly basis in the 1890s and early 1900s, probably based on the number of pupils.

In what may have been a typical year, William Hurt was Clerk of School District No. 4, Dry Creek in 1898. His district received an apportionment of $233.32 from Ada County Superintendent of Schools

John J. Blake in January of that year. Hurt was Clerk of the Dry Creek School District from at least 1896 to 1900.

In 1902, Ada County Superintendent of Schools Helen Coston sent a letter to Samuel P. Glenn, Clerk of the Dry Creek School District, informing him that the January funding for the school was $426.64, bringing the total funds in the District's account to $687.92. She directed him not to draw checks in excess of this amount and to spend three percent of the funds on books for the school library using two book lists provided by the District. She also informed him that U.S. schools were planning memorial activities for the late President McKinley on Friday afternoon January 24, 1902.

Books and some school supplies for the District were purchased from James A. Pinney & Co. in Boise City. The District ordered other supplies such as desks, blackboard canvas, and chalk from W.S. Pierce School Supplies in Salt Lake City. These were sent by stagecoach to Dry Creek.

Dry Creek School operated into the 1950s, when the building was incorporated into the home of Pete and Betty Echanove who came to own the Glenn ranch.

Health & Welfare

The U.S. Census does not record physicians living in Dry Creek or Green Meadow during the late nineteenth century. Families generally tended to their own minor medical needs, or made the trip into Boise City for major medical attention. Doctors from Boise occasionally traveled out to Dry Creek and other rural areas to address pressing medical issues.

Late nineteenth century newspapers mentioned medical conditions when the illness or the family was considered noteworthy. Folks then suffered many illnesses still common today like heart disease, stroke, tick fever, and pneumonia. Other diseases that are uncommon today, like typhoid, malaria, and tuberculosis, also occurred in late nineteenth century Dry Creek and Green Meadow. Childbirth was not usually mentioned as a cause of death but can be inferred from the written record when the death of a mother quickly followed the birth of a child. The deaths of newborn infants were sometimes not reported.

Accidents were common in agricultural operations and were generally treated at home unless they presented a major health threat. Some intentional gunshot wounds in eastern Green Meadow and the nearby Eagle area were written up in the local newspaper. *Statesman* accounts described the area as excessively violent during the 1860s and 1870s.

19th Century Dry Creek & Green Meadow Residents
Unable to Read or Write

Born	Name	Born In	Occupation
1804	John Blagg	N. Carolina	Farmer
1805	Judith Blagg	N. Carolina	Kept house
1812	Thomas Mann	Rhode Island	Farmer
1820	John Miller	Pennsylvania	Farmer
1828	Felix Johnson	Ireland	Farmer
1831	Elizabeth Shoffner	Ohio	Kept house
1835	Marg. McGauley	Ireland	Kept house
1835	Thos. McGauley	Ireland	Farm worker
1837	James Heren	Ireland	Farmworker
1837	Elizabeth Stewart	Ireland	Kept house
1839	Sarah Clemmens	Indiana	Kept house
1840	Catherine Heren	Ireland	Kept house
1840	Mary B. Johnson	Ireland	Kept house
1843	John Heren	Ireland	Farmworker
1843	William Kennedy	Illinois	Laborer
1847	Rosa Heren	Ireland	Kept house
1847	Mary E. Kennedy	Indiana	Kept house
1847	Alexander Mencer	Pennsylvania	Farmer
1848	Hannah Rockhill	Indiana	Kept house

Source: U.S. Census Records 1870-1900.

Funding for School District No. 4, Dry Creek

Date	Funds	Clerk	Cour
April 4, 1896	$ 117.00	William Hurt	John
Oct. 1, 1896	$ 18.40	William Hurt	H.S.
July 17, 1897	$ 21.61	William Hurt	John
Jan. 10, 1898	$ 233.32	William Hurt	John
Year 1899	No record		
July 18, 1900	$ 70.38	William Hurt	Kate
Year 1901	No record		
Jan. 17, 1902	$ 426.64	Samuel P. Glenn	Heler
July 30, 1904	$ 101.46		

Sources: Schick-Ostolasa Farmstead Archives; Idaho Statesman 1904.

Reported Accidents & Injuries, Dry Creek & Green Meadow

Individual	Accident/Injury	Caused death?	Year
Johnny Roberts	Gunshot	No	1863
Minnie Burmester	Gunshot	Yes	1869
Jacob Drake	Head run over by wagon	No	1860s
Thomas H. Kingsbury	Gunshot	No	1871
Phillip Paul	Frostbite	No	1874
David Clemmens	Fall from cliff	Yes	1877
A.H. Robie	General trauma	Yes	1878
Thomas West	Hand run over by wagon	No	1880
Lizzie Adams	Laudanum	Yes	1882
Thomas Mann	Kicked by horse	Yes	1888
John V. Wilson	Gunshot	No	1892
Dora Pope	Rape	No	1899
Jeanne Jullion	Blood poisoning	Yes	1901
Phillip L. Schick	Burns	Yes	1902
Fritchman infant	Thrown from wagon	Yes	1905

Sources: Idaho Statesman; family obituaries.

Crime & Punishment

Dry Creek and Green Meadow homesteaders spent a fair amount of time in court settling property, livestock, political, and personal disputes with their neighbors. For minor disputes, they had access to hearings by local justices of the peace such as Dry Creek homesteader Barrett Williams. For more important issues they hired attorneys and sought hearings in district court at Boise City. Reported crimes over the decades included theft of livestock, water, crops, and personal property; assault; land claims and mining issues; and rape. Domestic disputes, divorce, and personal grievances also came before the courts.

Locals considered certain ranches to be headquarters for criminal activities. The Robie ranch, when owned by gunslinger Hank Vaughn and his wife Martha Robie Vaughn, was reportedly home to a group of cattle thieves who ranged throughout the Boise area in the early 1880s. At another ranch near the mouth of Goose Creek, several members of the Burd family had a reputation for encounters with the law in the 1890s and early 1900s. They were variously charged with assault, theft of personal belongings from their neighbors, and livestock theft over several years in the early twentieth century.

Civic & Social Life

Most Dry Creek and Green Meadow homesteaders, men and women

alike, spent at least some time engaged in civic activities. They served as delegates to political party conventions, as election judges, as voting registrars, and as school board officials. Both Republicans and Democrats were active in the communities, in about equal numbers. As elsewhere in Idaho, most Democrats hailed from southern states, while most Republicans had ancestral ties to the northern U.S.

Local social life was at its height during the winter months when the farm was quiet. Fall and winter were the seasons of parties, dances, and weddings. Social gatherings took place at local schools and at the homes of the more prominent families. Groups of young people traveled to town for social events, and families enjoyed plays and musical performances by traveling artists.

Farming & Ranching

Over the decades, the early practice of farming a variety of crops to sell locally gave way to a focus on livestock and feed crop production in the Dry Creek Valley. The western conflict between sheep and cattle ranching played out in the valley as it did elsewhere in Idaho. Dry Creek and Green Meadow farmers who took up sheep ranching in the 1870s came into conflict with cattle producers who were concerned that sheep in the foothills around Dry Creek would overgraze the range leaving little summer pasture for their cattle. However, sheep production in the valley overtook cattle production by the 1890s and ranchers grazed sheep in the Dry

Creek foothills and in Boise County to the north. Buyers combined many of the forty to 160-acre homesteads into larger spreads with major sheep operations. By the turn of the century, sheep producers owned the most valuable ranches in the valley.

The arrival of the railroad in the 1880s allowed livestock to be shipped to market more easily and more profitably than in the past, further enhancing the shift to livestock production. According to an early twentieth century historian, cattle raised in western territories brought $8 a head in 1878, increasing to $12 a head, and later to more than $20 a head.[2]

The shift to livestock production is also evident in land use changes over the decades. The acreage of improved farmland (crop production) in Idaho grew steadily from 1870 to 1890, but then began to decline as livestock production increased and ranchers left more land unimproved for grazing as compared to earlier decades.[3] By 1900, Ada County (including Dry Creek and Green Meadow) had more than 750 farms whose average size was 120 acres, compared to the early homestead ranch of 160 acres.[4]

The End of the Settlement Era

In 1911, Boise City held another history parade featuring some of the area's elder pioneers. Among them were Green Meadow settlers Angeline Aiken, Godfrey and Grace Rhodes, Hugh Rutledge, and Fidelia Heron. The honorees, who had come to Idaho on horseback and in wagons, now rode on the "best automobiles that the city could provide" according to the *Statesman* (October 13, 1911).

At that time, the Dry Creek Valley was still rural farmland. Green Meadow, though well outside the small town of Boise, was more densely settled. The Boise & Interurban Railway had laid trolley tracks along the north side of the old Valley Road (State Street) with stops at Pierce Park and Saxton in Green Meadow. Investors made money in real estate along the route as the descendants of the early homesteaders subdivided their farms into residential and business properties.

The city would finally arrive at

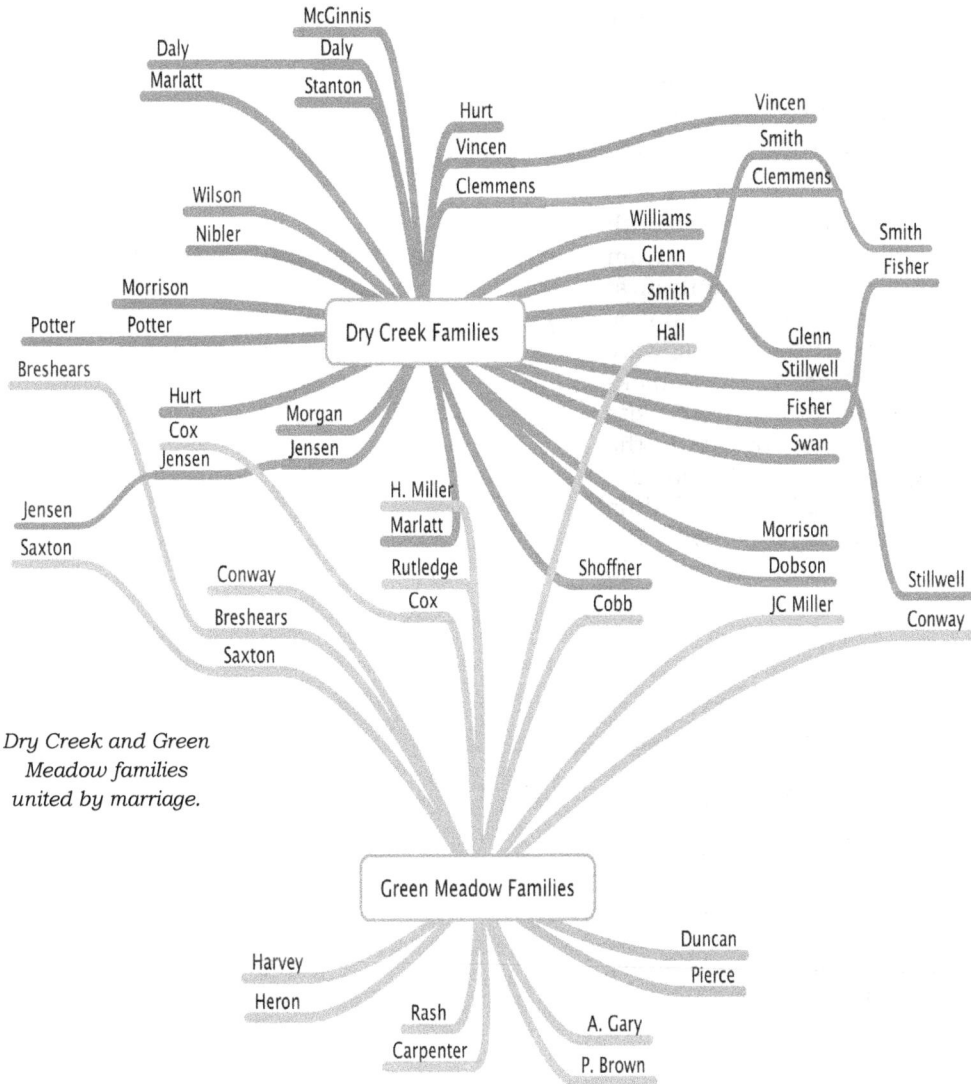

McGinnis
Daly
Daly
Marlatt
Stanton
Hurt
Vincen
Vincen
Smith
Clemmens
Clemmens
Wilson
Williams
Nibler
Glenn
Smith
Fisher
Morrison
Smith
Potter
Potter
Dry Creek Families
Hall
Glenn
Breshears
Stillwell
Hurt
Fisher
Cox
Morgan
Jensen
Jensen
Swan
Jensen
Saxton
H. Miller
Marlatt
Morrison
Conway
Rutledge
Shoffner
Dobson
Stillwell
Breshears
Cox
Cobb
JC Miller
Conway
Saxton

*Dry Creek and Green
Meadow families
united by marriage.*

Green Meadow Families

Harvey
Duncan
Heron
Pierce
Rash
A. Gary
Carpenter
P. Brown

Green Meadow during the twentieth century, ending its agricultural era. Denser settlement of Dry Creek would not occur until 100 years later, during the twenty-first century. By that time, farming concepts had come full circle and the value of small farms providing local foods was again in the forefront. This idea was re-introduced in the Dry Creek Valley during the early years of the twenty-first century with a community supported agriculture operation on the old Schick and Crawford homesteads, by then part of the planned community of Hidden Springs.

Although most of the nineteenth century buildings were gone from the valley by the twenty-first century, the old Schick farmhouse and some of its outbuildings were preserved in place. The Schick-Ostolasa Farmstead historic site now stands as a silent tribute to the history of agriculture in Idaho and the Dry Creek Valley, reminding succeeding generations of the significant rural heritage of Ada County and southwestern Idaho.

Endnotes
[1] John S. Billings, *U.S. Census 1880, Mortality and Vital Statistics of the United States*, (Washington D.C.: U.S. Government Printing Office, 1885), XX.
[2] Albert Hart Sanford, *The Story of Agriculture in the United States* (New York: D.C. Heath & Co., 1916), 241.
[3] 12th Census of the United States, Bulletin 185, Agriculture: Idaho (Washington D.C.: United States Census Office, 1902), 103.
[4] Ibid., 104.

Bibliography

Ada County. Tax Assessment Records, 1868-1870. Card Catalog Index. Idaho Historical Society Archives.

_____. Instrument Numbered 665, May 16, 1903. Idaho Historical Society Archives.

_____. Instrument Numbered 78717, March 26, 1919. Idaho Historical Society Archives.

_____. Instrument Numbered 87473, April 19, 1920. Idaho Historical Society Archives.

_____. Instrument Numbered 221837, November 16, 1942. Idaho Historical Society Archives.

_____. Instrument No. 220480, July 16, 1943. Idaho Historical Society Archives.

Ada County Commissioners. Minutes of the meeting January 3, 1866. Card Catalog Index. Idaho Historical Society Archives.

_____. Minutes of the meetings, January 10 and October 8, 1867. Card Catalog Index. Idaho Historical Society Archives.

Ada County Court Records 1888. Idaho Historical Society Archives, Boise, Idaho.

Ada County Deed Books I, II, III. Idaho Historical Society Archives, Boise, Idaho.

Ada County Homestead Abandonment, 1879. Card Catalog Index. Idaho Historical Society Archives, Boise, Idaho.

Ada County Land Claims Book I. Idaho Historical Society Archives, Boise, Idaho.

Ada County Marriage License Books 1-8, 1865. Card Catalog Index. Idaho Historical Society Archives.

Bake, B.R., ed. *1910 Idaho Census Index.* Compiled by the Upper Snake River Valley Family History Center volunteers and McKay Library employees at Ricks College. Bountiful, Utah: Precision Indexing, Inc., 1993.

Baker, Laurie L., City of Eagle, and Ronald J. Baker. *Images of America: Eagle.* Charleston, South Carolina: Arcadia Publishing, 2012.

Baker, Ronald J. *A Brief History of Eagle, Idaho.* Eagle, Idaho: Eagle Public Library, 2005.

Bancroft Hubert Howe. *The Works of Hubert Howe Bancroft Volume XXXI, History of Washington, Idaho, and Montana 1845-1889.* San Francisco: The History Company, Publishers, 1890.

Bardwell, A.A., D.C. Eggleston and M.A. Palmer. "Appraisal of Land and Resources Malheur Indian Reservation, Grant, Harney & Malheur Counties, Oregon," 1958.

Barghouti, Kim, comp. "Nevada State Journal, 1878." Washoe County Library, Reno, Nevada. The Generations Network, Inc., 2000.

Bauer, Barbara Perry and Madeline K. Buckendorf. *A History of Dry Creek Valley, 1860s to 1940s.* Report prepared for Grossman Family Properties. Boise, Idaho, July 1994.

Beal, Merrill W. "Rustlers and Robbers: Idaho Cattle Thieves in Territorial Days." *Idaho Yesterdays* 7:1, Spring 1963.

Billings, John S. *U.S. Census 1880, Mortality and Vital Statistics of the United States.* Washington D.C.: U.S. Government Printing Office, 1885.

Bird, Annie Laurie. *Boise, the Peace Valley.* Canyon County Historical Society. Caldwell, Idaho: Caxton Printers, Ltd., 1975.

Boise City Directory, 1891. Boise: Leadbetter & Walterbeek, 1891.

Boise City Land Office Records Homestead Application No. 45, 1874.

Brigham Young University (BYU) Idaho. Western States Historical Marriage Record Index, 2004. abish.byui.edu/ specialCollections/ fhc/newMarriage

Brosnan, Cornelius J. *History of the State of Idaho.* New York: Charles Scribner's Sons, 1918.

Bureau of Land Management (BLM). Land Patent Details, Accession/Serial # IDIDAA 030189. General Land Office Records, 2004. www.glorecords.blm.gov/PatentSearch

_____. *Emigrant Trails of Southern Idaho.* Idaho Cultural Resource Series Number 1. Boise: BLM Idaho State Office, 1999.

Carr, Ezra S. *The Patrons of Husbandry on the Pacific Coast.* San Francisco: A.L. Bancroft and Company, 1875.

Chaffee, Eugene B. *Early History of the Boise Region 1811-1864.* M.A. Thesis, University of California, 1927.

Clarke, S.J. Publishing Co. *Idaho Deluxe Supplement.* "Hon. Henry Chiles Riggs" and "John R. Carpenter." Chicago: S.J. Clarke Publishing Co., 1920.

Delgado, Max A., III. *Jesus Urquides: Idaho's Premier Muleteer.* Master of Arts in History, Boise State University, 2010.

Dunbar, J.E. and J.M. Hollister. "Map showing approximately all the agricultural lands in Ada County, Idaho, 1904."

Durham, N.W. *History of the City of Spokane and Spokane County, Washington From Its Earliest Settlement to the Present Time*, Volume I. Spokane: The S.J. Clarke Publishing Company, 1912.

Elliott, Wallace W. *History of Idaho Territory.* San Francisco: Wallace W. Elliott & Co., 1884.

Fairhurst, R. *Fisher's Landing. Images of America.* Charleston, South Carolina: Arcadia Publishing, 2008.

Freeman, Paul. "Abandoned and Little Known Airfields: Southwestern Idaho," 2010. www.airfields-freeman.com/ID/ Airfields_ID_SW.htm#floatingfeather

French, Hiram T. *History of Idaho. A Narrative Account of Its People and Its Principal Interests, Volumes I & II.* Chicago: The Lewis Publishing Company, 1914.

"Growing a Nation. The Story of American Agriculture." In *A History of American Agriculture*, 1860-1890. www.agclassroom.org/gan/timeline

Hailey, John. *The History of Idaho.* Boise: Syms-York Company, Inc., 1910.

Hart, Arthur A. *Life in Eagle, Idaho.* Eagle, Idaho: Eagle Historic Preservation Commission, 2008.

Hasko, John J. "Cattle v. Sheep: The Idaho Experience." *The Crit* 3, no. 2, Summer 2010. www.thecritui.com.

Hawley, James H. *History of Idaho, Volumes I-IV.* Chicago: S.J. Clarke Publishing Company, 1920.

Hockaday, James. *History, Payette National Forest.* USDA Forest Service Intermountain Region, 1968.

Idaho Department of Water Resources (IDWR). Adjudication Claim Report 63-383, 2004.

Idaho Digital Atlas. "Stagecoach Routes in Idaho." www.imnh.isu.edu/digitalatlas/geog/historic

Idaho Statesman. 1865–1906. *The Idaho Statesman* Boise, Ada County, Idaho. Deaths 1865-1906.

Idaho Daily Statesman. "Mount Hood Saloon." March 1, 20 and October 6, 1866.

_____. "Mount Hood Saloon." February 14, 1867.

_____. "Toll Road." May 28, 1869.

_____. "Lumber for Currency." December 3, 1869.

_____. "A.J. Wyatt's Farm." September 20, 1873.

_____. "Frozen." January 3, 1874.

_____. "Dissolution Notice." April 2, 1878.

_____. "Proceedings of the Board of County Commissioners for Ada County." July 10, 1878.

_____. "Proceedings of the County Commissioners." April 1, 1882.

Idaho Tri-Weekly Statesman. "Lumber for Currency." December 21, 1869.

_____. "Lumber for Currency." January 1, 1870.

_____. "Honorable A.H. Robie Masonic Resolutions." August 10, 1878.

Idaho Statesman. "Still Sits the Dry Creek Schoolhouse by the Road." January 11, 1953.

_____. "Echanove 50th Anniversary." January 16, 2005.

Idaho State Historical Society. "The Boise City Assaying and Refining Works." Idaho State Historical Society Reference Series Number 3, 1962.

_____. "Ada County." Idaho State Historical Society Reference Series Number 30, 1964.

_____. "Bigfoot." Idaho State Historical Society Reference Series Number 40, 1970.

_____. "New Union Ditch Company Canal." Idaho State Historical Society Reference Series Number 513, 1974.

_____. "New Dry Creek Ditch Company." Idaho State Historical Society Reference Series Number 529, 1974.

_____. "Eagle Island Ditches." Idaho State Historical Society Reference Series Number 507, 1974.

_____. "Placer Mining in Southern Idaho, 1862-1864." Idaho State Historical Society Reference Series Number 166, 1980.

_____. "Albert H. Robie." Idaho State Historical Society Reference Series Number 596, 1981.

_____. "Alexander Rossi." Idaho State Historical Society Reference Series Number 597, 1981.

_____. "Boise Valley Electric Railroads." Idaho State Historical Society Reference Series Number 220, 1982.

_____. "A Look at the Boise Valley." *Idaho Yesterdays* 28, no.4: 1985.

_____. "Boise-Kelton Stage Service Past City of Rocks, 1869-1883." Idaho State Historical Society Reference Series Number 849, 1995.

_____. Naturalization Index, 2005. www.idahohistory.net/naturalization.html

Idaho Transportation Department (ITD). Transportation Background, 2003. www.idahofuturetravel.info/PDFs/IDTransBkg.PDF

Illustrated History of the State of Idaho. Chicago: The Lewis Publishing Company, 1899.

Indiana Marriage Collection. Bartholomew County, Indiana. 1850–1920 Inclusive. Vol. WPA, Book C5. The Generations Network, 2005.

Intermountain Map Company. Ada County, Idaho: complete ownership, 1917.

Jackson, Orville E. *Idaho Mining Rights Revised and Enlarged*. Boise: Jackson, 1906.

Land Office Boise City, Idaho. "Proof Required under Homestead Acts" and "Affidavit Required of Homestead Claimants." Homestead Application No. 45, Boise City, Idaho, 1874.

Langley, Henry G. *Pacific Coast Business Directory for 1867*. San Francisco: H.G. Langley, 1867.

Legends of America. "Hank Vaughn–An Unhappy Horse Thief," 2006. www.legendsofAmerica.com

Lindgren, Waldemar. Description of the Boise Quadrangle, 1897.

McConnell, William J. *Early History of Idaho*. Caldwell, Idaho: Idaho State Legislature, 1913.

Metsker, Charles F. *Metsker's Atlas of Ada County*. 1938.

Michno, Gregory. *The Deadliest Indian War in the West: The Snake Conflict 1865-1868*. Caldwell, Idaho: Caxton Press, 2007.

Monahan, A.C. "Consolidation of Rural Schools and Transportation of Pupils at Public Expense." U.S. Bureau of Education Bulletin No. 30. Washington D.C.: Government Printing Office, 1914.

Monroe, J. "Germans." In *Idaho Encyclopedia*. University of Idaho and the Idaho Humanities Council, 2003. www.webs.uidaho.edu/idahoencyclopedia/art icles/people/germans.htm

National Park Service (NPS). "Civil War Soldiers & Sailors," 2005. www.itd.nps.gov/cwss

Olson, J. "The Detailed Work of the GLO Surveyors in Chronological Order," 2008. www.olsonengr.com

Ontko, A.G. *And the Juniper Trees Bore Fruit, Volume V*. Bend, Oregon: Maverick Publications, Inc., 1999.

Oregon Historical Society, "News Article, State Robbery," The Oregon History Project, 2012. www.ohs.org/education/oregonhistory/histori cal_records

Pacific Reporter Volume 51. St. Paul: West Publishing Co., 1898.

Payette Independent. "Death of Alexander Rossi." Obituary, March 2, 1906.

Polk, R.L. *Boise City and Ada County Directory 1909-1910, Vol. VI*.

_____. *Boise City and Ada County Directory 1917, Vol. XI*.

Prickett, H.E. *Reports of Cases Argued and Determined in the Supreme Court of Idaho Territory*. San Francisco: A.L. Bancroft and Company, 1882.

Rich, Burdett A. and Henry P. Farnham, eds. *The Lawyers' Reports Annotated*. New Series Book 34. New York: The Lawyers Co-operative Publishing Company, 1911.

Rossi & Lambing. "Daily Accounts Journal, 1873-1876. " Idaho Historical Society Archives.

Sanford, Albert Hart. *The Story of Agriculture in the United States*. New York: D.C. Heath & Co., 1916.

Schwantes, Carlos A. *In Mountain Shadows: A History of Idaho*. Lincoln: University of Nebraska Press, 1996.

_____. *The Pacific Northwest: An Interpretive History*. Lincoln: University of Nebraska Press, 1996.

Smith, Roxann Gess. "Boise City Elections 1867 to 1885." City of Boise, 2000. gesswhoto.com/idaho/boise-elections.html

_____. "Ada County officials, 1865-1885." gesswhoto.com/idaho/ada-county-officials.html

Social Security Death Index, 2003. ssdi.rootsweb.com

State of Idaho. Ponderosa State Park General Development Plan. Idaho State Parks and Recreation, no date. http://parksandrecreation.idaho.gov/assets/content/docs/Ponderosa

State of Washington. *The Mashel (sometimes Maxon) Massacre (March 1856)*. Washington Department of Archaeology and Historic Preservation. www.historylink.org

Twelfth Census of the United States. *Census Bulletin No. 18*. Washington D.C.: November 28, 1900.

University of Washington. *"Report of A.H. Robie, special agent for the Indians between the Columbia River and the Cascade Mountains. July 31, 1857."* University of Washington Digital Collections, 2009.

U.S. Census Office. *Report on Population of the United States at the Eleventh Census: 1890, Part I*. Washington D.C.: Government Printing Office, 1895.

U.S. Federal Census. Ada, Idaho Territory. Agricultural Schedule, 1870.

_____. Ada County, Idaho, District 2, Agricultural Schedule, 1880.

_____. Fourteenth Census of the United States: 1920—Population Schedule. Dry Creek Precinct.

U.S. Office of Indian Affairs. *Annual report of the commissioner of Indian affairs, for the year 1857*, Oregon and Washington Superintendency, 1858.

U.S. Tax Assessment, 1869. Annual, Monthly and Special Lists. NARA Series T1209, Roll 1.

U.S. IRS Tax Assessment Lists for Idaho Territory, 1865.

Washington State Historical Society. "Treaties and Councils: Stevens' Entourage, Blackfeet Treaty." In *The Treaty Trail: U.S.–Indian Treaty Councils in the Northwest*, 2009. www.washingtonhistory.org.

Weisshaupt, Rudy J. "Cartwright Road." Student Research Paper, 1977. Idaho Historical Society Archives.

Whitney, Orson F. *History of Utah Volume 3*. Salt Lake City: George Q. Cannon & Sons, 1884.

Williams, Barrett. "Ledgers of Business Transactions, 1872-1880, Volumes 1–5." Idaho Historical Society Archives.

Woods, Shelton, ed. *Valley County Idaho Prehistory to 1920*. Valley County History Project. Donnelly, Idaho: Action Publishing, 2002.

Wyman, Dorothy Stiff. *Light Upon the Mountain*. Bend, Oregon: Maverick Publications, 1989.

Yaryan, Del. Personal recollection of Del Yaryan told to Claudia Druss, 2009.